In the Land of
INVENTED

SPIEGEL & GRAU
New York
2009

{ ESPERANTO ROCK STARS,
KLINGON POETS, LOGLAN
LOVERS, AND THE MAD
DREAMERS WHO TRIED TO BUILD
A PERFECT LANGUAGE

LANGUAGES

Arika Okrent

PUBLISHED BY SPIEGEL & GRAU

Copyright © 2009 by Arika Okrent

Published in the United States by Spiegel & Grau, an imprint of The Random House Publishing Group, a division of Random House, Inc., New York.

SPIEGEL & GRAU is a trademark of Random House, Inc.

Chapters 22 and 23 were originally published as "Among the Klingons" in *Tin House* magazine, Summer 2007, and subsequently appeared in *The Week* magazine in both the U.S. and the U.K.

Chapters 6 and 8 were originally published as "Letter from Esperantoland" in *The American Scholar*, Winter 2006. Copyright © 2006 by Arika Okrent. By permission of the publishers.

Library of Congress Cataloging-in-Publication Data
Okrent, Arika.
In the land of invented languages : Esperanto rock stars, Klingon poets,
Loglan lovers, and the mad dreamers who tried to build a perfect language /
Arika Okrent.
p. cm.
Includes bibliographical references and index.
ISBN 978-0-385-52788-0
1. Languages, Artificial. I. Title.
PM8008.O37 2009
499'.99—dc22   2008038732

PRINTED IN THE UNITED STATES OF AMERICA ON ACID-FREE PAPER

www.spiegelandgrau.com

10 9 8 7 6 5 4 3 2 1

First Edition

Book design by Nicola Ferguson
Illustrations by Jackie Aher

To Derrick

CONTENTS

Nine Hundred Languages, Nine Hundred Years

   1. Scaring the Mundanes   *3*

   2. A History of Failure   *10*

John Wilkins and the Language of Truth

   3. The Six-Hundred-Page Rewrite   *21*

   4. A Calculus of Thought   *26*

   5. A Hierarchy of the Universe   *38*

   6. The Word for "Shit"   *51*

   7. Knowing What You Mean to Say   *58*

Ludwik Zamenhof and the Language of Peace

   8. A Linguistic Handshake   *79*

   9. *Un Nuov Glot*   *86*

  10. Trouble in Volapükland   *94*

  11. A Nudist, a Gay Ornithologist, a Railroad Enthusiast, and a Punk Cannabis Smoker Walk into a Bar . . .   *110*

  12. Crank Pride   *124*

Charles Bliss and the Language of Symbols

13. Word Magic   *135*
14. Hit by a Personality Tornado   *151*
15. Those Queer and Mysterious Chinese Characters   *160*
16. The Spacemen Speak   *173*
17. The Catastrophic Results of Her Ignorance   *183*

James Cooke Brown and the Language of Logic

18. The Whorfian Hypothesis   *199*
19. A Formula for Success   *208*
20. Suitable Apologies   *215*
21. Meaning Quicksand   *231*
22. To Menstruate Joyfully   *241*

The Klingons, the Conlangers, and the Art of Language

23. Flaws or Features?   *255*
24. The Go-To Linguist   *264*
25. What Are They *Doing*?   *272*
26. The Secret Vice   *282*

Appendix A: The List of Languages   *295*
Appendix B: Language Samples   *315*
Notes   *323*
Acknowledgments   *331*
Index   *333*

NINE HUNDRED LANGUAGES, NINE HUNDRED YEARS

Language,—human language,—after all, is but little better than the croak and cackle of fowls and other utterances of brute nature,—sometimes not so adequate.

—*Nathaniel Hawthorne*

Language, the most valuable single possession of the human race.

—*Charles Hockett*

Scaring
the Mundanes

Klingon speakers, those who have devoted themselves to the
study of a language invented for the *Star Trek* franchise,
inhabit the lowest possible rung on the geek ladder. Dungeons &
Dragons players, ham radio operators, robot engineers, computer
programmers, comic book collectors—they all look down on
Klingon speakers. Even the most ardent *Star Trek* fanatics, the
Trekkies, who dress up in costume every day, who can recite
scripts of entire episodes, who collect *Star Trek* paraphernalia with
mad devotion, consider Klingon speakers beneath them. When
a discussion of Klingon appeared on Slashdot.org—the Web site
billed as "News for Nerds"—the topic inspired comments like "I'm
sorry but it's people like this that give science fiction a bad name."
Another said that Klingon speakers "provide excellent reasons for

forced sterilization. Then again being able to speak Klingon pretty much does this without surgery."

Mark Shoulson, who has a wife and two children, doesn't enjoy being talked about this way. "It's okay to laugh about it, because it's funny. It's legitimate to laugh. Klingon has entertainment as part of its face value. But I do get annoyed at some of the ruder stuff." Mark was my unofficial guide to the world of Klingon. When I met him, we lived in the same New Jersey town. I discovered this browsing the Internet, where I also found that he was assistant director of the Klingon Language Institute (KLI) and editor of the Klingon translation of *Hamlet*. I wrote him, and he e-mailed me back the same day, saying he was so excited by the prospect of another Klingon speaker so close by that he didn't even finish reading my message before he responded.

I wasn't yet a Klingon speaker, and I wasn't really planning on becoming one. I was a linguist who had developed a side interest in the subject of artificial languages, and I wanted to talk to Mark for research purposes. People really spoke Klingon—so claimed the Klingon Language Institute materials anyway—and I wasn't sure what that meant. When people "spoke" Klingon, was it playacting? Spitting out little words and phrases and putting on a show? A charades-like guessing game where someone sort of cobbled together a message and someone else sort of understood it? Or was it actual language use?

If it was the latter, then this was something I needed to see for myself, because that would make Klingon something so remarkable as to be almost unheard of—a consciously invented language that had been brought to life.

Although we like to call language mankind's greatest invention, it wasn't invented at all. The languages we speak were not created according to any plan or design. Who invented French? Who invented Portuguese? No one. They just happened. They arose. Someone said something a certain way, someone else picked up on it, and someone else embellished. A tendency turned into a habit, and somewhere along the way a system came to be. This is how pidgins, slangs, and dialects are born; this is the way English, Russian, and Japanese were born. This is the way all natural languages are born—organically, spontaneously.

The variety of shape, pattern, and color found in the languages of the world is a testament to the wonder of nature, to the breathtaking array of possibilities that can emerge, tangled and wild, from the fertile human endowments of brain and larynx, intelligence and social skills. The job of the linguist, like that of the biologist or the botanist, is not to tell us how nature should behave, or what its creations should look like, but to describe those creations in all their messy glory and try to figure out what they can teach us about life, the world, and, especially in the case of linguistics, the workings of the human mind.

In libraries organized according to the Library of Congress call number system, linguists can usually be found in the stacks classified in the first half of the Ps, anywhere from subclass P, which covers general linguistics, to subclass PN, where "literature" starts. When I was in graduate school, I used to wander this territory, in a procrastinatory haze, noting how the languages covered by the intervening categories became more and more "exotic" the farther I got from PA (Greek and Latin). I would first pass through aisles and aisles of Romance languages, then Germanic, Scandinavian, English, Slavic. There at the end of the Slavic section, at PG9501, things would start to get interesting, with Albanian, followed by the offerings of PH—the Finno-Ugrics (Veps, Estonian, Udmurt, Hungarian), the mysterious Basque. By the time I got to PL, I would be far from Europe, drifting through

Asia and Africa, lingering over *A Grammar of the Hoava Language, Western Solomons* or *The Southern Bauchi Group of Chadic Languages: A Survey Report.*

The final subclass, PM, was a tour through the New World, starting with the Eskimo languages of Greenland and Alaska and proceeding southward through Tlingit, Kickapoo, and Navajo to the Mayan and Aztecan languages of Mexico and Central America, down across the Amazon, through the Andes and the plains of Brazil, until I reached the islands off the southernmost tip of South America with *Yámana-English: A Dictionary of the Speech of Tierra del Fuego.* From there, there was nowhere to go but to the borders of language itself—the contact, or "mixed," languages, the pidgins and creoles of the PM7800s: *Spanish Contact Vernaculars in the Philippine Islands*; *Le créole de Breaux Bridge, Louisiane: Étude morphosyntaxique, textes, vocabulaire.*

At the very end of this lush orchid garden of languages there was one more section, where linguists don't generally care to visit—a few lonely shelves of faded plastic flowers, the artificial languages. *The Klingon Dictionary* was here, among other books on languages I had never heard of: Babm, aUI, Nal Bino, Leno Gi-Nasu, Tutonish, Ehmay Ghee Chah. These were not lighthearted language games, like pig Latin, or the spontaneous results of in-group communication, like Cockney rhyming slang or surfer jargon. They were invented on purpose, cut from whole cloth, set down on paper, start to finish, by one person. They had chapters and chapters of grammar and extensive dictionaries. They were testaments not to the wonder of nature but to the human impulse to master nature. They were deliberate, painstakingly crafted attempts to tame language by making it more orderly, more rational, less burdened with inconsistencies and irregularities. There were hundreds of them. And they were all failures, dead in the water, spoken by no one.

Well, of course they were. If you plant a plastic flower, will it grow? So I was skeptical about the claims that Klingon—*Klingon?*— had really defied the odds and sprouted roots. In the name of research, I registered for the annual Klingon conference, or *qep'a'*, to occur in Phoenix at the end of the summer. I wanted to be prepared, and so I arranged to meet with Mark.

For our first meeting Mark showed up in a T-shirt with the International Phonetic Alphabet printed on it, and I soon discovered that all his T-shirts were a form of self-expression. In fact, everything he owns somehow advertises his interests to the world. On his minivan he has a KLI license plate holder and an LNX sticker (proclaiming himself a user of the Linux operating system). On the vest he wears most days, he displays his three Klingon certification pins; membership pins for the Dozenal Society ("they advocate switching to a base 12 system from the base 10 system we use for numbering"), Mensa ("it's a way for insecure people to feel better about themselves"), and the Triple Nine Society ("a more extreme kind of Mensa"); and a button he made that says "If you can read this you are standing too close" in Braille.

I usually met with Mark at a kosher pizza place. He's an Orthodox Jew who follows all the rules, but jokes that he would be an atheist "if I weren't such a scaredy-cat." He is slender and jittery, one knee constantly bouncing as he talks in a speedy patter. His eyes convey both friendliness and sadness, as if he hopes you will like him but wouldn't be surprised if you punched him. He never finished his Ph.D. in computer science, and he has had trouble holding down a job, to which he credits his attention deficit disorder ("It's not an excuse; it's an explanation"). He cares for his children while his wife, a physician, works, and he teaches computer programming part-time at a yeshiva in Newark. While many bright people like Mark tend to blame the world for not rewarding them more heartily for their smarts, he accepts his own responsibility in the matter. He knows a lot, but not much of it is career making. He is, as he might put it, a polymath of esoterica. His other interests include knot making, typography, mathematical knitting, and calendrical systems. We flew to Phoenix together, and when the plane took off, he pulled a book out of his duffel bag titled *Science from Your Airplane Window*.

Mark is an extreme case of the Klingon-speaker type—a computer guy with an interest in languages and a slightly hurt pride in his status as an outsider. He doesn't fear being called a geek, even by the geekiest, because what is happening with Klingon is just too damn interesting. "So-called normal society," Mark says, "spends all these resources figuring out new and exciting ways to drape cloth on our bodies. What's so bad about having fun with this little language?" While his life has been marked by some unpleasant run-ins with so-called normal society, he has no desire to appease it. The part of the *qep'a'* he was most looking forward to was going out to restaurants with the participants (some in costume), speaking Klingon, and "scaring the mundanes."

I wasn't looking forward to that as much. Not as brave as Mark, and probably more of a mundane myself, I felt conflicted about whether to call the conference hotel to request the special conference rate. In order to do this, I would have to, as the registration materials stated, identify myself as a conference attendee. I rehearsed in my head: "Hi, I'm with the Klingon conference . . ." I tried to get up the nerve to call, but in the end I reserved my room online from a comfortable cushion of anonymity.

And then I got to work on my verb charts and lists of affixes. I needed to study in order to pass the first language certification exam. The Klingon Language Institute, what you might call the academy of the Klingon language, runs the *qep'a'* and also administers the Klingon Language Certification Program. Passing the first certification exam earns you a bronze pin and the title of *taghwI'* (beginner). The second test confers a silver pin and the title *ghojwI'* (intermediate), and the third test earns a gold pin and the title *po'wI'* (advanced).

I didn't know about the tests until Mark told me. I had been casually studying the Klingon dictionary, intending to familiarize myself with the grammar from a clinical distance. But the idea of a test stirred something in me. A feeling every school-loving egghead who ever got a secret thrill from a spelling quiz knows. I was going to take that test and pass it. To get ready, I began the KLI's online postal course. I completed the first lesson and e-mailed it in. It came back with the words that sealed my fate: "Perfect— first time I've seen someone get every question right. Keep it up!" I felt the drug of overachievement rush through my veins. I didn't want to pass that test anymore. I wanted to ace it.

*A History
of Failure*

I did take the test, and (I'm rather proud to say) I did ace it. That achievement, however, is not the beginning of the story I wish to tell with this book, but the end of it. The true significance of what I saw and participated in at the conference, the lessons the Klingon phenomenon can teach us about how language does and doesn't work (trust me on this), can be fully appreciated only in the context of the long, strange history of language invention, a history that encompasses more than nine hundred languages created over the last nine hundred years, a history of human ambition, ingenuity, and struggle that, in a way, culminates with Klingon. You can get a brief overview of this history in appendix A, where I have provided a list of five hundred of these languages.

The earliest documented invented language is the Lingua Ignota of Hildegard von Bingen, a twelfth-century German nun.

Scholars have long puzzled over the purpose of this language, presented in a manuscript as a list of about a thousand words, with Latin and German translations. Because Hildegard was known to experience visions, which she recorded in theological texts, it has been assumed that her Lingua Ignota was some type of glossolalia, or "speaking in tongues." But the product of glossolalia tends to be a string of repetitive nonsense, without system or organization, and without any sign of deliberate planning. Though Hildegard's language may have been motivated by some kind of divine inspiration, the fact that it was written down, with the words carefully organized into meaningful categories and with some structural relationships between words indicated by endings, makes it look more like the intentional work of an inventor with a plan than the channelings of a spiritual medium.

The purpose of Hildegard's language may be lost to history, but through the chancy luck of document preservation the language survives. How many others were not so lucky? The nine hundred languages, over nine hundred years, we do have evidence for suggest that the urge to invent languages is as old and persistent as language itself.

It is at least as old and persistent as the urge to complain about language. The primary motivation for inventing a new language has been to improve upon natural language, to eliminate its design flaws, or rather the flaws it has developed for lack of conscious design. Looked at from an engineering perspective, language *is* kind of a disaster. We have words that mean more than one thing, meanings that have more than one word for them, and some things we'd like to say that, no matter how hard we struggle, seem impossible to put into words. We have irregular verbs, idioms, and exceptions to every grammatical rule—all of which make languages unnecessarily hard to learn. We misunderstand each other all the time; our messages are ambiguous despite our best efforts to be clear. Most of us are content to live with these problems, but over the centuries a bold idea has bloomed again and again in the minds of those who think these problems can be solved: Why not build a better language?

The history of invented languages is, for the most part, a history of failure. Many of the languages involved years of work and sacrifice. They were fueled by vain dreams of fame and recognition, or by humble hopes that the world could be made a better place through language, or, most often, by a combination of the two.

Language inventors, it hardly needs to be said, have usually been eccentric types. Often a plan for an improved language was not the only, or the most unusual, idea an inventor pursued. Paulin Gagne, the creator of Monopanglossc (1858), was well-known in Paris for, among other things, proposing that the French help out the famine-struck Algerians by donating their own bodies for food (or just an arm or leg, if one preferred not to die for the cause). Joseph Schipfer, who presented his Communicationssprache in 1839, when he was nearly eighty years old, also worked to promote his idea for preventing people from being accidentally buried alive (a common concern in the nineteenth century). Schipfer had been a relatively prosperous landowner in the German town of Niederwalluf who served on a state government council for a time. He moved among nobles and acted as an adviser to the prince of Salm-Salm. But by 1830 his fortunes had changed and he had somehow lost his estate. He continued to work, as he said, "for the general welfare of mankind," by petitioning government officials to consider his proposals for the prevention of premature burial, the establishment of mortuaries in small villages, the improvement of fire brigades, and the promotion of his language, Communicationssprache. He asked only that the duchy take on the cost of printing his Communicationssprache grammar and that any profits received from sales of the booklet go to aid the distressed people in France who had recently been afflicted by a major flooding of the Rhône.

His requests were not granted, and in a subsequent letter he asked instead for a loan with which he might pay off the printing costs he had already incurred. He promised to repay the loan once he received an expected pension from Prague. Or, should his request be denied, he had a couple of oil paintings to sell, if anyone was interested.

The lot of the language inventor was almost always a hard one, and those who set out with the most confidence invariably ended up full of bitterness. Ben Prist, the Australian creator of Vela (1995), simply could not understand why his language was being ignored, and blamed some kind of anti-Australian conspiracy. "Why aren't we allowed to have the easiest language possible?" he complains. "A child can go to a library and pick-up a book on pornography. Why can't a grown-up person pick-up a book on the easiest language possible? Is this democracy? Is this human? Where are our human rights?" He has no doubt that his work is an unrecognized masterpiece for which he has become a persecuted martyr. "What is going to be prohibited next: best soup, best cakes, best clothes, best cars, or what?"

It was this overblown ridiculousness that first attracted me to the artificial-language section of the library. It was entertaining to read the unreasonable boasts, like "Mondea! The New World Language! Unequalled! Unsurpassable! New system easy to learn in one minute!" and "In a few years, we will all use Ehmay Ghee Chah . . . the greatest boon of the twenty-first century."

But it was curiosity about the authors of these projects that kept me there. Why did people invest so much effort in this pursuit?

What made them think they could succeed? Who were these inventors? They usually provided very little information about themselves in their books, but I gleaned what I could from the way they presented their languages. Early in my wanderings through the invented-languages section of the library, I became particularly absorbed in the backstory alluded to by Fuishiki Okamoto, who in 1962, when he was seventy-seven years old, published a description of Babm, a "man-made language" for the "future World Society" and also "a theoretical system of the supreme good, which is assured by my philosophical Learning of Knowledge (not yet translated into English)." Since it is designed to be used easily by everyone from "the natives in the Himalayas" to "the inlanders of African ravines," Babm is "planned most simply but perfectly." Really? Here's an example:

V pajio ci htaj, lrid cga coig pegayx pe bamb ak cop pbagt.

It means:

> "I am reading this book, which is very interestingly written in
> Babm by a predominant scholar."

More is revealed by the translation of his sentence than by the sentence itself. It shows something of his human yearnings. That he hopes to be found interesting. That he hopes to be considered a predominant scholar, and that perhaps he hopes that other predominant scholars will one day use his language. He does seem quite sure that "many experts in Babm are expected to appear one after another, who will present abundant and excellent examples of literary works."

He is, of course, gravely mistaken.

But why? Why does this enterprise seem doomed to fail? After all, what do people do when they identify a problem with an existing tool? They try to invent a better one. Is it so crazy to apply this impulse to language? Hundreds of years ago dreamy souls were ridiculed for drawing up plans for vehicles that could travel underwater or fly to the moon. They have since been vindicated. But it's also been hundreds of years since less dreamy, sometimes quite respected souls started drawing up plans for a better language. They and their successors are still ridiculed—if anyone has heard of them at all.

Maybe they deserve it. There is no shortage of arrogance or foolishness in the history of language invention. But after reading into the story of Mr. Okamoto and his beloved Babm, I didn't feel much like ridiculing him. Of his own life he says little beyond that he was "born an extremely weak baby in the most miserable of circumstances," but he unwittingly reveals more in the sentences he uses to illustrate the rules of his language:

V kog cald mtk, lrek deg cjobco ca mnom.
"I hope for an important matter, which is the consummation of
  the whole of humankind."

V kij kdopakd aj modk.
"I choose a healthful meal rather than a delicious one."

Sasn muq in ve hejp.
"No money is in my pocket."

Vli cqeo.
"I have nothing of myself."

Ox udek pbot.
"He does not carry out his original mission."

Y uhqck V.
"I request you not to reproach me."

Dedh cjis beg kobp.
"Time causes youth to be old."

It seemed as if he had suffered enough. And he had worked so hard. "In spite of the fact that my physical body has so much weakened so that even walking annoys me," he writes, "I am every day engaging in theoretical writings and compositions of Babm without even one holiday all the year round, from the early dawn of morning till the dark of evening." He made me feel guilty. I had been born a strong baby in good circumstances, and yet here I was, lazing the day away, producing nothing but new procrastination strategies, and here was Mr. Okamoto, his body aching, his meals non-delicious, working all day every day to produce this book. He deserved a little respect for that, I thought.

Didn't they all? Didn't their hard work deserve at least a look? As I started piecing together the history of invented languages, I discovered amazing feats of work ethic that made me wish I could muster that kind of productive dedication. Of course, my respect was tried by the nutty claims made about these languages: It can be learned in twenty minutes! It can express anything you wish to say with a vocabulary of only fifty items! It is logically perfect! It will make you think more clearly! It will reveal the Truth! (And variations on these themes.) I didn't have to believe these claims, but I thought it was only fair to at least test them for myself.

And so I entered the land of invented languages. I read the books and made a sincere attempt to learn the languages. I studied example texts line by line to figure out how the rules worked. I scoured vocabulary lists and composed translations. I dug up information on the lives of the inventors and got drawn in by their hopes and struggles. My journey also took me beyond the land of books, to gatherings of Esperantists, Lojbanists, and Klingonists, where I witnessed (and participated in) the unexpected phenomenon of invented languages brought to life.

What follows is not just a collection of stories about individual languages. The way people think about language is influenced by the times they live in, and it is possible to show how changing times led, in a general way, to changes in the types of languages that inventors came up with. There are trends, or eras, in language invention that reflect the preoccupations of the surrounding culture, and so, in a way, the history of invented languages is a story about the way we think about language.

It is also a story about natural language. In answering the question of why invented languages fail (and indeed, why they sometimes succeed), we will touch on topics like the relationship of concepts to words, the revival of Hebrew, Chinese writing, sign language, the role of logic in language, and the effect of language on thought. We will see what happens when you attempt to take the flaws out of language, and those "flaws" will be revealed as more important than we realize.

This is a story of why language refuses to be cured and why it succeeds, not in spite of, but because of, the very qualities that the language inventors have tried to engineer away.

JOHN WILKINS AND THE LANGUAGE OF TRUTH

Hαı coba 88 ıa ril dad,
ha bαbı ıo s8ymtα,
ha salba ıo velcα,
ha tαlbı ıo vemg8,
m8 ril dady me ril dad,
ıo velpı lαl αı ril ı poto hαı sαba vαty,
na ıo s8eldy8s lαl αı hαı bαlgas
me αı ıa s8eldy8s lαl eı 88 ıa vαlgas r8 αı
na mı ıo velco αı, rαl bedodl8
nil ıo c8αlbo aı lal vαgasıe
nor αl salba, na αl tado, na αl tadalα ıa ha
pı8by8
m8 ıo

—*The Lord's Prayer in John Wilkins's Philosophical Language*

1600	*Developments in mathematical notation on the rise*
1629	*Descartes considers a "universal language"*
1647	*Lodwick publishes* A Common Writing
1651	*Urquhart publishes* Ekskubalauron *(Gold out of Dung)*
1657	*Dalgarno moves to Oxford*
1660	*Royal Society founded*
1661	*Dalgarno publishes* Ars signorum
1665	*The plague reaches London*
1666	*The Great Fire of London*
1668	*Wilkins publishes* An Essay Towards a Real Character and a Philosophical Language
1672	*Wilkins dies*
1852	Roget's Thesaurus *published*

The Six-Hundred-Page Rewrite

Sixteen sixty-six was a hard year for John Wilkins. It was a hard year for everyone in London. The previous summer the Plague had swept through the city, killing thousands. Wilkins, like most who could afford to, had fled to the countryside. The emptying of London brought the activities of the Royal Society—the scientific academy that Wilkins had recently helped to found—to an abrupt halt. This was a minor inconvenience, of course, compared with the Black Death, but still an inconvenience, and Wilkins did what he could during that time to continue advancing the cause of science. He and a couple of fellow Society members used the various instruments they had hauled up from the city with them to carry on with their experiments. By the summer of 1666 the epidemic appeared to have run its course, and the streets of

London began to fill with people again. Then a baker neglected to extinguish his oven fire one night and the city went up in flames.

The Great Fire of London burned for four days and destroyed most of the city. Wilkins lost his house. And because the church where he was vicar was also destroyed, he lost his job. A few years before, when he had been pushed out of his position as master of Trinity College for political reasons, he had bounced back relatively quickly with the help of influential friends. But the disruption to his life was more severe this time, and his friends were concerned about his low spirits.

This time he had lost something much more difficult to replace than living quarters or income. The fire had also claimed his "darling"—his universal language. He had been working on it for a decade, through the vagaries of national political upheaval and the pain of chronic kidney stones. His manuscript—hundreds of pages, finally complete, already at the printer's shop—was now reduced to ashes.

Wilkins was at the very center of scientific life in his day, but his particular gifts were not of the type that go down in history. He was a mentor, an organizer, a promoter, a peacemaker, and a soother of egos. He befriended and encouraged the innovators who would gain more lasting fame. Robert Hooke (of Hooke's law, the relationship of force to stretch in springs) said of him, "There is scarce any one Invention, which this Nation has produc'd in our Age, but it has some way or other been set forward by his assistance." He collaborated with Robert Boyle (of Boyle's law, the relation of pressure to volume) and John Ray (father of natural history in Britain). He noticed the extraordinary talent of the young Christopher Wren (mathematician, astronomer, architect of St. Paul's Cathedral) and took a special interest in promoting his career.

Wilkins's own work was not groundbreaking (it was suggested that he got along so well with everyone because he didn't arouse jealousy), but it did display a unique kind of creative verve. He drew up plans for land-water vehicles and flying machines. He designed an early odometer and a rainbow-producing fountain. He built a hollowed-out statue for playing practical jokes on people; he would speak through the statue's mouth by means of a long pipe that allowed him to stand at a distance and observe the bewildered reactions of his targets. He constructed an elaborate glass beehive, outfitted like a palace with tiny decorations. Whimsical but also practical, it permitted the scientific observation of bee behavior. He presented a report on the differences between queens and drones at a meeting of the Royal Society.

Wilkins took a secondary role in the greater achievements of others both as an inspirer (his suggestions led to pioneering research on skin grafting and blood transfusion) and as a publicizer. He was perhaps the first popular science writer. Exasperated by dense, overly theoretical presentation styles, he made the promotion of plain language a lifelong cause. He wrote one book to explain Copernican astronomy to a general audience and another to explain mechanical geometry to people who might want to benefit from its practical applications. All applications of scientific theory were interesting to him; many of his own experiments veered toward the domestic (more efficient methods of embroidery, quicker ways to roast meat). He took great joy from science, and he knew how to make it accessible. Boyle may have been the true innovator when it came to the principles of air pressure, but it was Wilkins who thought to demonstrate the power of those principles in an experiment where, by blowing into a series of connected pipes, he levitated "a fat boy of sixteen or seventeen years" a clear two inches off the ground. The Society members were so entertained by his presentation that they agreed it should be performed for the king's proposed visit.

Wilkins didn't actively court fame for its own sake, but as generous and diplomatic as he was (one colleague said that he never met anyone else who "knew how to manage the freedom of speech so inoffensively"), he could not have been completely unconcerned with his own place in posterity. He did have one project that was exciting, important, and unquestionably his. It was a man-made language free from the ambiguity and imprecision that afflicted natural languages. It would directly represent concepts; it would reveal the truth.

Others had talked about creating such a language, or made preliminary attempts at it. Wilkins had collaborated with some of them and, in characteristic fashion, encouraged their efforts. But no one had put in the work he had. No one but Wilkins had been brave or industrious enough to take on the massive task that the creation of such a language required—a complete and ordered cataloging of all concepts, of everything in the universe. And now, after the Great Fire, the pages on which he had set down the universe were gone, along with his shot at immortal fame.

He was lower than he had ever been. But he was not one to indulge too long in self-pity. He got back to work, and within two years he had rewritten the whole thing. It came to over six hundred pages. When he presented it to the Royal Society in 1668, he acknowledged that he was "not so vain as to think that I have here completely finished this great undertaking," and requested that a committee be appointed to "offer their thoughts concerning what they judge fit to be amended in it" so that he could continue to make improvements.

A committee was appointed. There was excitement, praise, and plans for translating the work into Latin. The king expressed an interest in learning the language. Robert Hooke suggested it should be the language of all scientific findings and published a description of the mechanics of pocket watches in it. The mathematician John Wallis wrote letters to Wilkins in the language and claimed that they "perfectly understood one another as if written in our own language." Newton, Locke, and Leibniz read Wilkins's book with interest.

Wilkins continued to work on perfecting his masterpiece, suffering with ever more frequent "fits of the stone." In the summer of 1672 he sought a cure at Scarborough spa, but found no relief. In November, dying from "suppression of the Urine," he told the friends and admirers who came to visit him for the last time that he was "prepared for the great Experiment" and that his only regret was that he would not live to see the completion of his language.

But he had seen it as complete as it ever would be. The king would not get around to learning it. The committee would never issue its report. Gradually, even Wilkins's close friends and collaborators would stop talking about it. No more scientific reports would be written in it. No more letters. There is no evidence that anyone ever used it again.

What happened? Did it get lost in the shuffle of history? A case of wrong time, wrong place? Or was there a problem with the language itself? There was only one way to find out. I settled in for a long weekend with *An Essay Towards a Real Character and a Philosophical Language*. I emerged blinking and staggering, unsure of whether any word in any language meant anything at all.

*A Calculus
of Thought*

Wilkins's project was the most fully developed of all the many linguistic schemes hatched in his day. Language invention was something of a seventeenth-century intellectual fad. Latin was losing ground as the international lingua franca, and as the pace of advancement in philosophy, science, and mathematics picked up, scholars fretted about the best way to propagate their findings. Talk of universal language was in the air. It was not the first time. The search for a cure for Babel was as old as the story of Babel, but the cure proposed before this point usually involved the discovery of the original language of Adam as crafted by God. Now, in the throes of the scientific revolution, people started to think that perhaps a solution could be crafted by man.

It seems that any self-respecting gentleman of the day could be expected to have some sort of universal language up his sleeve. Of all the works published on the idea during this time, the one with my favorite title is by Edward Somerset, the second Marquis of Worcester: *A Century of the Names and Scantlings of Such Inventions as at Present I Can Call to Mind to Have Tried and Perfected, Which (My Former Notes Being Lost) I Have, at the Instance of a Powerful Friend, Endeavoured Now in the Year 1655, to Set These Down in Such a Way as May Sufficiently Instruct Me to Put Any of Them in Practice.*

There among his inventions ingenious (the steam engine), overly optimistic (an unsinkable ship), and fanciful ("a floating garden of pleasure, with trees, flowers, banqueting-houses, and fountains, stews for all kinds of fishes, a reserve for snow to keep wine in, delicate bathing places, and the like") is a mention of "an universal character methodical and easie to be written, yet intelligible in any language." He doesn't, however, say much more about it.

Another gentleman inventor, who never missed a chance to say more about anything, was the eccentric Scotsman Sir Thomas Urquhart of Cromarty. He made a name for himself as the English translator of Rabelais, and not, as he had hoped, as the inventor of "a new idiome of far greater perfection than any hitherto spoken." In a characteristic display of his excessive lack of humility, he likened his universal language to "a most exquisite jewel, more precious than diamonds inchased in gold, the like whereof was never seen in any age."

He described his language as a sort of arithmetic of letters by which every single thing in the universe could be given a unique name that, through a simple computation, showed you its exact and true definition. What's more, every word meant something read both backward and forward—or in any permutation of the letters. He published two works on this language: *Ekskubalauron*, or "Gold out of Dung," in 1652; and *Logopandecteision; or, An Introduction to the Universal Language* in 1653. (He was an avid coiner of exotic Greco-Latin-based terms, often taken to—to use a phrase of his—*quomodocunquizing*, or "any-old-way-ing," extremes.) Both of these works include an indictment of natural languages for their gross imperfections and a trumpeting of praise for the solution that he had devised. But he never gets around to the details. The remainder of the first work is taken up with an invective against greedy Presbyterians and a history of Scotland. The largest part of the second work consists of a chapter-by-chapter complaint against the "impious dealing of creditors," "covetous preachers," and "pitiless judges" who were compounding his money troubles.

He claimed to have completed a full description of his language, but the manuscript pages had been destroyed when they were appropriated for "posterior uses" by the opposing army after he was taken prisoner at the battle of Worcester. Seven pages from the preface, however, were rescued from under a pile of dead men in the muddy street (thus, "gold out of dung").

Urquhart was such a shockingly self-aggrandizing hack that some scholars have concluded that he must have been joking. He had earlier published a genealogy of his family, placing himself 153rd in line from Adam, and a book on mathematics, which an "admirer" (who happens to use words like *doxologetick* and *philomathets*) said explained the subject in so clear and poetic a manner that it conferred the ability to solve any trigonometry problem, no matter how difficult, "as if it were a knowledge meerly infused from above, and revealed by the peculiar inspiration of some favourable Angel."

The book in question begins:

Every circle is divided into three hundred and sixty parts, called degrees, whereof each one is sexagesimated, subsexagesimated, resubsexagesimated, and biresubsexagesimated.

Ah, the voices of angels. Though Urquhart did have a sense of humor (in fact, he died from laughing too hard at the news that Charles II had been restored to the throne), he was no satirist. If you take the time to beat your way through his suffocating prose, you will find quite earnest (and humorless) proposals.

It is easy to mistake his universal language proposal for satire because it appeared at a time when such proposals were the latest thing. Seventeenth-century philosophers and scientists were complaining that language obscured thinking, that *words* got in the way of understanding *things*. They believed that concepts were clear and universal, but language was ambiguous and unsystematic. A new kind of rational language was needed, one where words perfectly expressed concepts. These ideas *were* later satirized by Swift in *Gulliver's Travels*, when Gulliver visits the "grand academy of Lagado" and learns of its "scheme for entirely abolishing all words whatsoever." Since "words are only names for things," people simply carry around all the things they might need to refer to and produce them from their pockets as necessary.

Gulliver observes especially learned men "almost sinking under the weight of their packs, like pedlars among us; who, when they met in the streets, would lay down their loads, open their sacks, and hold conversation for an hour together: then put up their implements, help each other to resume their burthens, and take their leave."

This scenario illustrates a major problem with the rational language idea. How many "things" do you need in order to communicate? The number of concepts is huge, if not infinite. If you want each word in your language to perfectly express one concept, you need so many words that it will be impossible for anyone to learn them all.

But maybe there was a way around this problem. After all, by learning a few basic numbers and a system for putting them together, we can count to infinity. Couldn't the same be done for language? Couldn't we derive everything through a sort of mathematics of concepts?

This was a tremendously exciting idea at the time. In the seventeenth century, mathematical notation was changing everything. Before then, through thousands of years of mathematical developments, there was no plus sign, no minus sign, no symbol for multiplication or square root, no variables, no equations. The concepts behind these notational devices were understood and used, but they were explained in text form. Here, for example, is an expression of the Pythagorean theorem from a Babylonian clay tablet (about fifteen hundred years before Pythagoras):

> 4 is the length and 5 the diagonal. What is the breadth? Its size is not known. 4 times 4 is 16. 5 times 5 is 25. You take 16 from 25 and there remains 9. What times what shall I take in order to get 9? 3 times 3 is 9. 3 is the breadth.

And expressed a little more abstractly by Euclid a couple millennia later:

> In right-angled triangles the square on the side subtending the right angle is equal to the squares on the sides containing the right angle.

And Copernicus, over fifteen hundred years after that, taking advantage of the theorem to solve the position of Venus:

> It has already been shown that in units whereof DG is 303, hypotenuse AD is 6947 and DF is 4997, and also that if you take DG, made square, out of both AD and FD, made square, there will remain the squares of both AG and GF.

This is how math was done. The clarity of your explanations depended on the vocabulary you chose, the order of your clauses, and your personal style, all of which could cause problems. Here, for example, is Urquhart, in his "voices of angels" trigonometry book, doing something somehow related to the Pythagorean theorem—it's hard to tell:

> The multiplying of the middle termes (which is nothing else but the squaring of the comprehending sides of the prime rectangular) affords two products, equall to the oblongs made of the great subtendent, and his respective segments, the aggregate whereof, by equation, is the same with the square of the chief subtendent, or hypotenusa.

It is possible to do mathematics like this, but the text really gets in the way. *Wait, which sides are squared? What is taken out of what? What was that thing three clauses ago that I'm now supposed to add to this thing?* Late-sixteenth-century scientists who were engaged in calculating the facts of the universe had a sense that the important ideas, the truths behind the calculations, were struggling against the language in which they were trapped. The astronomer Johannes Kepler had turned to musical notation (already well developed at that time) in an effort to better express his discoveries about the motions of the planets, yielding "the harmony of the spheres." But musical notation could only go so far. The development of mathematical notation in this context was nothing short of revolutionary.

The notational innovations of the seventeenth century—symbols and variables instead of words, equations instead of sentences—not only made it easier to keep track of which thing was which in a particular calculation; they also made it easier to see fundamental similarities and differences, and to draw generalizations that hadn't been noticed before. In addition, the notation was universal; it could be understood no matter what your national language was. The pace of innovation in science accelerated rapidly. Modern physics and calculus were born. It seemed that the truth was finally being revealed through this new type of language. A tantalizing idea took hold: just imagine what might be revealed if we could express all of our thoughts this way.

But how do you turn the world of discourse into math? Three primary strategies emerged from the competitive flurry of schemes whipped up by this challenge, two so superficial they allowed the illusion of success (leaving the egos of the authors undisturbed), and one so ambitious that those who attempted to implement it could only be humbled by the enormity of the task it revealed.

The first strategy was to simply use letters in a number-like way. When you combine the letters or do some sort of computation with them (the nature of that computation being very vaguely described), you get a word and—voilà!—a language. This was Urquhart's approach. He had tried a version of this strategy in his trigonometry book when he assigned letters to concepts, such as *E* for "side" and *L* for "secant," and then formed words out of the letters to express statements like *Eradetul*, meaning "when any of the sides is Radius, the other of them is a Tangent, and the Subtendent a Secant." He thought a similar approach could be used to make precise, definition-containing words for everything in the universe. All you needed was the right alphabet, and he claims to have devised one so perfect that not only can it generate distinct words for all possible meanings, but the words for stars will show you their exact position in the sky in degrees and minutes, the words for colors will show their exact mixture of light, shadow, and darkness, the names of individual soldiers will show their exact duty and rank. What's more, in comparison with all other languages, it produces the best prayers, the most elegant compliments, the pithiest proverbs, and the most "emphatical" interjections. And besides all that, it is the easiest to learn. He stops short of claiming that it whitens your teeth and cures impotence, but he might as well have. His claims can't be disproved, because he doesn't provide any examples.

The second strategy was to turn words into numbers. This was the approach of Cave Beck, an Ipswich schoolmaster who published his invention (*The Universal Character: By Which All the Nations in the World May Understand One Anothers Conceptions*) in 1657. He assigned numbers to concepts: 1 was "to abandon," 2 "to abash," 3 "to abate," 742 "to embroider," q2126 "gogle-eyed," r2654 "a loosenesse in the belly," p2846 "hired mourners at funerals." (Letters appearing before the numbers were used to indicate part of speech and grammatical concerns such as tense and gender.) He provided a pronunciation key for the numbers so that the language could be spoken out as words (for example, 7 is pronounced "sen"). Though the book opens with a series of poems (by his friends) praising Beck and his invention, his confidence is far less blustery than Urquhart's; he presents his system as merely a practical tool for translating between languages. However, with an ambitious gleam in his eye, he adds that if it should happen to become a universal language that could unlock "Glorious Truths," he will "judge this pains of mine happily bestowed." He provides only one example of the language in action, the fifth commandment. Honor thy father and thy mother, "leb 2314 p2477 & pf2477," to be pronounced, "Leb toreónfo, pee tofosénsen et pif tofosénsen."

There is an assumption in these approaches that all you have to do to build a perfect language is find the right set of symbols— whether letters, numbers, or line drawings. The focus on symbols was influenced by other, related popular pursuits of the time such as cryptography, shorthand, and kabbalism (seeking divine messages in patterns of letters in ancient texts). Another influence was the widespread interest in hieroglyphics and Chinese writing, which were believed to represent concepts more directly than alphabetic writing systems. But if your goal is to craft a language capable of mathematically exposing the truths of the universe, the form of the symbols you use is relatively unimportant. What is more important is that systematic relations obtain *between* the symbols. The number 1 stands for the concept of oneness, and 100 stands for the concept of onehundredness, but, more important, there is a relationship between oneness and onehundredness that is captured by the relationship between the symbols 1 and 100. And it is the same relationship that obtains between 2 and 200. In Beck's system there is no such relationship between 1 (abandon) and 100 (agarick—a type of mushroom), and if you do find a way to read a relationship into them, it won't be the same as the one between 2 (abate) and 200 (an anthem). The numbers are just labels for words. They might as well *be* words. Both Beck and Urquhart had a vague sense that symbols were capable of systematically capturing relationships between concepts, but they never did the hard work of applying this idea to language.

They could have learned a thing or two from the humble Francis Lodwick, a Dutchman living far from home in London whose 1647 book, *A Common Writing*, was signed simply "a Well-willer to Learning." In his preface he apologizes for the "harshnesse of [his] stile" and entreats "a more abler wit and Pen, to a compleate attyring and perfecting of the Subject." His modesty was partly due to a feeling of inferiority, life-station-wise. He was a merchant with no formal education, which, in the opinion of the author of a later scheme, made him "unequal to the undertaking." But his modesty was also of the hard-earned type—the modesty that all thoughtful and honest scholars must come to (whatever their life station) when their work reveals a vast, churning ocean of difficulty just beyond the charming rivulet they had glimpsed from afar.

The important insight of Lodwick's system wasn't in the symbols he chose (characters that look like capital letters, with various hooks, dots, and squiggles attached) but in the way his symbols expressed relationships between concepts. For example, as shown in figure 4.1, the symbol for "word," $8^⫣$, is the symbol for "to speak," 8, combined with a mark denoting "act of . . .": $⫣$. A word is essentially defined as an act of speaking. The symbol for God, $⸜8^⫣$, is the symbol for "to be," 8, combined with "act of . . . ," $⫣$, and "proper name," $⌣$. God is the proper name of the act of being (something like "The Embodiment of Existence"). The symbol for man, $⸝U^⌐$, is the symbol for "to understand," U, combined with "one who . . . ," $⌐$, and "proper name," $⌣$. Man is "The Understander." Lodwick's major insight was to derive more complex concepts by adding together more basic ones.

Lodwick had hit upon the third method for creating a mathematics of discourse. It was concerned not with mere letters or numbers or symbols but with the relationships between the con-

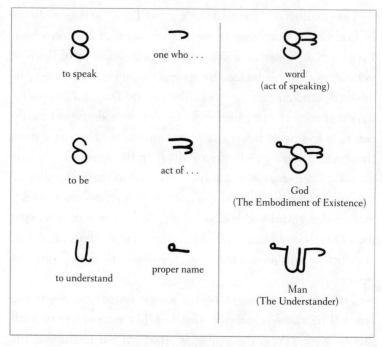

Figure 4.1: Lodwick's symbols

cepts they represented. From a limited set of basic concepts, you could derive everything else through combination. Leibniz would later describe this as a "calculus of thought." The first rule of this calculus was that numbers for concepts "should be produced by multiplying together the symbolic numbers of the terms which compose the concept." So, "since man is a rational animal, if the number of animal, *a*, is 2, and of rational, *r*, is 3, then the number of man, *h*, will be the same as *ar*: in this example, 2 × 3, or 6." The calculations work in reverse as well. If you saw that ape was 10, you could deduce that it was an animal (because it could be divided by 2) but not a rational one (as it can't be divided by 3).

Descartes had also considered this idea a decade or two before Lodwick. He mused that if you could "explain correctly what are the simple ideas in the human imagination out of which all human thoughts are compounded . . . I would dare to hope for a universal language very easy to learn, to speak and to write." But he never tried his hand at creating such a language, because he thought it would first require a complete understanding of the true nature of everything. While he did think it was "possible to invent such a language and to discover the science on which it depends," he also thought this was unlikely to occur "outside of a fantasyland."

Lodwick had hit upon a solution to the problem of how to make a mathematics of language, but the solution introduced a much bigger problem: How do we know what the basic units of meaning are? How do we define everything in terms of those units?

Well, you can start by figuring out the order of the universe. This was not a ridiculous proposition for the seventeenth-century man of science. It was a difficult proposition, and one that anyone could see would most likely never be adequately fulfilled. But that was no reason not to try. This was the age of reason, and so the rational animal got to work.

A Hierarchy
of the Universe

The bulk of John Wilkins's six-hundred-page description of his language is taken up with a hierarchical categorization of everything in the universe. Everything? When I first sat down to confront *An Essay Towards a Real Character and a Philosophical Language*, I did what any sensible, mature language scholar would do. I tried to look up the word for "shit."

But where to look? I was holding a dictionary of concepts, not words. They were arranged not alphabetically but by meaning. To get the word for "shit," I would have to find the concept of shit, which meant I had to figure out which of Wilkins's forty categories of meaning it fell under.

Wilkins's categories are organized into an overall structure of the type known as the Aristotelian hierarchy, or Porphyrian tree. This is the genus-species-difference organization we are most familiar with from taxonomies of plant and animal life. The higher positions in the tree are the most general categories, which are split into subcategories on the basis of some distinguishing feature. Daisies, spiders, woodpeckers, tigers, and porcupines all fall under the category of animate substances; they are all living things. But only some of them share the property of being sensate (bye, daisies) or of having blood (bye, spiders) or of being beasts (see ya, woodpeckers) or of being non-rapacious (so long, tigers). As we move down the tree, categories are narrowed and members more precisely defined by their membership.

Figure 5.1 shows Wilkins's tree of the universe, with his forty numbered categories as the bottom nodes. The first division, general versus special, separates the big abstract metaphysical ideas (notions like existence, truth, and good) from the stuff of the world (the notions those ideas can apply to). This division was consistent with the philosophy of categories, descended from Plato and Aristotle, as practiced at the time. The division between substances and accident (at the second node under "special") also comes from this tradition. Substances are answers to the question, What is this? and accidents are answers to the question, How/in what way/of what quality is this? A glance at the table will show that these distinctions do not always hold up very well, but, as Wilkins was quite aware, the philosophy was incomplete and this was as good a place to start as any.

The bottom nodes of this tree, the forty main categories, are themselves top-level categories in their own sprawling trees. For example, if we zoom in on category XVIII, "Beasts," we find it further divided into six subcategories, as shown in figure 5.2.

It doesn't stop there. Lift a subcategory and you find a tree of sub-subcategories that get even more specific. So under category XVIII (Beasts), subcategory V (oblong-headed), you will find six

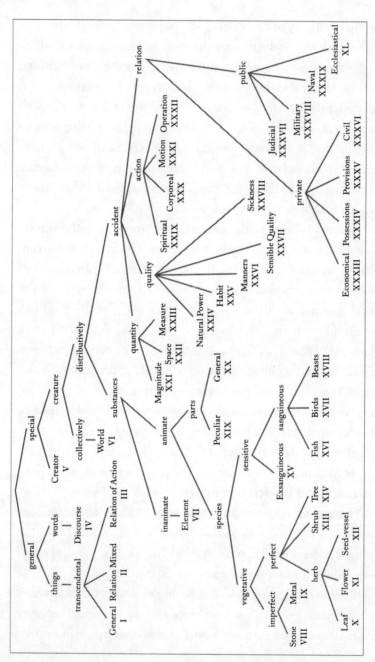

Figure 5.1: Wilkins's tree of the universe

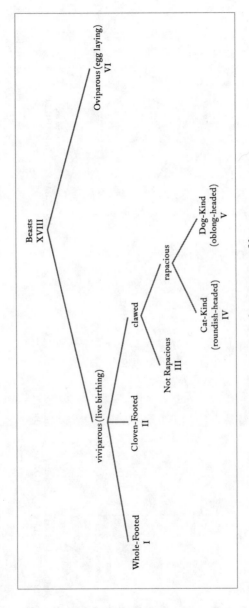

Figure 5.2: Subcategories of beasts

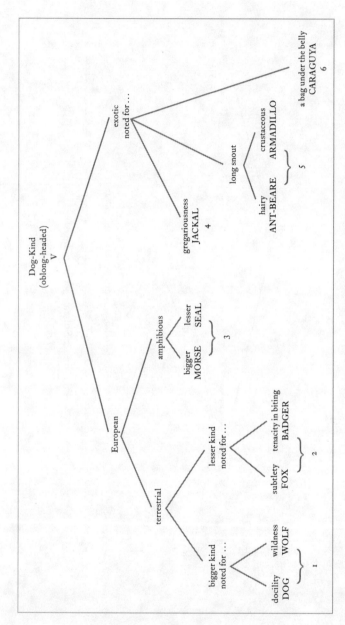

Figure 5.3: Subcategories of oblong-headed beasts

sub-subcategories under which specific animals are finally named (as shown in figure 5.3).

Each one of his forty top-level categories expands in this manner into multiple sub- and sub-sub trees. A place is provided for everything from "porcupine" (substances > animate > sensate > sanguineous > beast > clawed > non-rapacious) to "dignity" (accident > quality > habit > instruments of virtue > concerning our conditions in relation to others) to "potentialness" (transcendentals > general > quality > degree of being). We are dealing with an enormous magnum opus here.

But why was all this necessary? What does the idea of a mathematics of language have to do with a gigantic conceptual map of the universe?

We have seen that a mathematics of language required two things: a list of the basic units of meaning, and a knowledge of how everything else was to be derived from those units. In Lodwick's system "to understand," "one who . . . ," and "proper name" were primitives, and "man" was derived from the combination of those three primitives. Man was defined as the one who understands. For Leibniz the primitives were rational and animal, and man was derived by the combination of those primitives—the rational animal. Well, which is it? Is man the rational animal or the understander? It depends on the primitives you're working with. And finding the right set of primitives depends on finding the right definition. Now, the rational animal and the understander are pretty similar definitions for man—they both focus on man's capacity to think—but man *could* be defined in other ways. Why not the upright-walking animal? Or (after Plato) the featherless biped?

Upright walking does not work, because, while it is a pretty distinguishing characteristic of man, it is not *the* distinguishing characteristic. Apes walk pretty upright, and even a dog can walk upright if properly motivated. And as for the featherless-biped idea, Diogenes the Cynic responded to it by brandishing a plucked chicken and proclaiming, "Behold, Plato's man!" A description of man that lets you pick out man as opposed to something else is dependent not so much on the characteristics man *has* as on the characteristic that everything else does not have.

And that characteristic, it was commonly supposed, was the capacity to reason. Naturally, the people who were concerned with big questions like the essential nature of man—the philosophers—held this characteristic in high regard. After all, it was the tool of their trade. So they may have failed to focus on other human characteristics that are arguably just as distinguishing. Why is man not the vengeful animal or, in the words of G. K. Chesterton, "the animal who makes dogmas" or, in the words of Ambrose Bierce, the "animal so lost in rapturous contemplation of what he thinks he is as to overlook what he indubitably ought to be"?

Depends on what's important in your philosophy. Descartes thought the philosophical language idea was doomed because it required you to first figure out the *true* philosophy. Wilkins thought the philosophical language idea was possible because all you needed was a pretty good philosophy. Though he aimed to make his system "exactly suited to the nature of things," he acknowledged that it fell short. He didn't know the Truth, but he had some not completely unreasonable opinions about it. They were, however, still opinions, and therefore informed by his own idiosyncratic viewpoint and the particular preoccupations of the times he lived in. Had he been younger or older when he crafted his tables (he was in his early fifties when he finished), he may not have categorized the age "betwixt the 50th and 60th year" as the "most perfect for the Mind . . . the Age of Wisdom." Had he not lived in the seventeenth century, he may not have categorized "witchcraft" under judicial relations > capital crimes. Had he not lived in England, he may not have included a whole category of terms for ship rigging. The parrel, jeers, and buntline all get their rightful places in the universe of Wilkins.

So, to sum up the progression from "let's make a math for language" to "let's make a hierarchy of the universe":

1. To make a math for language, you need to know what the basic units of meaning are, and how we compute more complicated concepts out of them.

2. To figure both of these things out, you need an idea of how concepts break down into smaller concepts.

3. To break down the concepts, you need a satisfactory definition for those concepts; you have to know what things *are*.

4. In order to know what something *is*, you have to distinguish it from everything it is not.

5. Because you have to distinguish it from everything, you have to include everything in your system. So there you are, crafting your six-hundred-page table of the universe.

Do you get the sense that each step in this progression doesn't necessarily follow from the last one? So did George Dalgarno. He was a Scottish schoolmaster of humble means who moved to Oxford in 1657 in order to start a school. After attending a demonstration of a new type of shorthand that could express phrases in "a more compendious way than any I had seen," he was inspired to "advance it a step further." In the process of working out how to stuff the most meaning into the fewest possible symbols, he realized that such a system could be used not just as a shorthand for English but as a universal writing that could be read off into any language. He was "struck with such a complicated passion of admiration, fear, hope and joy" at this idea that he "had not one houres natural rest for the 3 following nights together."

His idea wasn't as original as he thought. Quite a few scholars of the time had become preoccupied with developing a "real character." This was the term used by the philosopher Francis Bacon to describe Chinese writing—it was "real" in that the symbols represented not sounds, or words, but ideas. Traveling missionaries of the previous century had noted that people who spoke mutually incomprehensible languages—Mandarin, Cantonese, Japanese, Vietnamese—could understand each other in writing. They got the impression that Chinese characters bypassed language entirely, and went right to the heart of the matter. This impression was mistaken (we will discuss how Chinese characters do work in chapter 15), but it encouraged a general optimistic excitement about the possibility of a universal real character.

Dalgarno was a nobody in Oxford, but it so happened that the only person he knew there, an old school friend, was in good with the vice-chancellor of the university. Dalgarno's work was read and passed around, and soon he found himself in the company of the most eminent scholars in town, a stroke of luck at which he was "overjoyed." One of these scholars was Wilkins, who had not yet begun to work on his own universal character.

Dalgarno's system provided a list of 935 "radicals"—the primitive concepts he judged necessary for effective communication—

and a method for writing them. They were not, however, organized into a hierarchical tree. They were not grouped by shared properties, or by any logical or philosophical system. Instead, they were placed into a verse composed of stanzas of seven lines each, so that they could be easily memorized. For example, if you memorize the first stanza, you know the placement of forty-two of his radical words (italicized):

When I *sit-down* upon a *hie place*, I'm *sick* with *light* and *heat*
For the *many thick moistures*, doe *open wide* my *Emptie* pores
But when sit *upon* a *strong borrowed* Horse, I *ride* and *run* most
    swiftly
Therefore if I can *purchase* this *courtesie* with *civilitie*, I *care* not the
    hirers barbaritie
Because I'm *perswaded* they are *wild villains*, *scornfully deceiving*
    modest men
Neverthelesse I *allowe* their *frequent wrongs* and will *encourage*
    them with *obliging exhortations*
Moreover I'l *assist* them to *fight* against *robbers*, when I *have* my *long*
    crooked sword.

He developed a written character where the placement and direction of little lines and hooks referred to a specific place in a line of a stanza (as shown in figure 5.4).

To write "light," for example, you draw the character representing the first stanza modified by a small mark indicating first line, fifth word. The pattern is repeated for the fourth through sixth lines, but with little hooks added to the marks, and for the seventh line the mark is drawn through the character (as shown in figure 5.5).

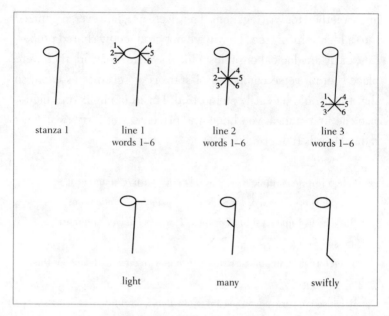

Figure 5.4: Dalgarno's system

Additionally, the opposite of a word was represented by reversing the orientation of the stanza symbol.

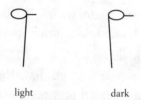

He also provided for a way for the system to be spoken by assigning consonants and vowels to the numbered stanzas, lines, and words. So if *B* = stanza 1, *A* = line 1, and *G* = word 5, then the word for "light" would be *BAG*.

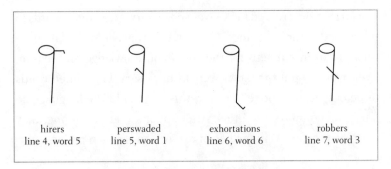

Figure 5.5: Dalgarno's system, lines 4–7

Wilkins admired Dalgarno's system, but he thought it needed to include more concepts, and took it upon himself to draw up an ordered table of plants, animals, and minerals. Dalgarno respectfully declined to use those tables, arguing that the longer the list of concepts got, the harder they would be to memorize. He thought that specific species, like elephant, didn't need their own, separate radical words, but that they could be referred to by writing out compound phrases, such as "largest whole-footed beast."

Dalgarno's method was another way to get a mathematics of language. No need to determine a universe of categories and distinguishing features—you simply decide what the primitives are (no need to systematically break everything down; just ask yourself what makes sense) and assume everything else can be described by adding those primitives together to make a compound. For Dalgarno, "coal" is "mineral black fire," "diamond" is "precious stone hard," and "ash tree" is "very fruitless tree long kernel."

Wilkins thought this method lacked rigor. Dalgarno hadn't chosen his basic concepts in a principled way, and, worse, the words in his language told you nothing about their meanings, just their arbitrary placement in a nonsense verse. Wilkins was convinced that the ordered tables were necessary. He wanted words to reflect the nature of things—only in this way could the language serve as an instrument for the spread of knowledge and reason. Dalgarno thought the tables were unnecessary. He wanted words to be easy to memorize—only in this way could the language be a useful communication tool. After about a year of arguing, they parted ways, and Wilkins began to work on his own project.

The Word for "Shit"

The problem with natural languages, as Wilkins saw it, was that words tell you nothing about the things they refer to. You must simply learn that a dog is a "dog" in English or a *chien* in French or a *perro* in Spanish or a *Hund* in German. The sounds in those words are just sounds to be arbitrarily memorized. They tell you what to call a dog, but they do not tell you what a dog is.

In Wilkins's system, the word for "dog" does tell you what a dog is. Like Dalgarno, Wilkins worked out a way to refer to a specific position in his tables with a character or a word. Since the concept dog is located in category XVIII (Beasts), subcategory V (oblong-headed), sub-subcategory 1 (bigger kind) (refer to figure 5.3), the character for "dog" would be formed with the symbol for category XVIII, along with modifications indicating subcategory V, and sub-subcategory 1.

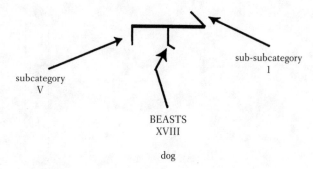

subcategory
V

sub-subcategory
1

BEASTS
XVIII

dog

The character for "wolf," being paired with "dog" on the basis of a minimal opposition (docile versus not docile), requires an additional marking for opposite.

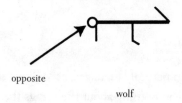

opposite

wolf

Wilkins's scheme for forming pronounceable words follows the same plan. "Dog" is *zitα*:

category XVIII	subcategory V	sub-subcategory 1
Zi	t	α (pronounced as in "fought")

$$\Downarrow$$

Zitα

and "wolf" is *zitαs*.

The words of both Dalgarno's and Wilkins's systems direct you to a position in a table, but only in Wilkins's case does that position mean something. Dalgarno's word for "light," *BAG*, shows you where in his verses the word "light" may be found (stanza 1, line 1, word 5), but it does not tell you what light is. *Zitα*, on the other hand, gives you a definition of a dog: a clawed, rapacious, oblong-headed, land-dwelling beast of docile disposition.

A word in Wilkins's language doesn't *stand for* a concept; it *defines* the concept. So, to return to the important business at hand, what is the definition of "shit"? Where might I find it in Wilkins's tree of the universe? Wilkins does provide an index to his tables, where you can look up specific English words and find out where they fall in the hierarchy. If you look up, say, "rabble," you will find written next to it RC.I.7 (relations, civil > political relations of rank > of the lower sort, in the aggregate). Sometimes the word directs you to another word; if you look up "parsimony," it will tell you to see "frugality" (which then directs you to Man.III.3—manners > virtues relating to our estates and dignities > in regards to keeping as opposed to getting). But "shit" doesn't appear in the index, nor does "feces." So I set out to find it by figuring out its true definition. To begin, I turned to what seemed to be the most promising category for my quest, number XXX, "Corporeal Action." But I did not find what I was looking for. The concepts included in this category ranged from quite general (living, dying) to quite specific (itching, stuttering). I noted that some of them, contrary to the indications of their category title, didn't seem very corporeal (editing, printing) or very action-like (dreaming, entertaining). But this category did include the concept politely known as coition, listed along with a colorful collection of synonyms: "coupling," "gendering," "lie with," "know carnally," "copulation," "rutting," "tread," "venery." The word for all this, by the way, is *cadod* (a corporeal action > belonging to sensate beings > of the kind concerning appe-

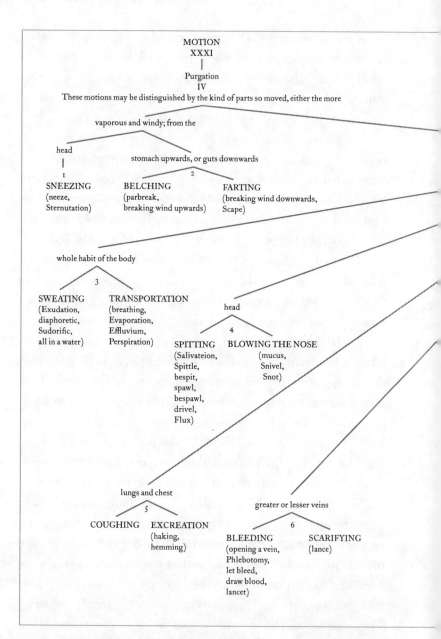

Figure 6.1: Category XXXI (Motion), subcategory IV (Purgation)

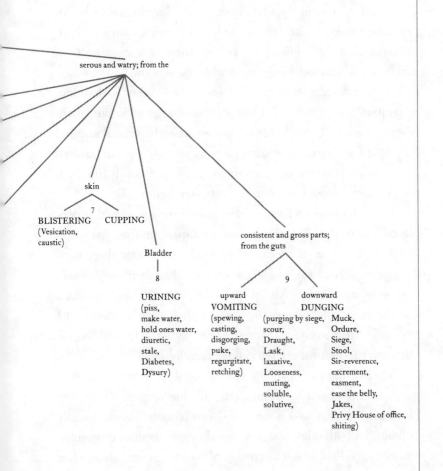

serous and watry; from the

skin

7

BLISTERING   CUPPING
(Vesication,
caustic)

Bladder

8

URINING   upward
(piss,   VOMITING
make water,   (spewing,
hold ones water, casting,
diuretic,   disgorging,
stale,   puke,
Diabetes,   regurgitate,
Dysury)   retching)

consistent and gross parts;
from the guts

9

downward
DUNGING
(purging by siege, Muck,
scour,   Ordure,
Draught,   Siege,
Lask,   Stool,
laxative,   Sir-reverence,
Looseness,   excrement,
muting,   easment,
soluble,   ease the belly,
solutive,   Jakes,
                     Privy House of office,
                     shiting)

tites and the satisfying of them > relating to the preservation of the individual > as regards the desire of the propagation of the species).

Sexual matters being a bit above my level of dictionary maturity, I continued my search in the next category, number XXXI, "Motion." After skimming past the first three subcategories (animal progression, modes of going, and motions of the parts), which rather haphazardly encompassed everything from "swimming" to "ambling" to "yawning," I came to subcategory IV, purgation, where I found: "Those kinds of Actions whereby several animals do cast off such excremetitious parts as are offensive to nature." This was a seven-year-old boy's dream catalog of bodily function, and it bears reproducing in its entirety (see figure 6.1).

What a window on the past! How interesting to note that people once talked of "breaking wind upwards," or that you could just as well "neeze" as sneeze. How much less distant three hundred years ago seems when one realizes that then, too, people said "snot" and "puke." And there it was, not just "shiting," but a fascinating array of alternatives, which, being the scholar that I am (immaturity notwithstanding), sent me to the *Oxford English Dictionary* to look for origins and explanations.

"Muting," for example, is a special word for "bird poop." And "sir-reverence" used to mean "with all due respect" (from the Latin *salva reverentia*—"save [your] reverence"). People usually pull out "with all due respect" when they are about to drop some bad news, so I suppose the change of meaning came about after enough people, upon hearing the phrase, thought to themselves, "Oh, great. Here comes another pile of sir-reverence."

Once I had located my target concept in the tables, I could finally piece together the word for it:

category XXXI	subcategory IV	sub-subcategory 9	opposite
(Motion)	(purgation)	(from "gross" parts)	(of vomiting)
Ce	*p*	*yꝺ* (pronounced "uhw")	*s*

$$\Downarrow$$

Cepyꝺs

Cepuhws. A serous and watery purgative motion from the consistent and gross parts (from the guts downward). That's how you say "shit" in Wilkins's language. By the time I figured it out, I was too tired to giggle.

Knowing What
You Mean to Say

Even though Wilkins's universe was supposed to be a more organized, rational place than the one I was living in, I sometimes found it disorienting. Animals could be categorized according to the shapes of their heads, their eating preferences, or their general dispositions. I didn't really understand why emotions were classified as simple (hope) or mixed (shame), or why tactile sensations could be active (coldness) or passive (clamminess). Entertaining was a bodily action, but shitting was a motion—so was playing dice. While things as different as irony and semicolon were grouped together (under discourse > elements), things as similar as milk and butter were placed miles apart (milk with the other bodily fluids in "Parts, General," and butter with other foodstuffs in "Provisions").

There is an absurdity to Wilkins's categorization of the universe that was best highlighted in an article by Borges titled "The Analytical Language of John Wilkins":

> These ambiguities, redundancies and deficiencies remind us of those which doctor Franz Kuhn attributes to a certain Chinese encyclopedia entitled "Celestial Empire of benevolent Knowledge." In its remote pages it is written that the animals are divided into: (a) belonging to the emperor, (b) embalmed, (c) tame, (d) suckling pigs, (e) sirens, (f) fabulous, (g) stray dogs, (h) included in the present classification, (i) frenzied, (j) innumerable, (k) drawn with a very fine camelhair brush, (l) et cetera, (m) having just broken the water pitcher, (n) that from a long way off look like flies.

Borges's point is not to ridicule Wilkins's attempt to impose a pattern on the universe (he later concedes that Wilkins's is "not the least admirable of such patterns"), but to call attention to the hopelessness of all such attempts.

"It is clear," he says, "that there is no classification of the universe not being arbitrary and full of conjectures. The reason for this is very simple: we do not know what thing the universe is."

I thought it would be appropriate, in a slyly ironic way, to attempt a translation of these lines into Wilkins's language.

This translation was no simple matter. The sentiment expressed in these lines is quite correct. In Wilkins's tables I found arbitrariness and conjecture all around. He did not know (as we do not) what thing the universe is. But he took a heroic stab at it. Over the four days I worked on my translation, sly irony gave way to surprised admiration. As a language of its own, Wilkins's work was unusable, but as a study of meaning in English it was brilliant.

I started by looking up the word for "clear." Where, in the universe of ideas, might this one fall? What does "clear" mean, in the grand scheme of things? Well, lots of things. In the index I found over twenty-five options listed. Do you mean "not mingled with another"? Then see "simple." Do you mean "visible"? Then see "bright," "transparent," or "unspotted." Do you mean "as refers to men"? Then see "candid." Do you mean "not hindered from being passed through"? See "accessible" or "empty." Do you mean in the sense of "clear weather"? That would be El.VI.1 (elements > condition of the air > being transparent). "Not guilty"? That's RJ.II.6 (relations, judicial > concerning proceedings > decision regarding party's lack of transgression).

Near the end of the list I found the particular sense of "clear" that I was after: "not hindered from being known." This entry referred me to two possibilities, "plain" or "manifest."

So I turned to the entry for "plain." It referred me to many senses I could reject—"simple," "mean," "homely," "frank," "flatlands"—but two offerings seemed promising: "not obscure" and, once again, "manifest." I was hovering over the right meaning area now, re-spotting landmarks and getting oriented.

"Not obscure" was located in the tables at D.III.9 (discourse > complex grammatical notions > concerning the form or signification of words, with regard to their understandability). Figure 7.1 shows that section of the table (presented with the first eight sub-subcategories condensed).

Here, as in the table of bodily functions provided in chapter 6, words are followed by a list of synonyms. Wilkins considered synonymy to be one of the defects of natural language—a rational language should be free from redundancy; it should have one word for one meaning. A particular position in his table of concepts would be represented by a single word, and he intended all

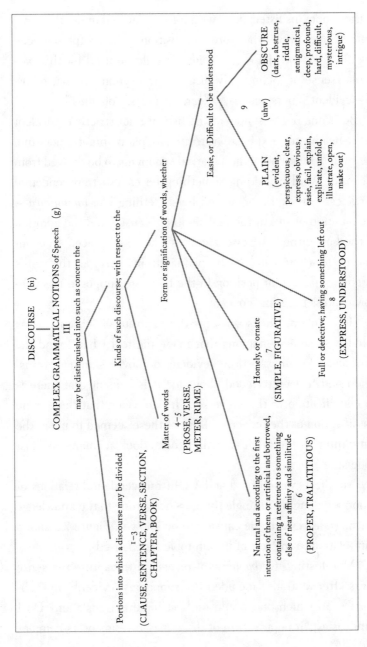

Figure 7.1: Category IV (Discourse), subcategory III—condensed

of the synonyms listed along with it to be covered under the same word. For example, the word for position 9, *bigy8* (pronounced "biguhw," D = *bi*, III = *g*, 9 = *uhw*) would be used for this particular sense of "plain," as well as for the synonyms that follow it—"evident," "perspicuous," "clear," "express," "obvious."

But some of the synonyms he lists are not strictly equivalent to the headword. "Explicate" is related to "plain," but it is not quite the same. He intended these partial synonyms to be derived from the basic word by adding something he called "transcendental particles." So "explicate" would be something like *bilguhwwa*—the addition of *-wa* at the end signifies "cause," and the addition of the *l* after the first vowel signifies "the active voice." To explicate is "to act to cause to be plain." In any case, all the words listed at a particular position in the table are supposed to somehow express the same concept.

Here, "plain," in its sense as the opposite of "obscure," was listed with some synonyms that made me feel I had found the right place. I could substitute "evident" or "obvious" into my translation and feel pretty good about it: "It is evident that there is no classification of the universe." "It is obvious that there is no classification of the universe." Both of these seemed to mean the same thing as the original. Still, I took a look at "manifest," just to be sure.

"Manifest" was located at TA.I.9 (transcendental relations of action > belonging to single things > pertaining to the knowledge of things, as regards the causing to be known). Figure 7.2 shows it in relation to the rest of its sub-table (condensed).

"Manifesting" (or *bebuhw*) also seemed to capture the sense I was after (and also included the synonyms "evident" and "obvious"). So which one would be best for this translation? Do I want to say, "It is [a feature of discourse in terms of its complex

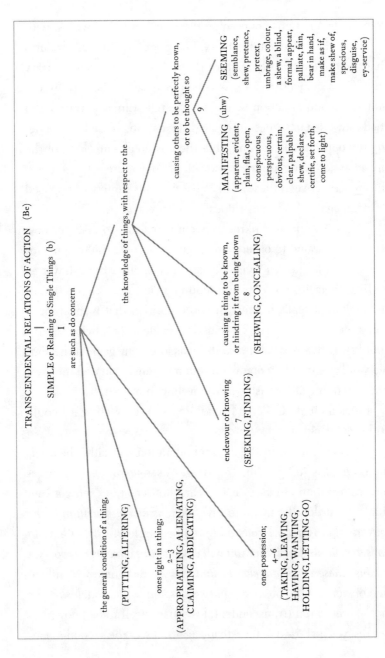

Figure 7.2: Category III (Transcendental Relations of Action), subcategory I—condensed

grammatical notions concerning the signification of words, with regard to their understandability, being the opposite of obscure] that there is no classification of the universe not being arbitrary and full of conjecture"? Or is it better to say, "It is [a transcendental relation of action belonging to single things pertaining to the knowledge of things, as regards the causing to be known, being the opposite of seeming] that there is no classification of the universe not being arbitrary and full of conjecture"? Is there any difference between these two? What was this sentence supposed to mean again? Wait, what does "clear" even mean?

To get it right in Wilkins's system is not just to discover how words correspond to other words, but to discover the true meaning of a word. The synonyms he lists are just other English words, with all their little defects and redundancies; it is the position in the table that really matters. It is the position that is meaning. I could see that "clear" corresponded to "evident" or "obvious," but I couldn't really say what it *meant*. I was losing my grip on the simple word "clear." Only one word into my translation and my solid understanding of English was unraveling in my hands.

I took a break. Called a friend. Reassured myself that I could still speak English.

Then I returned to the original quotation (actually, the *original* original is in Spanish, and Borges uses *notoriamente*, "notably," rather than *es claro*, "it is clear," but let's not even get into that). What does he mean to say? *There is no classification of the universe that is not arbitrary and full of conjecture. All you have to do is look around a bit and you will come to this conclusion too. Not because these words are easy to understand* (discourse > signification of words > not obscure), *but because this is the conclusion the facts reveal to you* (transcendental > causes itself to be known).

Yes, yes. I started to feel steady again. It was the second meaning, "manifest," that best captured the intention of "clear" in this case. I felt more than steady—satisfied, in fact. It was a particular kind of satisfaction, the kind you feel when you've finally wrangled control over a wide range of linguistic shade and nuance. It was a familiar feeling. Where did I know it from . . . ?

Then it hit me; I was using a thesaurus. Wilkins, without intending to, had invented the thesaurus.

I pulled down the old *Roget's* and turned to "clear." I perused the long list of senses, from "acquit" to "transparent" to "audible." Wilkins had covered them all.

Now I must make an admission. I have always used a thesaurus in the way that most people use one. You go to the alphabetical index, look up a word, find some synonyms, and pick the one that best expresses the sense you're going for. If you don't see something you like, you look at the little number next to the closest sense, turn to the numbered list, and find more alternatives to choose from. You make a choice, stick it in your sentence, and close the book until next time.

I never gave a thought to how the numbered list was organized. I never even thought about whether it *was* organized. But of course it has to be. The words near each other in this list are related in meaning. There must be some basis for considering them related.

That basis, it turns out, is a conceptual classification not all that different, in raw outline, from that proposed by Wilkins. My thesaurus, *Roget's International Fourth Edition*, groups words into eight major classes (physics and sensation were added, in later editions, to the six originally provided for by Roget):

abstract relations
space

physics
matter
sensation
intellect
volition
affections

Each of the major groups is further divided into sub- and sub-subcategories. There are ten kinds of abstract relations, three kinds of matter. "Beauty" is under affections. It is a personal affection, a discriminative one. "Truth" is under intellect. It is an intellectual faculty, a conformity to fact.

And guess where "shit" is? When I looked for this word in Wilkins's table, I had expected to find it grouped with corporeal actions, but was surprised to find it under motion instead (a purgatory motion, from the guts downward)—another example of Wilkins's charmingly arbitrary and absurd categorization scheme. In the thesaurus I thought it might be under organic matter, but instead I found it listed under class two > subclass IV > sub-subclass D > 311. Which is to say, space > motion > motion with reference to direction > excretion. Here, too, "shit" is classed under directional motion. Arbitrary? Yes. Absurd? Perhaps. But also—importantly—useful.

Usefulness is all the thesaurus demands of its classification system. It should be useful to someone who is trying to find a word. It should group words with other words in a way that will help a person locate the one that most accurately expresses a particular meaning.

But it does not need to explain that meaning. It assumes you already know it (when this assumption fails, a thesaurus can be a dangerous thing, as anyone who has ever graded a freshman essay can attest). The classification is useful, but not definitive. What you come away with at the end of a session with a thesaurus is not a meaning but a word, a plain old imprecise English word. It means whatever it means because, well, that's what English speakers generally use it to mean. At the end of the day, shit is not an excretory downward motion; shit is that thing we mean when we say "shit."

Wilkins's classification, on the other hand, *was* meant to be definitive. You use it to produce not an English word but a universal word. A word that bypasses messy human languages and gets right to the concept. Shit is not "shit" but *cepuhws*. And *cepuhws* is . . . Well, perhaps it's time for me to restore a little dignity to the discussion here.

This demand for conceptual precision makes Wilkins's language very hard to use. Before you can say anything, you have to know exactly what you mean to say. I never realized what an imprecise word "clear" was until I tried to translate it into Wilkins's concepts. I learned that what I meant to say was "manifest" (or rather *bebuhw*), and for that I give him credit. He did an impressive job of unpacking and analyzing the many senses of the words. But I couldn't imagine carrying on a conversation using these unpacked senses. If the word "clear" is imprecise, it is mercifully so. And not necessarily to the detriment of meaning. "It is clear that . . ." carries with it a bit of transparent glass, the bright ring of a bell, a sunny day, a candid conversation, an uncluttered table. *Bebuhw* has left these senses separately imprisoned in their own categories, and it seems the poorer for it.

My translation of the rest of the words proceeded along the same lines of my "clear" experience: muddled confusion punctuated by flashes of insight. A few words lent themselves to an easy translation ("universe"—"the compages or frame of the whole creation"), but most of them were as difficult as "clear." The more I worked on "arbitrary," "reason," and "simple," the more slippery and ungraspable they became.

Once I had decided where each word was placed in the tables, I had to figure out how to pronounce it. This should have been straightforward—each category, subcategory, and sub-subcategory provides a sound or syllable—and it would have been, if not for the addition of all sorts of complications. You have to add syllables or change letters depending on whether you want the noun or the adjective, and whether it's active, passive, plural, and so on. *Bebuhw,* for example, must be changed into *vebuhw* if you want the adjective "manifest" (rather than the verb "is manifesting").

Language, after all, is more than just a bag of words. The words have to be put together into sentences, and we need a way to keep track of what roles the words play in sentences—we need things like suffixes, prepositions, or word-order rules to tell us how the individual words are contributing to the big picture. Wilkins (unlike some of his modern successors) was quite aware of this, but his ideas on grammatical points like parts of speech don't exactly match current linguistic ideas, and he doesn't provide much explanation. All I had to go on in figuring out how to put words together (and put them into sentences) was the two example translations he provides—the Lord's Prayer and the Creed. These don't provide a very wide range of sentence types.

Latin was the model language for most ideas about grammar at the time, and some of Wilkins's translation betrays a Latin influence. For example, "forgive us our trespasses" becomes "forgive to us our trespasses" (to show that "forgive" takes the dative case, which English doesn't have). But in other ways his grammar is very English-like: He generally sticks to English word order. He uses the articles "a" and "the," and prepositions like "of" and "for," which you wouldn't find in a language like Latin. Sometimes he does things that look like neither English nor Latin. "Lead us not into temptation" becomes "not maist-thou-be leading [marked for adjective active] us into temptation ['trying' marked for 'corruptive' sense]," and "he shall come to judge the quick and the dead" becomes "he shall-be coming [marked for adjective active] for judging [marked for noun of action] the living persons and the having-died persons."

Well, I did the best I could. I hereby present you with, as far as I know, the first sentences to be written in Wilkins's language in over three hundred years:

> ya vebуδ ya mi valbα bagуs lα αl da mi ya cδαpуɪ na cδimbу lα cααthуδ. αl bαd lo i ya vαgуɪlα: ay mi cδαldo δδ baba αl da ya
>
> "ya vebuhw ya mi valba baguhs la al da mi ya cwapuhy na cwimbuh la caathuhw. al bad lo i ya vaguhyla: ay mi cwaldo oo baba al da ya"

Here is the word-by-word translation:

> is manifest is no existing catalog of the universe no is arbitrary and filled of conjectures. the reason for this is very-simple: we no knowing which thing the universe is.

And here is what this translation *means*:

> It is [a transcendental relation of action belonging to single things pertaining to the knowledge of things, as regards the causing to be known, being the opposite of seeming]

that there is no [mixed transcendental relation of discontinued quantity or number concerning the position of things numbered, denoting their order, belonging either to things or to words]

of the [compages or frame of the whole creation]

which is not [having the quality of a spiritual action of the will belonging to the affections of the will in itself in its actions, consisting in its having power of applying itself to the doing or not doing]

and [a completed action of operation of the mixed mechanical type of putting things nearer together or farther asunder, with reference to the capacity of fluid bodies such as are supposed to be contained in something]

of [spiritual actions of the understanding and judgment of the speculative type such as do concern the various exercise of our understanding about the truth and falsehood of things, with respect to secondary judging of the truth, found as to the consequence of it in respect of other things to be concluded from it, or to follow upon it].

The [general transcendental of that which in any way contributes to the producing of an effect]

for this is [augmentative transcendental of the opposite of mixture]

we do not [spiritual action of understanding concerning primary judgment of the special type proceeding from intrinsic causes]

what [transcendental, namely of those more universal and comprehensive terms which fall under discourse relating to those beings which are truly such, or those which our senses mistake for beings]

the [compages or frame of the whole creation]

is.

Got that?

Whether or not Wilkins's language could improve your ability to reason (and I have my doubts), it would certainly do little for your ability to communicate. What had seemed so exciting a possibility when presented in sketch form—a language of concepts rather than words!—turned out to be less exciting in its fully realized form. Wilkins's project effectively put an end to the era of the universal philosophical language. He produced something brilliant and valuable. As a study of English at a particular moment in time, it is remarkable. His work gave rise to the thesaurus, to new methods of library classification, and to the taxonomy of the natural world later perfected by Linnaeus. But as a language, it was simply unusable.

It seemed clear to me (manifestly so), as I emerged from my long weekend with *An Essay Towards a Real Character and a Philosophical Language*, that Wilkins had performed another valuable service in taking the philosophical language idea as far as it could go. He had shown that it was a ridiculous idea. And so the idea could be put to rest.

But, alas, it would not be. History forgets. The philosophical language idea persisted, and would from time to time plant itself in the minds of ambitious types who had never heard of Wilkins. The graveyard of invented languages is littered with their efforts.

But even those who had heard of Wilkins were not always deterred. They thought the idea was good, but Wilkins had just done it wrong. Leibniz thought that he could do it right, but he never figured out how. And 180 years after Wilkins's death, Roget, in the introduction to his thesaurus, expressed the hope that *his* classification scheme would lay the groundwork for a universal philosophical language. He was familiar with Wilkins's work, but declared it, in true thesaurus-writer fashion, to be "too abstruse and recondite for practical application."

I wondered if any of those who thought they could do better than Wilkins ever tried their hand at a "practical application" of his system. It is easy to take issue with his tables or his grammatical apparatus or his general view of the universe. You barely have to look at any of these things before you can find something to criticize. But if you sit down and make a sincere attempt to use the language, you discover the really important flaw, not in *his* language, but in the whole idea of a philosophical language: when you speak in concepts, it's too damn hard to say anything.

People find something very comforting about the notion that *words* are the problem, not concepts. When words fail us, we tend to blame the words. We've all experienced the frustration of not being able to say what we mean to say. When we struggle with language, we have the sensation that our clean, beautiful ideas remain trapped inside our heads. We accuse language of being too crude and clumsy to adequately express our thoughts. But perhaps we flatter ourselves.

Sometimes we do find the words to express an idea, and only then realize what a stupid idea it is. This experience would suggest that our thoughts are not as clean and beautiful as we would like to believe. Instead of blaming language for failing to capture our thoughts, maybe we should thank it for giving some shape to the muddle in our heads.

I'm no philosopher, and I am not qualified to make claims about whether thought is possible without language (although I think it is), or whether there may be other means than language by which we can give shape to the muddle (sure, why not?). I'm just saying that when it comes to expressing ourselves, we need some fuzzy edges, a chance to discover what we're trying to say even as we say it. We should be grateful to our sloppy, imperfect languages for giving us some wiggle room.

To be fair, Wilkins didn't assume our thoughts were as organized as his language. But he did assume there was a truth "out there" that his language could help us to see "by unmasking many wild errors, that shelter themselves under the disguise of affected phrases." His system would help us *learn* to think clearly. To know the word would be to know the thing. We would be able to see everything for what it was. And if we suspected something wasn't what it seemed, we could call it what it was—the serous and watery purgative motion (from the guts downward) of the consistent and gross parts of a male, hollow-horned, ruminant, cloven-footed beast.

The "language as mathematics" idea, as we will see, had a resurgence in the late 1950s, another era of science and computation. It would be used as a tool of inquiry and experiment, a way to discover how language might work, how our minds might work.

But the goals of the seventeenth-century language inventors went beyond that. They were after a cure for Babel. They wanted a real, working language that people could use. They neglected, however, to think much about usability.

Except for poor George Dalgarno. Remember him? The stubborn schoolmaster whose disagreements with Wilkins had resulted in the end of their collaboration? He wanted to keep the number of root words in his language to a minimum. He wanted them organized in verses that were easy to memorize. Wilkins pushed for philosophical perfection. Dalgarno pushed back for usability. They came to an impasse.

Dalgarno left Oxford for a few months to work alone. He returned to find that scholarly interest was now solely focused on

Wilkins's emerging project. His own work was ignored or undermined by accusations that he was plagiarizing from Wilkins. In his disappointment he resolved to "make haste to cast it lyke an abortive out of my hands."

But instead, "after bemoaning myself and my unfortunate labors I made all haste possible." He worked frantically, hoping to beat Wilkins to publication. In his anxiousness, his confidence faltered. He reorganized his root words, doing away with the mnemonic verses and replacing them with a hierarchical table of the type Wilkins had argued for. His list of root words grew. But he clung to his principles by presenting a method to aid memorization (a sort of word-association strategy that he doesn't elaborate on very much), and he was sure to emphasize that *he* did not provide root words for the enormous range of natural species (like he knew Wilkins would). He instead promoted his compounding strategy (for example, elephant = largest whole-footed beast; coal = mineral black fire).

Dalgarno managed to publish *Ars signorum* (The Art of Signs) in 1661, seven years before Wilkins's *Philosophical Language* came out. His rush to publication went unrewarded. The one detailed review he received mocks him for his poor skills in Latin, implies that his benefactors supported him only because they felt sorry for him, and concludes by using his own language to call him *nŋkpim sʊfa* (the greatest ass).

Because of Dalgarno's haste and his obvious discomfort with some of the Wilkins-influenced features he had decided to adopt, *Ars signorum* was, in fact, kind of a mess. And a great deal harder to figure out how to use than Wilkins's system ultimately was. But Dalgarno deserves credit for having been unique in at least thinking about the usability of his language in practical terms. The other language inventors of the time had their heads in the philosophical clouds. They assumed that if you got your theory of concepts right, the language would automatically be easy to learn and to use. Dalgarno, ever the teacher, gave a little more consideration to the poor soul at the other end of that assumption. And in doing so, he was a very early pioneer of the next major era in language invention.

LUDWIK ZAMENHOF AND THE LANGUAGE OF PEACE

En la komenco la Senkorpa Mistero kreis volapukon. Kaj Volapuko estis senforma kaj kaosa, kaj mallumo estis en ĝi. Kaj la Senkorpa Mistero diris: Estu lumo; kaj fariĝis Esperanto. Kaj la Spirito vidis Esperanton, ke ĝi estas bona; kaj la Spirito apartigis Esperanton de Volapuko. Kaj la Spirito nomis Esperanton Eterna Tago, kaj Volapukon nomis Nokto. Kaj estis vespero, kaj estis mateno—unu tago.

In the beginning the "Incorporeal Mystery" created Volapuk. And Volapuk was without form and chaotic, and darkness was within it. And the "Incorporeal Mystery" said: Let there be light; and he made Esperanto. And the Spirit saw Esperanto, that it was good: and the Spirit divided Esperanto from Volapuk. And the Spirit called Esperanto Eternal Day, and Volapuk he called Night. And it was evening, and it was morning—one day.

—From Izrael Lejzerowicz's satirical Esperanto *Verda Biblio*

1786	*Field of comparative philology begins*
1797	*Maimieux publishes* Pasigraphie
1815	*Nationalism on the rise in Europe*
1829	*Ruggles publishes* A Universal Language
1830s	*Sudre tours with Solresol*
1868	*Pirro's Universalglot*
1879	*Schleyer's Volapük*
1882	*Revival of Hebrew begins*
1887	*Zamenhof's Esperanto*
1905	*First international Esperanto congress*
1907	*Esperanto refomers propose Ido*
1914	*WWI begins*
1917	*Zamenhof dies*

A Linguistic
Handshake

By the time Wilkins, Dalgarno, and the rest of the intellectual circle of the philosophical language inventors were dead, French had become the international language of culture and diplomacy. Scientific academies in Berlin, St. Petersburg, and Turin adopted French as an official language. Treaties were drafted in French, even when neither party was a French-speaking nation. The elites of all European nations could conduct their business in French. Scientists and philosophers no longer focused their attention on creating a new universal language—they had one that worked well enough.

Language projects cropped up here and there, of course, especially after the work of Leibniz came into fashion among scholars in the 1760s. French was fine for communication purposes, but it was no perfect mathematical system. A couple of projects attempted to make French a bit more orderly, while others continued the tradition of starting from scratch with letters, numbers, and symbols in the quest for that perfect system. One of these, the Pasigraphie of Joseph de Maimieux, gained a bit of success—for a few years around 1800, it was taught in schools in France and Germany, and Napoleon was reported to have admired it. But probably only in theory. Had he actually tried to use it, his assessment may have been different. He would have found himself lost in a thicket of tables, sub-tables, columns, and lines, all serving to carve up the world of experience into arbitrary categories, all filled with odd-looking symbols that were hard to distinguish from each other.

Maimieux, like most language inventors at the beginning of the nineteenth century, was still using a method that was now old and tired and, after two hundred years, had never resulted in a language that people wanted to use. When he died in 1820, no doubt dismayed that his brief brush with success had remained so brief, he might have comforted himself with the thought that he had tried to do something that was simply impossible. If the establishment of an international network of teaching programs was not enough, if the endorsement of an emperor was not enough, then nothing was enough. No one would ever be able to get people to use an invented language.

But if he could have seen not even very far into the future, to the end of the nineteenth century, he would have been amazed. Not only would he have seen fierce new enthusiasm and optimism for the prospects of a universal language, he would have seen people, thousands of people, speaking to each other, writing to each other, and most of all arguing with each other in invented languages. The arguments were over which version of which language was the one best suited to be the universal language. Hundreds of projects and revisions of projects appeared during this time. In the end, none of them would become the universal language. But one of them, perhaps even more surprisingly, would become a living language.

Kim Henriksen is way cooler than you'd expect an accordion-playing Esperantist to be. Tall, lean, and muscular, with creative facial hair and a European-cowboy style, he looks younger than he is. In Esperantoland, he is something of a rock star. Through the 1980s, his band Amplifiki played international youth congresses all over Europe, releasing hits like "Tute ne gravas" (No Big Deal) and "Sola" (Alone). The band's name came from an old Esperanto dictionary word for "amplify," but a prurient mind might read it as *am-pli-fiki* (love-more-fucking). He later formed the Danish/Bosnian/Polish group Esperanto Desperado, which came out with party starters like "Ska-virino" (Ska Woman) and "La anaso kaj la simio" (The Duck and the Monkey). I wasn't prepared to encounter anyone like him when I set out on my first trip to Esperantoland.

"Esperantoland" sounds a lot sillier in English than it does in Esperanto. There is no land of Esperanto, of course, though not for lack of trying on the part of the Esperantists. In 1908 the tiny neutral state of Moresnet, the orphan of a border dispute between the Netherlands and Prussia, rose up to declare itself the first free Esperanto state of Amikejo (Friendship Place). More than 3 percent of the four thousand inhabitants had learned the language (a higher percentage of Esperanto speakers has never been achieved in any other country), and their flag, stamps, coins, and an anthem were ready to go. But in the increasingly tense and nationalistic atmosphere of prewar Europe, there was no place for a friendship place, and Esperanto never got its piece of terra firma. Instead, the proponents of Esperanto have made do with a virtual homeland. Esperantoland is located wherever people are speaking Esperanto. And contrary to what I had assumed, they really are speaking Esperanto.

The earthly setting of my first Esperanto experience was the MIT campus, the 2003 venue for the annual congress of the Esperanto League of North America. As I drove from New Jersey through hellish Fourth of July traffic toward Cambridge, the clearest mental picture of an Esperanto congress I could muster was five gray-haired radicals on folding chairs bantering about the Spanish civil war and their stamp collections. I imagined they would be speaking Esperanto, but not for everything. Surely, as soon as something worth saying came up, they would lapse back into English. Just in case, though, I studied up. I brought my dictionary and grammar book and practiced having the maturity not to giggle when I spoke the textbook phrase for "How are you?" or more specifically "How are you faring?" which is rendered as *"Kiel vi fartas?"*

More than eighty people turned up at the conference, and I can say that almost all of them spoke only Esperanto the entire weekend. Some were the retired teachers and spry socialist grandpas I was prepared for. Their emotional proselytizing about the noble ideals of "our dear language" clicked right into the Esperanto landscape I'd imagined. But there was no place in that landscape for Kim (known as Kimo in Esperantoland) and his 3:00 p.m. presentation on the importance of rock music in the history of Esperanto culture.

I really wanted to hear what he had to say on the subject, but I had a terrible time understanding him. Three obstacles hindered my full comprehension. One was my incomplete grasp of the language. I had studied Esperanto for only six weeks, by myself, from a book. I thought I was doing pretty well. I understood every word of the opening lecture on the future of the Esperanto movement. I held my own in conversations about topics ranging from the language imperialism of English to Esperanto haiku. In fact, I was doing so well that I started to enjoy meeting my fellow conference goers so I could chitchat about my meager Esperanto experience. "Oh, I started a month and a half ago, no teacher, just a book," I would toss off casually. If I really wanted a pat on the head, I'd add, "This is actually the first time I've ever heard it spoken."

I can be a bit of a show-off when it comes to facility with language. I have an aptitude for it that is probably much less impressive than that of the average European, but I've figured out how to work it to my full advantage by picking languages with high impact-to-proficiency ratios. Pretty good Hungarian gets you a lot more love in Budapest than perfect French buys you in Paris, and one well-placed word of Ibo to a Nigerian taxi driver can reward you with enough compliments to beat back the insecurities from all other parts of your life for a week. I wasn't expecting an ego boost from Esperanto. We are all speaking a second language here. Who's to impress? So when I heard, "Only six weeks? You're doing wonderfully!" I might have milked it a little. But I grew suspicious after four or five speeches about how we must do everything possible to encourage young people and keep them in the movement. A quick look around told me that I qualified as a young person (I was thirty-three at the time). The flattery may not have been inspired by my dazzling language skills.

The second obstacle to my full understanding of the role of rock music in Esperanto culture was Kimo's impenetrable Danish accent. In one sense Esperanto pronunciation is standardized (each letter stands for one sound, no confusing *c* or *gh*), but it allows for a lot of bleed around the edges; my *r* sound and a French person's *r* sound will be different. Usually, this isn't a problem. I've since heard and fully understood British, Belgian, Spanish, Russian, Swedish, and Chinese Esperanto. But Kimo's consonants were nearly unrecognizable. The Danes have a saying about their peculiar phonology: *"Danskerne taler med kartoffler i munden"* (The Danes speak with potatoes in their mouths). Even the expert Esperantists were having trouble. One of them generously took me aside and said, "Don't worry if you can't understand the Danish guy. I can't either."

My final obstacle to Kimo comprehension had to do with the important sense in which he differed from all the other speakers at the congress. They were fluent, but he was rapid-fire fluent. I couldn't keep up with him. He spoke like a native. But this was not as confounding as the fact that he spoke like a native because he was a native. I discovered this when Kimo's son, a nine-year-old with purple hair and a skateboard tucked under his arm, wandered into the room to ask his father a question. The woman in front of me asked the man next to her, "Is his son a native speaker, too?" "Yes, second-generation," he answered. "Wonderful, no?"

When I cornered Kimo later in the day to find out everything I could about his no-doubt totally weird and fascinating upbringing, he met my falling-over-myself excitement with a shrug. Born in Copenhagen to a Danish father and a Polish mother who met through Esperanto, he appeared not to appreciate how bizarre it was to be a native speaker of an invented language. Esperanto was the medium of his parents' relationship and of the entire home life of their family. Before you start getting indignant on his behalf, know that growing up he had plenty of contact with the world outside his home and learned to speak Danish as a native, too. But he considered Esperanto his true mother tongue.

For Kimo, Esperanto was a completely normal fact of life in the same way that Polish would have been if both of his parents had been Polish.

Kimo didn't choose to learn Esperanto, nor did his son, but everyone else at the conference did. Somewhere along the way they'd decided it worth their time to learn this utopian pipe-dream language, and I wanted to understand why. The stated reason in pamphlets and speeches and passionate letters to the editor is too abstract: "Esperanto is a 'linguistic handshake,' a neutral ground where people of different nations can communicate as equals." Nice idea, but people don't speak languages for abstract reasons. The Irish feel a strong emotional attachment to the once-persecuted language of their heritage, but despite mandatory school instruction they don't speak Irish. So goes the story of hundreds of attempts by political and cultural organizations to convince people to speak a language. And the fact that Esperanto is an invented language makes the notion that anyone would speak it even more unlikely. By the time Esperanto came along, a couple centuries' worth of invented languages had failed to attract more than a handful of speakers. None of them at any point had anywhere close to fifty thousand speakers, the most conservative estimate for Esperanto (the least conservative is two million)—much less any native speakers.

"Success" is probably not the first word that comes to mind when you think of Esperanto, but in the small, passionate world of invented languages there has never been a bigger one.

Un Nuov Glot

The nineteenth century saw a complete change in both the purposes and the methods of language invention. The change in method can be clearly seen in the following examples, the first from the first half of the century and the second from the second half:

1. *Dore mifala dosifare re dosiresi.*

2. *Men senior, I sende evos un grammatik e un verb-bibel de un nuov glot nomed universal glot.*

The second example, from Jean Pirro's Universalglot, published in 1868, can be understood by anyone with a passing familiarity with the general shape of European languages. It can be guessed at pretty successfully even if you only know English or French. But how to guess the meaning of the first example, from Solresol, developed by Jean François Sudre in the 1830s? Knowing what we know about the categorization principles employed by the language inventors of the seventeenth century, you might guess that the words beginning with *do-* all fall into the same meaning category. You would be partially correct. In Sudre's system all four-syllable words beginning with *dosi-* refer to a type of food or drink. The sentence above means, "I would like a beer and a pastry." The sentence *"Dore mifala dosiredo, dosifasi, dosifasol, dosirela, dosiremi, dosidosi, dosirefa, re dosifasol"* means "I would like milk, sugar, coffee, fruit, butter, eggs, cheese, and chocolate." Universalglot has a slightly ridiculous ring to it, but Solresol just sounds crazy.

It had something, however, that for a time made Sudre the toast of Paris—or at least of Brussels. It had a performable gimmick. The syllables of his language were taken from the seven notes of the musical scale—do, re, mi, fa, sol, la, si. His language could be sung, whistled, or played on a violin. When he invited the press to a demonstration of his Langue Musicale Universelle in 1833, they arrived to find not a lecture but a show—he played phrases on his violin while his students translated them into French. If the audience members weren't impressed, they were at least entertained. A year later, Sudre took his show on the road.

As his performances grew more elaborate, his fame grew. He would take phrases from the audience to translate into Solresol; he would perform translations not just with French but with multiple languages; he might even do a little singing. Since his language was fundamentally a method of translating phrases using seven units, there was no reason why he had to be limited to the seven units of the musical scale. He could translate using seven hand signals, seven knocks, the seven colors of the rainbow. In an especially impressive demonstration, he would blindfold himself and request that an audience member give one of his students a phrase to translate. The student would then silently approach Sudre, take his hand, and transmit the message by touch alone, using seven distinct locations on Sudre's fingers.

Sudre's performances earned him popular attention and praise. He filled large concert halls. He met the king and queen of England. Everyone knew his name.

However, hardly anyone knew his language. People liked the idea, but not enough to learn the system or, crucially, to fund his work. Solresol was generally regarded, to Sudre's great frustration, as an ingenious parlor trick.

As Sudre toured and struggled to make his mark, the world was changing in such a way that made the need for a universal language seem more pressing than ever. While the elites of previous eras had always had the opportunity to engage in international contact, industrialization was now bringing this opportunity to regular folks. The steamship, the locomotive, and the telegraph narrowed distances and expanded the range of communication situations a person might find himself in. Language barriers became that much more noticeable.

And schemes to overcome those barriers started to proliferate. But these schemes looked nothing like the old ones. *Babibu* and *123* and *doremi* gave way to *un nuov* kind of *glot*. The new crop of language inventors built upon the recognizable roots of European languages. They took a little Latin, a little Greek, spiced it up with some French and German and a splash of English. The resulting systems were much easier to learn than anything that had come before. You didn't have to know the whole order of the universe to be able to guess that *nuov* meant "new."

So why hadn't anyone thought to do it that way before?

The idea to create a language out of existing languages wasn't completely new. An Arabic-Persian-Turkish mix called Balaibalan was designed sometime between 1400 and 1700 (the documents can't be reliably dated), probably for religious purposes. Projects aiming to create a Pan-Slavic language (using common Slavic word roots) for the promotion of Slavic ethnic unity had occurred as early as 1666. A simplified version of Latin by someone called "Carpophorophilus" had been published in 1732, and in 1765 Joachim Faiguet, the treasurer of France, published a sketch for a simplified French in Diderot's *Encyclopédie*.

But the intellectual climate—the preoccupation with mathematical notation, the quest to discover the true nature of the universe—led most early language inventors away from existing languages. They were after a self-contained, perfectly ordered system, not a stitched-together hybrid. Natural languages had too many problems, so they had to start from scratch.

The next era of language inventors focused on a more practical problem: people who spoke different languages couldn't understand each other. Quotidian concerns pushed philosophical questions about meaning and concepts into the background. These new inventors also worked in a different intellectual climate, one where the similarities between natural languages had come to the foreground.

In 1786, Sir William Jones, in an address to the Royal Asiatic Society, suggested that Latin, Greek, and Sanskrit, and perhaps the Gothic, Celtic, and Persian languages as well, all developed from a common ancestor language, and the field of comparative philology was born. In the following decades, an explosion of scholarly activity confirmed Jones's suggestion. The development of scientific techniques of comparison made it possible to show how languages as different as Bengali and Lithuanian were related. Those arbitrary differences between languages turned out to be not so arbitrary or different after all. They had sprung from a common well.

These discoveries were not necessarily useful to the man set on inventing a universal language. It is one thing to be able to show that a complicated history of sound changes produced both the Hindi word *cakka* and the English word "wheel" from the same source (the hypothesized Proto-Indo-European word *kweklo*: *kweklo* > *cakra* > *cakka*; *kweklo* > *hweogol* > *wheel*), but to call a wheel a *kweklo* wouldn't do much to help Hindi or English speakers. The new language inventors weren't influenced so directly by the findings of the academic linguists.

They were, however, influenced by a general awareness of common word roots and their histories. In its nineteenth-century heyday, the field of comparative philology (as sadly obscure a relic as it sounds today) made its way into popular culture in a widespread fashion for historical dictionaries and armchair etymology. Any reasonably educated person could be expected to know a bit about how languages were related to each other. Philology was in the air, and budding language inventors started paying attention to what languages already had in common with one another.

One of the earliest inventors to turn toward natural languages was an American named James Ruggles. In the 1820s, he set out to create yet another Wilkins-type philosophical language but decided it was more practical to base his word roots on Latin rather than "the analysis of ideas." The Latin roots were already somewhat intrinsically connected to the concepts they represented, he argued, echoing a popular linguistic belief of the time, because the sounds of all languages at one point had their origin in nature.

I found Ruggles's book, *A Universal Language, Formed on Phil-*

osophical and Analogical Principles, published in 1829, at a library of pre-twentieth-century American history in Philadelphia. I was surprised to find in it a pretty complete grammar and an extensive dictionary. I had never seen this language mentioned in any bibliography or overview or list of invented languages. No one seemed to know about it. But Ruggles had been one of the first to take a step toward the more naturalistic style of language construction that would become popular fifty years later. However, he still had a foot firmly planted in the previous era.

To his Latin roots he added arbitrary letters representing a range of other functions. For example, the root *hom-*, "man," participates in the following words:

ROOT	ARTICLE	GENDER	CASE	
hom-	*p*	*e*	*n*	"the man"
hom-	*b*	*a*	*nk*	"O woman!"

Pretty much every kind of relation he can think of gets its own ending. There is a system for expressing degrees in adjectives. Here are a few of the twenty-four possibilities:

bon-h-in	positive	"good"
bon-zs-in	comparative	"better"
bon-zrms-in	saturative	"too good"
bon-zrmy-in	Nega-saturative	"not good enough"
bon-zrly-in	Nega-contra-proximative	"not somewhat bad"

At a certain point, the endings pile on to the point where the Latin roots stop doing you much good at all:

pretzpxn ljbztur frateriorpur
"the price of the book of the brother of mine"

Vadcbhinpixs bixgs timzdxrcd pluvzdur
"We can go out now without fear of rain."

Sings, pixrt kznhenpiots
"Ladies and Gentlemen, will ye sup with us?"

And then things just get crazy:

lxmsgevjltshevjlpshev
"179 degrees 59 minutes and 59 seconds of west longitude within one second of reaching 180 degrees west"

pintjltstehjlpstehzponpx
"It is fifteen minutes and fifteen seconds after one o'clock p.m."

Ruggles's move toward practicality did not go far enough. He was still enamored with the idea of systematic, combinatorial completeness, as were most language inventors of his time. But unlike most of his peers, he had a refreshing humility about the prospects for the success of his project. He begins his 1829 book with a dedication to the Congress of the United States in which he expresses the hope that even if they do not find his project "of sufficient weight to be entitled to your legislative notice," some of them, as individuals at least, might take an interest in looking it over. If they do, he continues, "your voices . . . will either approve or condemn; and should condemnation, which is not improbable, consign these pages to oblivion or contempt," he will console himself that his own lack of time, resources, and "abilities for so great an attempt" was the "cause of the unworthiness of the production."

Congress never did anything with Ruggles's submission, but he did get a letter from President John Quincy Adams, who said that his "opinion long since formed, unfavorable to *all* projects of this character has perhaps influenced that formed with regard to yours. From the examination, necessarily superficial, which I have been able to give it, I consider it creditable to your ingenuity." Not exactly a ringing endorsement, but still something to be proud of.

Meanwhile, Europe was transforming itself from a loose collection of kingdoms, principalities, and duchies into an angry cluster of nations. After the French Revolution and the Napoleonic Wars, people began to organize themselves around feelings of shared identity and culture (rather than loyalty to local landholders and monarchs) and fight for their interests. Their new political identities were formed not according to the various empires they lived under—Russian, Austro-Hungarian, Ottoman—but according to the languages they spoke. As revolutions broke out and tensions increased, language inventors found not only a new strategy for building the structures of their languages but a new reason for building them in the first place.

Trouble in
Volapükland

Ludwik Zamenhof, the inventor of Esperanto, was born in 1859 in the city of Bialystok, now part of Poland. I have a historical atlas of eastern Europe that includes a map of "ethnolinguistic distribution" during this time. On the left side is a smear of Polish orange, speckled with tiny purple dots of German. On the right is a dramatic swath of Russian pink. Snaking down the middle is an irregularly shaped confusion of multicolored stripes. Bialystok sits in the center of it. Zamenhof wrote that his city of birth

> marked the way for all my future goals. In Bialystok the population consisted of four different elements: Russians, Poles, Germans and Jews. Each of these elements spoke a separate language and had hostile relations with the other elements. In that city, more than

anywhere, a sensitive person might feel the heavy sadness of the diversity of languages and become convinced at every step that it is the only, or at least the primary force which divides the human family into enemy parts. I was brought up to be an idealist; I was taught that all men were brothers, while at the same time everything I saw in the street made me feel that men as such did not exist: only Russians, Poles, Germans, Jews and so forth. This always tormented my young soul, though many might laugh at such agony for the world in a child. Because at that time it seemed to me that adults had a sort of almighty power, I kept telling myself that when I was grown up I would certainly destroy this evil.

Zamenhof began to develop his new language in earnest during his teenage years, after his rapidly growing family (he was the eldest of nine) moved to Warsaw, where his father, Marcus, took a position as the official Jewish censor. The job involved vetting all Hebrew publications for any statements that could be construed as insulting to the tsar, an ambiguous task requiring Marcus to gauge the paranoia of a government that was already disinclined toward him and other Jews. He was a strict father, and the pressures of his new responsibilities sometimes made him cruel. Ludwik responded by becoming dutiful and well behaved.

The family spoke Russian and Yiddish at home, but Ludwik was familiar with Hebrew through his father (more as a scholarly language than as a religious one). Young Ludwik picked up Polish on the street and Latin, Greek, French, and German at school. His first attempts at inventing his own language didn't go well. He began by developing a lexicon of one-syllable words, like *ba* and *ka*, but found that he couldn't remember the meanings he'd assigned to them. He made things easier on his memory by substituting roots from languages he had studied—such as *hom* for "man" and *am* for "love." However, the universe of things that require a name is large, and as his notebooks filled with his neat and careful script, he again lost his ability to keep track of them. This was a problem he had to solve. A language intended for all mankind wouldn't work unless all mankind could learn it.

Ludwik's solution arose from an accidental insight:

> I noticed the formation of the (Russian) word *shveytsarskaya* (porter's lodge) which I had seen many times, and of the word *kondityerskaya* (confectioner's shop). This *-skaya* interested me and showed that suffixes provide the possibility of making from one word a number of others which don't have to be learned separately. This idea took complete possession of me. I began comparing words and looking for constant, definite relations among them, and every day I threw large series of words out of my dictionary and substituted for them a single suffix defining a certain relationship.

At about the same time, he began to study English in school. For a speaker of Russian, with its complex systems of verb conjugation and noun agreement, its accusative, genitive, locative, and other sundry cases, English must have appeared a dream of simplicity. He felt the freedom of gliding over ice-smooth paradigms— "I had, you had, he had, she had, we had, they had"—and purged his nascent language of unnecessary grammatical markers.

On December 17, 1878, a Proto-Esperanto congress convened. Despite his shyness, Ludwik had convinced some of his schoolmates to involve themselves in his project. They gathered in his cramped apartment to celebrate over cake and take part in that most Esperanto of activities—the singing of hymns. On this day they sang a poem by Ludwik that succinctly captures the sentiment that inspired his diligence:

Malamikete de las nacjes
Kadó, kadó, jam temp' està
La tot' homoze en familije konungiare so debà.

Enmity of nations
Fall, fall, the time has come
May the whole of humanity be united as one.

This poem is an example of early Esperanto. The language was further tweaked and modified when Ludwik was forced to reinvent it from scratch. Before he left for university to study medicine, a colleague of his father's had remarked that Ludwik seemed awfully wrapped up in this language of his. Fearing that it would distract the young man from his studies, Marcus demanded that he leave it behind. The compliant son handed over his lovingly filled notebooks, and some time after he set out for Moscow, his father threw them on the fire. Ludwik didn't discover this until he transferred home to the University of Warsaw. But he had no time to brood. Soon the enmity of nations bubbled up into a wave of violent pogroms that swept through Russia, including a two-day spree of bloodshed in Warsaw. More determined than ever, he started all over again.

In the next five years he finished his education and began his practice as an oculist, general medicine having proved to induce debilitating guilt when he couldn't do anything to help a patient. He continued revising and refining his language, and he met his future wife, Klara. She embraced him and his language, and they used it to write love letters to each other.

The official birth of Esperanto occurred in 1887, the year that Zamenhof, using Klara's dowry, self-published a small book titled *Lingvo internacia*. He modestly declined to attach his own name to it, signing it instead Dr. Esperanto, meaning "one who hopes." He explained inside that an "international language, like every national one, is the property of society, and the author renounces all personal rights in it for ever." Ludwik and Klara packaged the books and sent them into an unsympathetic world.

Nothing says success like bitter, angry jealousy in the hearts of your competitors. In this case, the names read like the product of the perverted etymological strategies of the modern-day pharmaceutical industry: Interlingua, Ido, Glosa, Globaqo, Novial, Hom-Idyomo. These are just a few of the many languages proclaimed by their advocates to be simpler, more logical, and more beautiful than Esperanto. But Esperanto can afford to be smug. It's the only one you've heard of.

And this drives the other guys nuts. When I first became curious about the topic of constructed languages, I joined a Listserv called Conlang. The next day my in-box held 287 messages. After a few days of this, I decided I wasn't that interested and unsubscribed. I didn't know that I'd innocently stepped right into the "flame war" that ultimately led to the "great split," after which things calmed down considerably.

The split was between two groups. The first was composed of people interested in quietly developing and discussing the languages they crafted for science-fictional worlds, what-if-a-language-did-this playfulness, or Tolkienesque fun (the true conlangers). The second was composed of those who wanted to talk about an international auxiliary language for the real world (the auxlangers). The auxlang group included a few devoted Esperantists and a larger number of supporters of alternate projects. Most of the war was conducted within the auxlang group, as vitriol hurled at Esperanto for its "totally ridiculous spelling system," "the backward and confusing affix system," and "the accusative -n abomination." Additional fighting took place between the various Esperanto competitors—Ido took on Interlingua, and a new version of Novial took on an old version of Novial. The conlangers got fed up with "this stupid argument about something that is never, NEVER, going to happen anyway, FACE IT!!!" and the auxlangers, no doubt tired of being called "deluded lunatics" in the one place it was supposed to be safe to talk about invented languages, agreed to split off and form their own list. The conlangers went back to tame exchanges about tense-aspect marking and vowel harmony, and the auxlangers took it outside.

Every anti-Esperantist auxlanger is convinced that he (no need to fret about gender-neutral pronouns on this one) represents a superior product. Perhaps one of them does. Perhaps all of them do. It doesn't matter. At an Esperanto conference, I witnessed a tired-looking man in a gray T-shirt defiantly introduce himself as an Interlingua supporter. "I think it is a better language," he announced. "It's clearer, more logical, and more beautiful than Esperanto," and then, without the slightest trace of irony, "but I have no one to speak it with."

Esperanto may never have risen to its position of prominence if it hadn't suffered its own great split early on. In the lore of Esperantoland, it is called the Schism, and if this makes you think of religious wars, you aren't far off. The Schism served to draw off the people who were interested in the language itself (the prestigious scholars with linguistically sophisticated suggestions for improving and perfecting it) from the people who were interested in the idea behind the language (the idealistic true believers, or, depending on whom you ask, the kooks).

Zamenhof was an amateur. He had no training in philology, no university chair. But because he was driven by the serious (if naive) hope that his language would help society, he devoted his energy to persuading people to use it rather than convincing them to appreciate its design. His book had included a form for the reader to sign, agreeing to learn the language if ten million others also signed the form. Fewer than a thousand came back, but enough interest had been generated to inspire him to translate the original Russian text into Polish, French, and German. He left the English translation to a well-meaning German volunteer, who produced choice manglings such as "The reader will doubtless take with mistrust this opuscule in hand, deeming that he has it here to do with some irrealizable utopy." Before its chances were completely killed in the English-speaking world, an Irish linguist took interest and produced a more readable translation.

The book laid out a grammar of sixteen rules and a lexicon of about nine hundred words. Though the lexicon has grown considerably since then, the basic structure of the language has remained essentially unchanged to this day. Words are formed from roots and affixes. Nouns end in -o, adjectives in -a, adverbs in -e:

frat-o	brother
frat-a	brotherly
ver-o	truth
ver-a	true
ver-e	truly

The verb endings differ with tense:

far-i	to do
mi far-as	I do
mi far-is	I did
mi far-os	I will do

Other endings modify the meaning in different ways. The feminine is formed with *-in*, diminutives with *-et*:

frat-in-o	sister
frat-in-et-o	little sister

The Russian *-skaya* (place for) that had inspired Zamenhof to build words through affixation became *-ej* (pronounced "ey"):

kuir-i	to cook
kuir-ej-o	kitchen
preĝ-i	to pray (ĝ is pronounced as *j* in "jar")
preĝ-ej-o	church

The opposite sense of a word can be formed by prefixing *mal-*:

bon-a	good	*mal-bon-a*	bad
estim-i	to respect	*mal-estim-i*	to despise

These, among other affixes, extend the range of the relatively small vocabulary of roots provided in the book. The affixes never change their form, so they are always recognizable. You can always at least tell whether a word is a noun or an adjective, whether a verb is past or present tense. The roots never change their form when they join to an affix, so you can always find them in the dictionary. This is not the way most languages work. Zamenhof gives an example from German, with the translation you would get if you looked it up word for word in a dictionary:

Ich	weiss	nicht	wo	ich	den	Stock	gelassen
I	white	not	where	I	—	stick	dispassionate

habe;	haben	Sie		ihn	nicht	gesehen?
property	to have	she/they/you	—	—	not	—

The second word, *weiss*, can be an adjective meaning "white," but here it is the first-person-present form of the verb *wissen*—"to know." *Gelassen* is an adjective meaning "dispassionate," but also, as in this sentence, the past participle of *lassen*, "to leave." *Habe* can be "property" or the first-person-present form of *haben*, "to have." *Den* is a special form of *der* (the), and *ihn* is a special form of *er* (he, it). You need a lot of special knowledge about German to get this translation right.

But for the Esperanto version, you don't need special knowledge, just the meaning of each piece:

Mi	ne	sci-as	kie	mi	las-is	la
I	no	know-present	where	I	leave-past	the

baston-o-n;	ĉu	vi	ĝi-n	ne	vid-is?
stick-noun-(object)	(question)	you	it-(object)	no	see-past

"I don't know where I left the stick; have you not seen it?"

Zamenhof doesn't spend much time explaining the rules of word formation. The lost-stick sentence is the only example for which he provides a translation. He provides other demonstration texts without translation, expecting that the reader will be able to puzzle them out and learn by example. He wanted to show that it was possible to begin using the language with barely any explicit study. He suggested that people test the language by writing to a friend in a foreign land, enclosing a small leaflet with the translations of a few roots and affixes, and leaving it up to the recipient to make sense of it. One of his demonstration texts is an example of such a letter. Give it a try.

> *Kar-a amik-o!*
>
> *Mi present-as al mi✱ kia-n vizaĝ-o-n vi far-os post la ricev-o de mi-a leter-o. Vi rigard-os la sub-skrib-o-n kaj ek-kri-os: "Ĉu li perd-is la saĝ-o-n? Je kia lingv-o li skrib-is? Kio-n signif-as la foli-et-o, kiu-n li aldon-is al si-a leter-o?" Trankvil-iĝ-u, mi-a kar-a! Mi-a saĝ-o, kiel mi almenaŭ kred-as, est-as tut-e en ordo.*

al—to	*kaj*—and	*saĝ-*—wise	*don-*—give	*kiel*—as
kia—what kind	*ek-*—out	*je*—in	*si*—self	*almenaŭ*—at least
vizaĝ-—face	*li*—he	*kio*—what	*iĝ-*—cause	
far-—to make	*perd-*—lose	*kiu*—which	*-u*—imperative	

✱Mi present-as al mi (I present to myself) is the way "I imagine" is expressed in languages like German and Russian.

The translation:

> Dear Friend,
>
> I can only imagine what kind of face you will make after receiving my letter. You will look at the signature and cry out, "Has he lost his mind? In what language did he write? What's the meaning of this leaflet that is added to the letter?" Calm down, my dear. My senses, at least as far as I believe, are all in order.

The translation shows that Zamenhof understood what kind of reaction this little experiment was likely to provoke. However, once the recipient had translated this far, another kind of reaction often set in. If you just tried the translation yourself, perhaps you know what I'm talking about. Are you a secret lover of sentence diagramming? A crossword puzzle aficionado? Have you ever read the dictionary for pleasure? Yeah, you know what I'm talking about. If you are a certain type of language-interested person, decoding an Esperanto letter can be an enjoyable little challenge. Much more enjoyable than reading a screed about the language's virtues.

The letter-writing test helped the language to spread. Small clubs of enthusiasts formed. Zamenhof came out with another textbook, a dictionary, and a translation of *Hamlet*, bringing into the world yet another rendering of the melancholy Dane's soliloquy on existence: "*Ĉu esti aŭ ne esti,—tiel staras nun la demando.*" The first Esperanto magazine, *La Esperantisto*, was published in 1889 in Germany. The movement attracted some prominent supporters, including Tolstoy, who wrote an essay for *La Esperantisto* on "the value of reason in solving religious problems." When this resulted in a ban of the magazine in Russia, Tolstoy wrote to the authorities, promising not to contribute anything else to it. His plea couldn't prevent the magazine's downfall, but others were already rising to take its place.

Meanwhile, there was trouble in Volapükland. Volapük was the project of a German priest named Johann Schleyer, who got the idea to create a universal language directly from God during one sleepless night in 1879.

His system had great success in Germany and soon spread as far as the United States and China. By the end of the 1880s there were over two hundred Volapük societies and clubs in the world and twenty-five Volapük journals. Even people who didn't care to learn it at least knew about it. President Grover Cleveland's wife named her dog Volapük. The craze was big enough to be mocked in local papers such as the *Milwaukee Sentinel*:

A charming young student of Grük
Once tried to acquire Volapük
  But it sounded so bad
  That her friends called her mad,
And she quit it in less than a wük.

Within a few years, most of the Volapükists had switched to Esperanto.

Those umlauts, the focus of many a Volapük lampoon, no doubt cost Schleyer a good number of English- and French-speaking customers. Not only did they add a threatening air of foreignness to the appearance of a Volapük text (*"If ätävol-la in Yulop, äliladol-la pükik mödis"*—"If you should travel in Europe you will hear many languages"); they also helped disguise the fact that Volapük was for the most part based on English roots. *Pük* (language), for example, comes from "speak," but it's hard to tell. It's likewise hard to see the "love" in *löf*, the "smile" in *smül*, the "proof" in *blöf*, or the "explaining" in *seplänön*. The problem went beyond umlauts, though. Schleyer, in trying to adhere to his principles of easy pronunciation (no "th" sound, minimal use of *r*, one-syllable roots), turned "friend" into *flen*, "knowledge" into *nol*, and "world" into *vol*. (The word *volapük* is a compound meaning "world language.")

And for the childish mind the temptations of Volapük are great. If you think the word *pük* is funny, then you will love how it figures into all kinds of other words related to the concept of language:

mother tongue	*motapük*
sentence	*püked*
polyglot	*möpüked*
to speak	*pükön*

Because I have one of those childish minds, I can't help throwing in another example here. "To succeed"? *Plöpön*.

Like Esperanto, Volapük had a system of affixes that extended the meaning of a root in a regular way, but when the prefixes and suffixes piled up on the poor little roots, the roots became even harder to pick out.

Despite all this, people were using it. In 1889, the year *La Esperantisto* was first published, the third international Volapük congress was held in Paris, and the proceedings were entirely in Volapük. The language worked well enough.

The downfall of Volapük lay elsewhere. Some of the Volapükists, dissatisfied with this or that detail of the language, began to petition Schleyer to make changes. He adamantly refused, and when the members of the recently formed Volapük Academy proposed reforms and then denied Schleyer the right to veto them, he left in a huff to form his own academy. The reformists, each with his own idea of how to proceed, published their own colorfully named modifications of Volapük—Nal Bino, Balta, Bopal, Spelin, Dil, Orba—and pretty soon a person who wanted to learn Volapük had no idea which version was worth his or her time. Esperanto, with its growing numbers, started to seem like a better investment. The fourth Volapük conference never happened.

In 1905, 688 people from twenty countries convened in Boulogne-sur-Mer, France, for the first international Esperanto congress. They wore the symbol of Esperanto, a green five-pointed star, and so were able to identify each other upon arrival at Paris train stations, where they gathered into conspicuous, animated groups for the trip to the coast. Until then, Esperanto had primarily been a tool of written correspondence. Many of them were speaking it for the first time, excited to see it actually working. A reporter from the *New York Herald* noted that "all appeared to converse with great facility."

As a gesture of respect to the host country, the congress opened with a polite singing (in French) of the distinctly un-Esperanto-like call to violence of "La Marseillaise." ("To arms, O citizens! / Form up in serried ranks! / March on, march on, / May their impure blood / Flow in our fields!") An energetic, tearful singing of the Esperanto anthem, "La espero," followed ("On the foundation of a neutral language / people understanding each other / will agree to form one great family circle"), and then, after greetings from the mayor and the president of the chamber of commerce, Zamenhof took the stage to wild cheers and applause. He spoke of invisible, powerful spirits in the air and images of a new future, and he ended with a prayer to a "powerful, incarnate mystery" that "peace be restored to the children of mankind." The audience stood, waving handkerchiefs and shouting, "*Vivu Zamenhof! Vivu Esperanto!*"

Not everyone was pleased. Some of the intellectual French Esperantists, who had reviewed Zamenhof's speech prior to the congress, had urged him to focus on the practical side of the language, its utility in travel and commerce, its potential in the sharing of scientific knowledge. Sentimental and religious overtones would make their cause look foolish, they argued. They wanted to be taken seriously.

They were also becoming restless about language reforms they thought were necessary. Unlike Schleyer, Zamenhof did not declare his language his own property, but the property of its users. Zamenhof had welcomed critiques in the beginning, and he even published a reformed version of Esperanto, incorporating the requested changes, in 1894. But this new version was rejected, in a vote, by the growing community of committed Esperantists who were already using the language as it was. They had been inspired by his message of universal peace, and they saw the requests for changes as disrespectful heresy. The lesson of Volapük had also been learned by many of them—once you start with the reforms, it's hard to stop. From then on, Zamenhof refused to impose changes, even, in 1906, when some reformists offered him 250,000 francs to do so.

That same year, when Zamenhof addressed the second international Esperanto congress in Geneva, he angrily rejected the calls to divorce Esperanto from its ideals, saying, "We want nothing to do with that Esperanto which must serve only commercial ends and practical utility!" The Schism came in 1907, when a delegation of prestigious university professors, including one chemist who would later win the Nobel Prize, chose to back an anonymously submitted proposal for a revised version of Esperanto called Ido (Offspring). While many of the prominent, well-educated, and practical-minded Esperantists joined the Ido faction, the rest rallied around their betrayed hero. More than thirteen hundred unashamed idealists from forty countries showed up at the 1908 congress in Dresden. They wore green stars and waved green flags, attended Esperanto poetry readings and theatrical performances, sang hymns, and by all accounts had a grand time.

The Idists, meanwhile, focused on the much less enjoyable pursuits of being logical and respectable. The official slogan of the first international Ido congress was "We have come here to work, not to amuse ourselves." But the congress didn't occur until 1921, by which time most of Ido's momentum had been sapped by infighting about further reforms. Most of the original supporters had by then left to work on their own language projects, which they deemed superior.

A Nudist, a Gay Ornithologist, a Railroad Enthusiast, and a Punk Cannabis Smoker Walk into a Bar . . .

Esperantists today have it rough outside of Esperantoland. No matter how elegant their arguments, how calm and reasoned their defenses of the *internacia lingvo*, they are inevitably met with one of two responses: dismissive humor or sneering disgust. Here is a gentle example of the former, as meted out by the *Times Higher Education Supplement*:

> The hunt for outstandingly obscure journals has upset readers conversant in Esperanto. A number contacted us after the Australian publication *Esperanto sub la suda kruco* was nominated, informing us that the journal was neither academic nor, in their opinion, obscure. Jacob Schwartz, a student at the Massachusetts Institute of Technology, explained: "I hope you can understand why speakers of Esperanto, who battle against this daily ridicule

from misinformed people, would be offended to be considered 'obscure.' "

We would like to apologise to readers of *Esperanto sub la suda kruco*, and we await complaints from infuriated subscribers to *The Journal of Fish Sausage* with anticipation.

There is no possible way you could respond to this that would result in your being taken seriously. Often, the hopeful Esperantist doesn't realize he's doomed at this point and tries to make his case: "Well, look now, Esperanto is spoken by people in more than eighty different countries. It has a rich original literature of more than forty thousand works. It is easy to learn." His listeners' eyes glaze over as they mentally sort him into their nonsensical-people pile.

At least dismissive humor is not mean. Another frequent reaction to the idea of Esperanto is anger, especially from people who care about language. On an ask-a-linguist Internet message board, a place where laypeople can have their questions about language answered by a panel of professional linguists, one of these professionals responded to an innocent question about whether Esperanto can be a native language, writing: "I will not try to conceal my contempt for the basket cases who teach their unfortunate children Esperanto." Contempt? As far as I know, those children grow up to be slightly eccentric but well-adjusted musicians, not serial killers.

Still, it is not hard to understand why so many people find Esperanto so repellent. Language is not just a handy tool for packing up our thoughts and sending them along to others. It's an index to a set of experiences both shared and extremely personal. More than any other expression of our culture, it is the way we do things—the way we complain, argue, comfort others. We love our languages for this. They are the repositories of our very identities. Compared with them, Esperanto is an insult. It asks us to turn away from what makes our languages personal and unique and choose one that is generic and universal. It asks us to give up what distinguishes us from the rest of the world for something that makes everyone in the world the same. It's a threat to beauty: neutral, antiseptic, soulless. A Mao jacket. A concrete apartment block.*

Strange, then, that I don't think I've ever been anywhere more colorful than Esperantoland. On my second trip there, the sixth All-Americas congress in Havana, I was exposed to so much culture that I started to get a headache. We sang "Guantanamera" in Esperanto on ten separate occasions in ten different Cuban musical styles. At the Arta Vespero (Evening of the Arts)—a staple of Esperanto congresses where delegates from the host country get to strut their stuff—we watched a three-hour extravaganza of every performable art Cuba has to offer, from traditional dances by little girls in white dresses to rumba rap music. For the finale we made a hundred-meter conga line, weaving our way through the Museum of the Revolution. At another staple, the Nacia Vespero (Evening of Nations), attendees from twenty other countries took the stage. A contingent of Mexicans sang folk songs, a Costa Rican played the piano, a Frenchman did a comedy routine about escargots. No, Esperantists don't want to take away your unique identity. On the contrary, they can't get enough of it. They just want you to express it in Esperanto so that everyone can appreciate it.

But this doesn't mean Esperanto has an identity of its own. Isn't it just a soulless translation machine laid on top of this cultural mutual-appreciation society? If it is, then why did I so frequently think to myself, "God, that is sooo Esperantoland!"?

I started to notice ways of speaking that were hard to translate out of Esperanto. For example, to say *"La ĉielo estas blua"* (The sky is blue) is a perfectly understandable, functional way to communicate, but to say *"La ĉielo bluas"* (The sky is bluing)—taking advantage of the feature that lets any word root be made into a verb—now that is Esperanto. People also love to use the word *etoso* to describe the feeling in the air at events. "At my first congress in Toronto I experienced such a *bona etoso*" or "I met some Esperantists in Bulgaria, and we spent the evening chatting and playing music. What *bela etoso!*" The dictionary will tell you that *etoso* means "ethos" or "atmosphere," but it will not tell you that it connotes a sort of mystical, positive, Zamenhofian vibe. For the newcomer, dictionary in hand, this word will be interpretable and clear, but for the seasoned Esperantist it will evoke a history of gatherings where the spirit of the Esperanto ideal brought everyone a little closer together.

While there are many words that reflect nuances of the Esperanto experience not captured by their dictionary definitions, there are some words that make sense only within the context of Esperantoland. *Krokodili* (to crocodile) means to speak in your national language at an event where you should be speaking Esperanto (conjuring up the image of a reptilian beast flapping its big jaws). This behavior is frowned upon, and it is convenient to have it summed up in a word, so that saying, "Hey, stop crocodiling!" is enough to discourage it. The offending party may be an *eterna komencanto* (eternal beginner)—the name for that fellow who's been showing up to congresses for years but still can't speak the language. People may also quietly complain to each other about some *verda papo* (green pope), a guy who's always preaching and droning on about the ideals of Esperanto. He is a figure not unlike the Jewish mother—annoying at times, but ya gotta love him.

Because he is one of us. He is part of what makes us us. In other words, it's an Esperanto thing. You wouldn't understand.

A few months after I returned from the Havana congress, I was watching the news and a personal-interest segment about dog yoga came on. The footage showed attractive New Yorkers in expensive workout clothes doing yoga with their dogs (or rather, around and over their dogs). The attitude conveyed by the newscasters wasn't so much "How insane!" as "How cute!" I suddenly found myself yelling at the television, "What kind of world do we live in that has room for dog yoga but not for Esperanto!" My husband turned to me and raised his eyebrows in a way that precisely expressed, "Uh-oh. I think you're crossing over, dear."

No, no, I reassured him. No need to fear a lifetime of vacations spent in foreign auditoriums listening to an endless parade of speeches and comments on those speeches. The consciously egalitarian nature of Esperantoland means that everyone gets a chance to take the floor, as many times as desired. The two most commonly spoken phrases in Esperanto must be "*Mi opinias . . .*" (In my opinion . . .) and "*Mi proponas . . .*" (I propose . . .). Sitting through this can be funny, but it's not much fun. I've always hated meetings, and the Esperanto ones kind of perfectly embody many of the reasons why.

Of course there's more to it than the meetings. There are the sing-alongs and the camping trips and the green-themed Esperanto fashion shows. All of these also not really my thing. However, the youth congresses, which are often sex-booze-and-rock-and-roll debauches (of the friendly, international variety, of course), might have been my thing once upon a postcollege time.

And, if I were still entranced by the backpacking-through-

Europe idea (many Esperantists never leave this phase), *not* being an Esperantist would be almost stupid. The international youth organization maintains a list of Esperantists all over the world who are willing to put up other Esperantists in their homes, feed them, and show them around. You can stay with a painter in Tajikistan, a nudist in Serbia, or a "gay, vegetarian ornithologist" in Belgium. You might like to stay with an "anarchist who likes to go out to bars" in Brazil or a father of five and founder of the "club of light and peace" in Mozambique. On the west coast of Japan you will find "physicists and railroad lovers especially welcome." A "sports journalist" in Budapest requests, "No hippies, please," but if that excludes you, you can move on to a small town in Sicily where "rawfoodists and hippies are especially welcome." Or, if that sounds a little too tame, head to Ukraine, where hosting is provided "only for hippies, punks, freaks, and cannabis smokers."

Esperantists like to point to this international hosting service as a challenge to those who say Esperanto confers no practical advantages. "See? Here's a solid, utilitarian reason to learn Esperanto. English is not the only language that pays off in concrete benefits." But when it comes to concrete benefits, Esperantists do not help their cause by mentioning English.

Claude Piron, a Swiss psychologist and prominent "prestige" Esperantist, emphasizes a different kind of benefit that Esperanto has over English:

> A Swede who speaks English with a Korean and a Brazilian feels that he is a Swede who is using English; he does not assume a special identity as "a speaker of English." On the other hand, a Swede who speaks Esperanto with a Korean and a Brazilian feels that he is an Esperantist and that the other two are also Esperantists, and that

the three of them belong to a special cultural group. Even if non-native-speakers speak English very well, they do not feel that this ability bestows an Anglo-Saxon identity on them. But with Esperanto something quite different occurs.

Can the thing that Esperantists share with each other really be called a culture? Professional anthropologists might be insulted by the question. All I know is that if you told me you just saw a nudist, a gay ornithologist, a railroad enthusiast, and a punk cannabis smoker walking down the street together, I would be waiting for the punch line. But if you then told me they were speaking Esperanto, no punch line would be necessary. It would all make complete and utter sense.

At the beginning of the twentieth century, while the proponents of Ido, Ulla, Ilo, Auli, Ile, Ispirantu, Espido, Esperido, Mundelingva, Mondlingvo, Mondlingu, Europal, Europeo, Uropa, Perfektsprache, Simplo, Geoglot, and the rest of Esperanto's competitors were advertising the potential practical roles for their languages—science, commerce, diplomacy, and so on—Esperantists were busy creating not a potential but an actual role for their language. While projects like Anglo-Franca, published around the same time as Zamenhof's first book, were presented through examples like *"Me have the honneur to soumett to you's inspection the prospectus of me's objets manufactured, which me to you envoy here-inclued,"* Zamenhof's book presented Esperanto through poetry and personal letters. Then came the congresses and their associated rituals, the green stars, the hymns, the excursions. Everything that happened at these congresses became loaded with Esperanto-conscious significance. The most routine protocols—the types of things you would have seen at any meeting of an international association during that time—over the years solidified into Esperanto orthodoxy. Because of this, the congresses of today have a distinctly Victorian flavor, from the reading of the greetings ("The Esperanto teachers club of Halifax sends its heartfelt greetings and congratulations on the occasion of the twentieth congress"), to the formal ceremonies (in Havana I attended the "solemn" presentation of the special-issue Zamenhof phone card), to the closing of the congress (with the symbolic flag-passing ceremony from the current year's host to the next year's).

The Esperantists worked to create a community and a culture. Yes, they did this somewhat artificially and self-consciously, but it did work (forced tradition + time = real tradition), and it turned out that many people who may not have been inspired to learn a language in order to *use* it for something would learn a language in order to *participate* in something.

Nowhere is this more evident than in the case of Modern Hebrew, or, as some call it, the miracle of Modern Hebrew. Technically, Hebrew is not an invented language. There was no Zamenhof of Hebrew to sit down and draft its rules and vocabulary. But there was an Eliezer Ben-Yehuda, who, as one biographer put it, "made it possible for several million people to order groceries, drive cattle, make love, and curse out their neighbors in a language which until his day had been fit only for Talmudic argument and prayer."

By about A.D. 200, Hebrew had died as a spoken language. It survived as a liturgical language and as a written language for philosophy, poetry, and other elite intellectual pursuits. In 1881, when Ben-Yehuda and his wife, Devora, immigrated to Palestine from Europe, Hebrew also served as a sort of lingua franca of the marketplace for Jews from various language backgrounds, but it was nobody's mother tongue. In 1882, when Ben-Yehuda's first child was born, he declared that his household would be Hebrew speaking only, and thus raised the first native Hebrew speaker in over a thousand years. His friends thought the child was sure to be damaged by the experiment. His neighbors thought he was crazy. But three generations later their own great-grandchildren would be living their lives in Hebrew—at home, at school, at the beach, and in the sandwich shops.

Ben-Yehuda and Zamenhof grew up at the same time under similar circumstances (Ben-Yehuda in Russian-ruled Lithuania, and Zamenhof in Russian-ruled Poland). Both were deeply affected by the results of nationalist sentiment spreading through Europe. Zamenhof saw how it turned man against man and inspired people to violence. Ben-Yehuda saw how it strengthened and legitimized a feeling of common identity. Both saw that a fundamental element of a sense of nationhood was a shared language.

Unlike the Germans, Italians, Greeks, Poles, Hungarians, Ukrainians, and other peoples who asserted themselves as nations during this time by uniting and throwing off, or attempting to throw off, foreign rule, the Jews were a widely spread diaspora without a significant, nation-worthy concentration in any particular territory. Many of them felt that if they were to define themselves as a nation, they must relocate. Ben-Yehuda believed that they must also revive their ancient language, and he relocated to Palestine to begin his task.

After the terrible pogroms of 1881, Zamenhof also came to the conclusion that the Jews needed a state of their own. After first supporting the idea for a Jewish homeland in the United States, he began an active involvement in the Zionist movement. But he became disillusioned with it and decided that "despite the heartbreaking sufferings of my people, I do not want to link myself with Hebrew nationalism, but I want to work only for absolute human justice. I am profoundly convinced, that this way I will bring much more good to my unfortunate people than through the goals of nationalism."

Just as the growth of Esperanto was aided by fervent true believers who didn't care what others thought of them, Hebrew benefited from a passionate idealism. Ben-Yehuda was criticized for being a naive dreamer, and even when he could convince associates to use Hebrew in their day-to-day interactions, they were met with an impatient request to speak Yiddish "like a normal person."

Yiddish was the language of the European Ashkenazi Jews, and many of them argued that Yiddish should be the language of Jewish nationhood. Had they established a territory in Europe or the United States, rather than in Palestine, this is probably what would have happened. But in Palestine there were North African Jews, who spoke North African Arabic; Mediterranean Sephardic Jews, who spoke Judeo-Spanish; and local Jews, who spoke Palestinian Arabic. There were already significant cultural differences between these Jews and the Yiddish-speaking European Jews, who were viewed as not-always-welcome newcomers.

Ben-Yehuda saw that Hebrew was shared more broadly by the Diaspora and had more potential as a unifying force. His writings and actions inspired a small group of others to follow his lead. A few other families declared themselves Hebrew-only households, and a few more declared that they personally would only use Hebrew in all their daily interactions. These were the early years of the first aliya, an influx of over twenty thousand immigrants from Europe, and as they established small agricultural colonies in a new, strange place, many of them were receptive to new language habits. Some teachers began to teach Hebrew in these colonies through the direct method—just jumping in and speaking the language, without commentary or explanation in Yiddish, Russian, or any other better-known language.

They were all, to a certain extent, making it up as they went along. How do you say, in a language of obscure theological debate and ancient ritual, "washcloth" or "doll" or "typewriter"? If Ben-Yehuda wanted to do something as simple as ask his wife to pour him a cup of coffee with sugar, he was reduced to gesturing while saying, "Take such and such, and do like so, and bring me this and this, and I will drink." It takes a lot of work and patience to run a household or a classroom this way.

Some conscious intervention was required. Ben-Yehuda would comb through ancient Hebrew texts, looking for long-forgotten words that might serve for the needed concepts. He also looked through more recent Hebrew literature, which had already done a good bit of grappling with vocabulary gaps. But the solutions that had been proposed in this literature were often too conservative, clunky, and inappropriate for natural, fluent language use. A tuning fork was referred to as "a bronze fork with two teeth that produce a sound." A word for "telegraph" had been coined by adapting the following lines from Psalm 19:4–5: "There is no speech, there are no words, neither is their voice heard. Their line is gone out through all the earth and their words to the end of the world."

Ben-Yehuda sought simple, natural-sounding solutions, and he often resorted to making them up himself. Others did the same, and this led to a great deal of variation in the way Hebrew was spoken. A newspaper editorial complained: "Here they say *gir* 'chalk' and here *neter* and here *karton*. This one says *xeret* 'letter' and this one *mixtav*. One says *shemurat ayin* or *af'af* for 'eyelash' and another, *risim*. In one school it is called a *bima* 'teacher's podium,' in another a *katedra* and in another a *maxteva*. This one says *sargel* 'ruler' and that one *sirgal*, this one *safsel* and that one *safsal*." Pronunciation also varied between the Sephardic and the Ashkenazic styles.

Though language academies were established in 1890 and 1904, they accomplished very little in the way of top-down enforcement of language norms. There was no standard or accepted authority. Though Ben-Yehuda introduced many of the words he created into general circulation by using them in articles he wrote for his Hebrew-language newspapers, he did not draw attention to them or comment upon them at all. Though the language was being manipulated quite consciously by individuals in various places, it was difficult to determine who was pulling the strings, and so the process managed to avoid seeming imposed and artificial.

Beginning in 1904, another wave of immigration from Europe, the second aliya, brought thousands more Jews to Palestine, many of them from Russia, where another bout of violent pogroms was under way. They were fired up on socialism and full of optimistic energy. Office clerks and doctors learned to plow soil and shovel manure on the newly established collective farms. Teachers and accountants built roads and laid foundations for new Jewish towns. These immigrants were willing to change their lives in dramatic ways, and many of them (but by no means all of them) were willing to change their language, too.

They made Hebrew the language of formal education in kindergartens and schools throughout Palestine. There were still a number of schools that used French, English, or German, but after the 1914 "language wars," when teachers from schools across the land went on strike to protest the decision that German, not Hebrew, would be the language of instruction at the Technion (a modern technical school recently established by a German Jewish charitable organization), Hebrew became the dominant language of education. The kids took it from there. As modern studies of the development of creoles from pidgins, or of native sign languages from home sign systems, have shown, a generation (or two) of children can turn the effortfully produced, inconsistent input of the adults around them into a fully fledged, effortless native vernacular. The children of the second aliya were exposed to Hebrew early enough, and in a natural enough manner, that they were able to do this.

What accounts for the success of the revival of Hebrew? It certainly wasn't efforts on the part of any official institution. Putting a language into the schools or onto street signs is no guarantee of success (as illustrated by the Irish example). Nor was it a sense of cultural pride in the language. Maori (the native language of New Zealand) and Hawaiian fail to flourish, despite large-scale government support and a hearty emotional response from the people who are supposed to be reviving the languages (but aren't). In dozens of movements struggling to bring dying languages back to life, there have been people with passionate conviction working very hard. The revival of a language doesn't depend on one inspired crusader, or even a group of them. How do you get people to speak a language they don't speak? Invented or otherwise?

One thing that seems to be very important is circumstances— as in right time, right place. If the Jews had decided to establish a nation in Uganda or Texas (both serious proposals at the time), would they be speaking Hebrew today? Probably not. If the situation in Europe hadn't sent a second wave of immigrants to Palestine, would the small movement that Ben-Yehuda established have petered out? Perhaps.

Hebrew and Esperanto are very different languages with very different origins. But their successes—that of revival for Hebrew and that of being brought to life in the first place for Esperanto— overlapped in their timing and in their reasons for occurring. Esperanto also benefited from circumstances. If Zamenhof hadn't come on the scene just as the Volapükists were jumping ship, would anyone have paid attention? If the situation in Europe hadn't highlighted the violent perils of nationalism, would so many have been attracted to his message of unity? If both the Hebrew revival and the Esperanto movements hadn't begun during the golden age of socialism, when the prospects for grand social-engineering experiments looked so bright, would the Jewish immigrants have so willingly believed that it was possible to overhaul the language habits of an entire society? Would enough people have believed in the utopian dream of a universal language to try to make it happen?

Only it didn't happen. Esperanto did not become a universal language. It became instead a particular language of a particular community.

Crank Pride

A fter World War II, there was a push to rid the Esperanto movement of its eccentricities, spearheaded by Ivo Lapenna, a Yugoslavian Esperantist and academic lawyer. He held important positions: professor of international law at Zagreb University, counsel-advocate at the International Court of Justice at The Hague, and professor of Soviet and East European law at the London School of Economics. Peter Forster, in his book *The Esperanto Movement*, described Lapenna as having "the sophistication of the cultured cosmopolitan." He was "fluent in several languages" and had "distinguished himself as a sportsman and a musician." You can imagine why such a genteel character might not be happy with the public image of Esperanto. After attending the 1947 universal congress in Bern, he published an angry plea for respectability, lashing out against the "naivetés and frivolities which only compromise the cause of the International Language." He complained that "the dissemination of Esperanto among serious people" was threatened by the "cranks" he had observed:

> One woman with green stockings explained to me that every lady Esperantist should wear only green stockings for propaganda purposes. One came to the ball in a dress, like a nightdress, with masses of green stars, large, medium and small. I saw a loud yellow tie with an even louder green star woven into it. In general, one could see stars everywhere; on the chest, in the hair, on belts, rings, etc.
>
> People will say again that everyone has the right to dress as he wishes. Certainly; but could we not kindly request such cranks not to hinder the spread of Esperanto by their standpoint and external appearance? If that does not work, have we not at least the right to make a mockery of them, since they make a mockery of Esperanto?

War's end had ushered in a new era of international communication and organization, and Lapenna did not want Esperanto to sabotage once again its chance to enter the world stage in an official capacity. Proposals for Esperanto endorsement after World War I had received serious consideration at the League of Nations. There was enough opposition (the most vocal from the French delegation, which claimed that French was already the universal language) to prevent the League from taking up the cause of Esperanto, though it did accept a resolution to recommend that it be considered a regular language, rather than a code, in the determination of fees for telegraph messages.

The dislocations of World War II convinced Lapenna, among others, that there was a fresh chance for Esperanto, and after a petition bearing the signatures of more than 500,000 people and

450 organizations was submitted to the United Nations, UNESCO began to look into the matter. With great hopes for success, Lapenna presented an eloquent case for Esperanto. Ultimately, the UNESCO delegates adopted a resolution expressing affinity between the goals of Esperanto and the goals of UNESCO. The Esperanto community celebrated this as a victory, but no concrete measures had really been endorsed. UNESCO essentially only agreed that, yes, Esperanto is a nice idea.

Lapenna's attempts to put a respectable face on Esperanto were not appreciated by everyone, and the cranks had an ardent voice in John Leslie, a.k.a. Verdiro (truth teller), the secretary of the British Esperanto Association. Leslie is described in Forster's book as "an 'anarchist, freethinking, patriotic Scot' . . . He objected to supporting UNESCO, regarding it as a bulwark of financial capitalism . . . He also opposed formality in dress and defended deviations . . . He praised the informal equality among Esperantists of all walks of life and criticized the importance attached to attracting those famous in other spheres." In direct opposition to Lapenna, Leslie promoted an attitude of crank pride among the green-stocking crowd.

The 1947 congress that Lapenna found so disturbing was also important in the life of a young Hungarian named George Soros. His father, Tivadar, was an active Esperantist and had changed the family name from Schwartz to Soros, an Esperanto verb meaning "will soar." Tivadar had escaped from a Siberian prison during World War I and managed to keep his family away from the Nazis during World War II. When the communists took over in 1947, Tivadar and George escaped to Switzerland, where they attended the Esperanto universal congress in Bern. Afterward, the father returned to Hungary and the son went on to Ipswich, England, for the annual world youth congress. Young George decided he wanted to stay in England, but he had only a tourist visa. He appealed to his fellow Esperantists for help, and it was Verdiro (Leslie), through a relative in the British parliament, who arranged George Soros's more permanent visa.

On his way to becoming one of the world's richest men, Soros was for a time actively committed to the Esperanto movement. According to the minutes of the Ipswich conference, he wanted to organize a bicycle trip through Europe, spreading the word. He also extolled the virtues of Esperanto at Speakers' Corner in London's Hyde Park, where anyone with an opinion and the bravery to mount a soapbox can compete for an audience. But he has long since stopped having anything to do with it. A Belgian woman I spoke to at the Havana congress told me bitterly, "He could do so much to help now, but he is a traitor. He hates Esperanto."

I asked Humphrey Tonkin, who did the English translation of Tivadar Soros's memoir of survival during World War II, for which George wrote the foreword, why Soros had changed his mind. "He doesn't hate Esperanto," Tonkin said. "He hasn't given up on its ideals, but his position is that it had its chance and it blew it. Which is a perfectly respectable view."

Born in Britain and educated at Cambridge and Harvard, Tonkin is an Esperantist but definitely not a kook. He's a professor of English specializing in Spenser and Shakespeare, a former Guggenheim fellow, and president emeritus at the University of Hartford. "Staying sane while dealing with something that is so low in the popular esteem is problematic," he told me. "It's a distressingly marginal community. Sometimes when I'm at Esperanto meetings, I say to myself—and this sounds terrible—I say, 'Am I really like that?' But then I sit in a faculty meeting, and I think to myself, 'This is not terribly different from an Esperanto congress,' because it's true. The fact is that overall, people are wackier than one imagines. So perhaps Esperanto is not that far-out."

Tonkin knew about the fringe quality of Esperantoland from the moment of his first contact with it. On a trip to Paris when he was barely a teenager, he went to a meeting of the Paris Esperanto Society. When the meeting was over, Tonkin said, he was followed out by "your sort of typical 1950s Paris Marxist, and he bent my ear at enormous length about Marxism. The awful thing about it was that I discovered that Esperanto really works. I understood every word he said."

He was in it for better or worse. When he was not yet sixteen years old, Tonkin traveled, by himself, from England to an Esperanto congress in Denmark and fell into a world full of interesting things. "Not that I found Esperanto was a comfort exactly, but it provided me with opportunities that I couldn't find in the rest of my life," he said. "Everything I know about Latvian culture, for example, I know about as a result of Esperanto."

In 1959 he went to Poland. "Nobody went to Poland in '59 except crazy Esperanto people," he said, "and I traveled all over the place. I was in Iran right before the revolution with Esperantists, and what I heard the Esperantists saying about Iran was nowhere to be found in the newspapers. Here I was in direct contact with a collection of people who were not beholden to the United States or Britain or whatever, and were not going to tell me what they thought I wanted to hear. So I was able in a sense to get a particular notion of the truth that other people didn't have."

I mentioned a man I had met at the Havana congress, an Icelandic fisherman who couldn't be more gaunt, or more silent, or farther from home. He first learned about Esperanto from a radio broadcast, studied it from a book, and had been to every universal congress since—Berlin, Tel Aviv, Zagreb, Fortaleza, Gothenburg. That July, he was headed for Beijing. "You know," Tonkin said, "there are a lot of Esperantists out there who just haven't yet found their way to Esperanto."

Back where it all started for me, at that MIT conference, I never did gain an understanding of the role of rock music in Esperanto culture. But I did get to hear Kimo play. On a stage set up on the lawn in front of the student center on the main quad, he brought out his accordion while his friend Jean-Marc LeClerq, formerly of the group La Rozmariaj Beboj (the Rosemary's Babies), tuned his guitar. They began with the mellow strains of "Besame mucho": "Kisu min / Kisu min multe."

Two gray-haired women in matching green dresses twirled to the music, their feet bare in the grass. A large-bellied man with a big green star on both his cap and his belt buckle stood with his hands in his pockets, swaying awkwardly. Others joined the ladies, or perched on benches and sang along. Outsiders wandered by. The curious ones stopped to listen or to take a leaflet from a friendly college student in an Esperanto T-shirt. Others sniggered or rolled their eyes as they refused the leaflet and continued on. I sat at a careful distance from the stage, hoping it wasn't too obvious that I was part of this group but feeling guilty for thinking so. While Esperantoland has its share of people you don't want to meet—insufferable bores, sanctimonious radicals, proselytizers for Christ, communism, or a new kind of vegetarian healing—for the most part, the Esperantists I encountered were genuine, friendly, interested in the world, and respectful of others. Though I may not have fully crossed over myself, I did develop a protective defensiveness about them.

Is it crazy to believe that Esperanto has a chance in the age of

English? It's insane. Ask any businessman in Asia, any hotel operator in Europe. Is it ridiculous to believe that a universal common language will bring peace to the world? Of course it is. We have all the brutal evidence we need: the fact that Serbians and Croatians speak the same language did not prevent the bloodshed in Yugoslavia; the shared language of the Hutus and Tutsis did nothing to stop the massacres in Rwanda. Do Esperantists really believe either of these propositions? Whether they do or they don't, as far as they are concerned, they're doing their part. It can't hurt.

The world may not need Esperanto, but it does need people who, like Zamenhof, are moved to act against the "enmity of nations." Knowing Zamenhof's fate makes it difficult to dismiss his life's work with a chuckle. During the bloody peak of World War I, Zamenhof's brother Aleksander killed himself upon being ordered into the Russian army because he couldn't bear to face once again the horrors he had witnessed while serving as an army doctor during the Russo-Japanese War. Not long after that, in the midst of death and destruction on a scale he never could have imagined, Zamenhof's heart gave out. He was lucky. He would not have to know that his lineage would end in yet another world war with the murder of his children at Treblinka.

Kimo and Jean-Marc began another song whose tune was unfamiliar to me. An original Esperanto song. Normando, a slight man with a hint of gray in his beard, came and sat on the grass across from me, his legs folded under him, facing me with his back to the stage. He proved to be a sweet-natured Esperanto ambassador who had been kindly introducing me to people and explaining special phrases and vocabulary to me in a modest, non-pedantic way. He leaned forward and in French-Canadian-accented Esperanto explained that the song we were hearing was called "Sola." People closer to the stage began to sing along, and he said it is often played at youth congresses, where it is a sort of anthem. The lyrics tell the story of a young person who feels completely alone, but then goes to an Esperanto congress and feels such friendship and connection to the world that his loneliness leaves him . . . until he is back in his own nation in his own little room. "This song," he almost whispered, "is so meaningful for Esperantists. Sometimes, when it's played at the congresses, you see people crying."

CHARLES BLISS AND THE LANGUAGE OF SYMBOLS

now is the time for all good

men and women to come to the aid

of Charles' invention of Blissymbols

—*Charles Bliss*

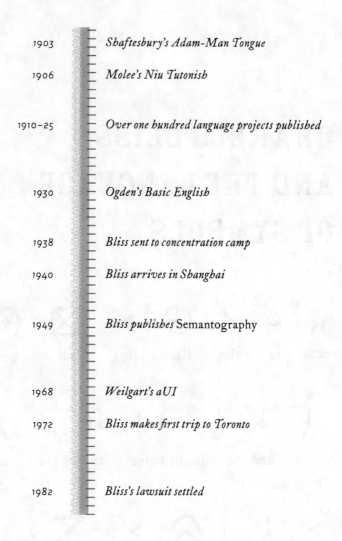

1903	Shaftesbury's Adam-Man Tongue
1906	Molee's Niu Tutonish
1910–25	Over one hundred language projects published
1930	Ogden's Basic English
1938	Bliss sent to concentration camp
1940	Bliss arrives in Shanghai
1949	Bliss publishes Semantography
1968	Weilgart's aUI
1972	Bliss makes first trip to Toronto
1982	Bliss's lawsuit settled

Word
Magic

Though Esperanto has survived into the present day, the era of the international language has not. In the years between 1880 and the beginning of World War II, over two hundred languages were published, most of them variations on the same theme: European roots, a set of grammatical endings, no irregularities. The number of projects, and the enthusiasm for them, began falling off in the 1930s, and by the end of the war the era of the international language was over.

There were a few reasons for this. One was the rise of a new lingua franca, on a scale more global than any had been before—English. The era of the international language coincided with the greatest period of growth and consolidation in the British Empire. English was spread to every continent. And Britain's position at the center of the Industrial Revolution ensured that wealth, status, and power became associated with English. The rising power of the United States during this time added fuel to the English fire, and it soon took over as the primary engine of spread.

In some ways, the noticeable expansion of English was good for the international language movement. The language inventors, looking at the growth of English, saw a threat to their own national languages (most of them were not native English speakers) and worked that much harder to convince the world that a universal *neutral* language was needed. They found a sympathetic ear. The most active international language supporters were in France and Germany—countries whose languages had the most to lose from the encroachment of English (French was losing its position as the primary language of diplomacy, and German as the primary language of science).

However, in most ways, the advance of English was very bad for the international language movement. The more common reaction was to stick up not for an invented neutral language but for your own home language, as France did in meetings of the League of Nations. Another alternative was to just accept English as the new lingua franca, as Sweden and Norway did in those same meetings. (Denmark wanted Ido.)

By the beginning of the 1920s, English had accumulated a heap of advantages—economic power, political power, large numbers of speakers—but it was not the only potential world language in town. French, Portuguese, Russian, and other colonial languages also enjoyed such advantages (though none on as grand a scale). However, by the end of the 1920s, English had added to its arsenal even more compelling advantages: jazz, radio, Hollywood. It became the language of a new, media-driven popular culture. It was the lingua franca not just of elite pursuits—diplomacy, business, science, belles lettres—but of good ol' entertainment. It swaggered around with a gum-cracking friendly confidence, shaking hands and winning people over.

It also seemed to already possess many of the qualities that the language inventors were after. When Count Coudenhove-Kalergi, son of an Austro-Hungarian father and a Japanese mother, founded the Paneuropean Union in 1923, he proposed that English be the language of its administration, claiming that the "ease with which the English language may be learned, and its intermediate position between the Germanic and the Romance language groups, predestine it to the position of a natural Esperanto."

The 1920s was the last decade of vigor in the second era of language invention. Though a few international language projects continued to crop up every year (as they still do today), even the language inventors were turning toward English. These inventors accepted English as an international language, but thought it could be made into a *better* international language by getting rid of some of its messy inconsistencies.

Some focused exclusively on spelling reform, as the Swede Robert Zachrisson did in his *Anglic* (1930):

Forskor and sevn yeerz agoe our faadherz braut forth on this kontinent a nue naeshon, konseevd in liberty, and dedicated to the propozishon that aul men ar kreaeted eequal.

Others sought to regularize the grammatical irregularities, as Ruby Olive Foulk did in her *Amxrikai Spek* (1937):

Pronouns and verbs:

I be	*Is be*
you be	*yous be*
he be	*hes be*

Plurals:

man, mans

Comparatives:

good, gooder, goodest

Other regularizations:

Frenchman, Americaman, Italiman, Mexicoman

historiman, scienceman, artman, musicman

The best-known project of this kind was C. K. Ogden's *Basic English*, first published in 1930. Ogden was a Cambridge-educated editor, writer, translator, and mischief maker. As a student, he opposed compulsory attendance at chapel and, with a few of his like-minded friends, founded a group called the Heretics Society, where he honed his skills in questioning authority and challenging dogma. He supported progressive social causes like women's rights and birth control, and generally enjoyed being on the wrong side of stuffy propriety. At his own request, his entry in *Who's Who* says that he spent 1946–48 "bedeviled by officials."

Basic English was his proposal for an international language based on a reduction of English to 850 words. Though he believed in spelling reform, he was practical enough to see how unlikely it was to be accepted (he called it "a problem waiting for a Dictator"), and instead tried as much as possible to build his Basic vocabulary around words that presented "no special difficulty." He claimed that of the 850 words he had chosen, "less than a hundred involve wanton violations of orthographical decency." He also objected to irregular plurals and past-tense forms, blaming their persistent existence on a dastardly cabal of "printers, lexicographers, and schoolmasters." However, realizing that an English that looked like English was more likely to succeed, he left the grammar alone.

Instead, he simplified the language by doing away with words like "disembark," "tolerate," and "remove" and replacing them with "get off a ship," "put up with," and "take away." In this way, he eliminated almost all verbs—including "to eat" ("have a meal") and "to want" ("have a desire")—from his list of 850, leaving them to be expressed with what he called "operators" like "get," "put," "take," "come," "go," "have," and "give." Ogden believed that such a recasting not only made English easier to learn and understand but also had the potential to cure our minds of some bad habits. He believed that much of the world's troubles could be traced to the negative effects of what he called "Word Magic," the illusion that a thing exists "out there," just because we have a word for it. When we are under the spell of Word Magic, we fail to see that "sin" is a moral fiction, "ideas" are "psychological fictions," "rights" are "legal fictions," and "cause" is "a physical fiction." (He also feels compelled to pick on "swing" by pointing out that it is a "saxophonic fiction.") Word Magic makes us lazy; we don't question the assumptions that are hidden in words, and so we allow ourselves to be manipulated by "press, politics, and pulpit." Ogden thought Basic English could work as an antidote to Word Magic by forcing people to express themselves in simple terms, thus forcing them to really think about what they are saying.

Winston Churchill, himself a tireless advocate of plain language, was a fan of Basic English and made efforts to promote it. He thought it could help create a different kind of empire, one based not on "taking away other people's provinces or land or grinding them down in exploitation" but on a shared language. He encouraged the BBC to take it to the airwaves and teach it far and wide.

He also appealed to President Roosevelt to join the cause of Basic English. Roosevelt promised to look into the matter, but he couldn't resist teasing that Churchill's inspiring speech about offering his "blood, toil, tears, and sweat" to his country may have been less effective if he "had been able to offer the British people only blood, work, eye water and face water, which I understand is the best that Basic English can do with five famous words."

For all they did to argue for its virtues, neither Churchill nor Ogden actually used Basic English in their own writings. They rather took luxurious advantage of English vocabulary. But Ogden didn't really intend for Basic English to replace full English. It was to serve as a second, auxiliary language, a utilitarian lingua franca. He advertised two other benefits. For foreigners, it would serve as an easy entrée into fuller English. For English speakers, it would serve as "an apparatus for the development of clarity of thought and expression."

I'm not so sure Basic English fit the bill on either point. Although sometimes the Basic English version is clearer ("First, God made the heaven and the earth." I like that. It's snappy), at other times it seems to strangle itself on its own restrictions:

> Seven and eighty years have gone by from the day when our fathers gave to this land a new nation—a nation which came to birth in the thought that all men are free, a nation given up to the idea that all men are equal.

"Came to birth in the thought that all men are free"? How does that clarify things? And if you don't speak English, how are you supposed to know that "given up to" means "dedicated to"? Just because you are familiar with the "operator" words that Ogden expected to bear the brunt of so much meaning, you don't necessarily have any idea what they mean when put together. It is precisely those words, and the huge number of idioms they participate in, that make English such a headache for the non-native speaker. You haven't really solved much by replacing "happen" with "come about," "tease" with "make sport," or "intend" with "have a mind to."

In 1943, Churchill touted Basic English in a speech at Harvard, and soon the reporters were at Ogden's doorstep. He received them wearing a mask and, over the course of the interview, exited and entered the room through different doors, each time wearing a different mask. This behavior was a symptom of his generally irreverent attitude and what friends called his "impish humor." He wore masks on other occasions, explaining that when the speaker wears a mask, the listener is forced to pay attention to the content of the speech. Whatever the content of his speech that day, he did nothing to dispel the impression that Basic English was kind of a kooky idea. When Churchill left office in 1945, officials at the BBC suggested that Basic English be left "on a high shelf in a dark corner."

Ogden's plan wasn't without merit. The promotion of plain language is a fine idea and I'm all for it. A simplified form of English is clearly a good thing for someone trying to learn the language. In 1959, two years after Ogden's death, the Voice of America began broadcasting news stories in something they called Special English, and these programs are still popular today in non-English-speaking countries all over the world. Special English is simplified, but not according to any particular theory or rules. It doesn't have anything against verbs, and while it has a core vocabulary of fifteen hundred words, other terms are introduced when they are needed, along with brief explanations. The few rules it does claim—no passive voice, one idea per sentence—are violated when they interfere with sensible judgment. It is what Basic English probably would have become if Ogden wasn't so hung up on grand philosophical justifications for his system. Or with having it be a "system" rather than a loose set of guidelines.

Basic English also might have had a better chance if Ogden had been a little less eccentric. But it almost didn't matter what his personality was like, for by the time he came along, the whole endeavor of inventing or even manipulating a language had been so thoroughly tainted with the eau de quackery that even the most sober, sensible language inventor had little hope of being taken seriously.

Language schemes had always been viewed a little skeptically. John Locke, a contemporary of Wilkins's, said he didn't think that anyone could "pretend to attempt the perfect reforming the languages of the world, no not so much as of his own country, without rendering himself ridiculous." But in the seventeenth century, highly prestigious people were working on the development of philosophical languages, and their work was circulated and discussed among the biggest names of the day.

And although at the beginning of the era of international languages, plenty of jokes were made at the expense of Volapük and Esperanto and other languages that came to public attention, they did get attention, and sometimes from quite esteemed sources. Respected institutions like the American Philosophical Association and the American Association for the Advancement of Science got involved in the international language question, and major papers reported on the different projects as they came out. Esperanto got a lot of press. In 1910, when the sixth universal Esperanto congress was held in Washington, D.C., the Washington *Evening Star* carried the headline "Zamenhof Alvenas" (Zamenhof Arrives), and the *Washington Post* ran daily stories on the program of events.

Public recognition of invented languages manifested itself in other ways, too. A Scottish company produced an Esperanto cigarette ("The international smoke"), and Cadbury manufactured an Esperanto chocolate. When the universal congress was held in Barcelona, the king of Spain sent a horse-drawn carriage to pick Zamenhof up on his arrival. Later, as Zamenhof traveled south to Valencia, groups of people came out to greet his train at different stations, waving and cheering him on.

As time went on and the crackpot element of Esperanto society became more pronounced, people concerned about their public image became less willing to be associated with it. And as the number of invented languages increased to the point where the language inventors were (in the words of one newspaper editorial) fixing to "out-Babel Babel," the newspapers and the scientific academies stopped paying attention.

Hundreds of language projects were published at the beginning of the twentieth century, and many of them were second or third attempts by people who weren't quite satisfied with their own original "optimal" solutions. Language inventors are, after all, motivated by the urge to reform and improve, and many of them, once they got going, found it hard to stop. They grew dissatisfied with their own projects and continued to tinker and adjust, publishing revised versions of their languages. Ernst Beermann, not satisfied with his Novilatiin (1895), later created Novilatin (1907). Woldemar Rosenberger (onetime director of the Volapük Academy) created Idiom Neutral (1902), followed by Idiom Neutral Reformed (1907), followed by Reform-Neutral (1912). Some of the most prolific producers were former Volapükists, such as Julius Lott, who gave us Verkehrssprache (1888), Compromiss-Sprache (1889), Lingua Internazional (1890), Mundolingue (1890), and Lingue International (1899); or Esperantists, such as René de Saussure (brother of Ferdinand, the father of modern linguistics), who gave us Antido I (1907), Antido II (1910), Lingvo Kosmopolita (1912), Esperantida (1919), Nov-Esperanto (1925), Mondialo (1929), Universal-Esperanto (1935), and Esperanto II (1937).

One particularly productive multiple offender was Elias Molee, the author of American Language (1888), Pure Saxon English (1890), Tutonish (1902), Niu Teutonish (1906), Altutonish (1911), Alteutonik (1915), Dynamic Language (1921), and Toito Spike (1923). Molee was born in Muskego, Wisconsin, to recently arrived Norwegian immigrant parents. In his autobiography, *molee's wandering* (written without capital letters, which he considered "cruel, non-ethical, non-artistic, and non-scientific"), he describes an idyllic childhood spent listening to tales of Norse mythology in his family's log cabin, eating "good pancakes with milk in e dough n much egg n butter in it," and roaming the fields picking fresh berries, plums, and nuts with the local children. Most of the neighboring families were Norwegian, but there were also quite a few Germans, as well as one or two English-speaking American households. As the children played, they developed their own little dialect, which they used to communicate with one another: "1 day we caught hold of 1 or 2 english words from henry n mary adams. at another time, 1 or 2 words from otto n emma shumaker in low german, sometimes they learned 1, 2, or 3 words from e tveite or e molee children in norwegian. as e norwegian n german children were e most numerous, e new union language leaned largely toward e teutonic side with very few latin words." They called their language "tutitu" and even used it to act as interpreters between their parents.

Molee later attended Luther College in Iowa and studied languages at Albion Academy and the University of Wisconsin. He did not like having to study Latin and Greek, and resented the way their influence made English more difficult than it needed to be. He once read a sermon and didn't understand the word "cacophonous." He "felt chagrined and humbled to think that after graduating at an American Academy and after having studied so as to speak and enjoy several languages, after having learned considerable Latin and a little Greek, yet I could not understand so popular a production as a sermon." As far as he was concerned, English had ceased to be a great language with the Norman Conquest. Why couldn't it be more like the "teutonic" languages, he thought, such as German, which instead of the Greek-based "cacophonous" has its own word, *übellautend* (ill sounding), formed out of its own Germanic roots?

Molee began to work on a language with a consistent spelling system and a regular grammar that was based on common Germanic roots. He started with American Language or Germanic English (1888):

ʃen drod nɪr untü hɪm ol dɪ tɶlɪra and sündɪra for tɑ hör hɪm.
"Then drew near all the publicans and sinners for to hear him."
(Luke 15:1)

This then became Pure Saxon English (1890):

yur heili welkom brɪf was bringen tu mɪ yesterdai.
"Your highly welcome letter was brought to me yesterday."

This was followed a little more than a decade later by Tutonish (1902):

dau shal not kil,

dau shal not stiel

dau shal not baer falsh vitnesu gegn dauo nabor.

This turned into Niu Teutonish (1906):

m seen eena d likt af ds velt een kold vintri morgn an d 3a dag of
eenam.

"I saw first the light of this world one cold wintry morning on
the 3rd day of January."

While Molee did seek "to re-unite all teutonic people into one
language within fifty years," he emphasized that his goal was not
to dominate over others but to stick up for a language heritage
that was under threat. He didn't think it was fair that Esperanto
and other heavily Latin-based languages were the most popular
proposals for an international language. These "commerce languages," as he called them, were geared toward people who did a
lot of international business and could probably afford translators
anyway. He wanted to help out the poor and uneducated American workingman who was being held back because he could read
only "cheap newspapers and light stories of romance" because everything of higher value was full of fancy Greek words like "cacophonous" that necessitated a college education or an expensive
dictionary.

By the time he published Niu Teutonish, Molee was sixty-one
years old and had suffered through a series of disappointments. He
had married, lost an infant son, and divorced. He moved through
Minnesota, the Dakotas, and Iowa, occasionally investing in tracts
of land but always selling just before prices went up. At one point

he took up with a widow of means, but she got tired of supporting him, and he went on his way. He traveled to the South with a plan for establishing a Norwegian colony there, but nothing came of it. He later moved to Washington State, where he tried his plan again in the town of LaCrosse by advertising in the Norwegian newspapers of the Midwest. He did attract many Norwegians to the area, and the settlement eventually became a success, but only after he had left it to try his fortunes in Tacoma.

In 1907 he sold off some land and sailed for Europe, where he traveled for a few years, meeting with language professors and discussing his Teutonic language ideas. A professor in Oslo helped arrange an audience for him with King Haakon of Norway. Molee reported in his autobiography that "e king ws very friendly t me, who ws only a student v language n a newspaper correspondent. he bid me sit down in a costly cushion chair. we talked together for half an hour mostly about uniting together e swedish, norwegian n danish languages."

After Molee returned to the States, he published Altutonish and then a few more versions of his language. In the last paragraph of his autobiography, which he completed in 1919, he endorses the right of a person to end his own life when he is no longer useful to society. As he entered his eighties, he apparently felt that he had done all he could. According to his 1928 obituary, "He ended his life with a shot on the 28th of September in the hotel in Tacoma where he had spent the past ten years."

The politeness of the Norwegian king notwithstanding, Molee could not interest anyone in his language projects, but that did not stop him from devoting his life to them. He was a man of big plans, one of many such men at the dawn of the twentieth century and one of many who never saw their plans go anywhere.

The language invention craze had attracted all sorts of hucksters, charlatans, and dreamers. Edmund Shaftesbury, who was all three, published his Adam-Man Tongue in 1903. Shaftesbury's real name was Webster Edgerly, but he was also known as Dr. Ralston, the founder of Ralstonism, a health food cult that advised its followers to eschew hot baked goods, walk on the balls of their feet, and eat "bacterial" foods, like raw eggs. (He also promoted whole-wheat cereal, and when the Purina Company asked him to endorse their wheat cereal, he agreed on the condition that it be named after him. The success of the product led to the company being renamed Ralston Purina.) He wrote over fifty self-help books on subjects from "sex magnetism" to "immortality" to "the Ralston brain regime"—and they were chock-full of racist rants, naive pseudoscience, and curmudgeonly attacks on modern society.

He also dabbled in real-estate speculation and the theatrical arts, though without much success. His book *Lessons in the Art of Acting*—a catalog of the emotions and how to portray them—recommends "Frenzy" be indicated "by inclining the head backward, looking up; and clutching the hair with both hands." This may help explain why a critic for the *New York Times*, in reviewing a play that Edgerly wrote, produced, and starred in, said the "originator, concocter, and financial backer of this forlorn enterprise is a misguided person, who evidently labors under the triple hallucination that he is a poet, a dramatist, and an actor."

His Adam-Man Tongue—so named because it is "the language of man (the human race) founded upon the primitive (Adam) roots and terms that are the watchwords of universal speech"—is nothing more than a bizarre-looking version of English. He provides a sample dialogue:

MR. GENTLE: It bɜ preti wqm tsdɑ
   (*It be pretty warm today.*)
MR. BLUFF: Wut bɜ preti wqm?
   (*What be pretty warm?*)
MR. G: W4, du wedu.
   (*Why, the weather.*)
MR. B: Wut wedu?
MR. G: Dis wedu?
MR. B: WΔl, hθ bɜ dis wedu eni difrunt frqm eni udu?
MR. G: It bɜ wqmer.
MR. B: Hθ ds ys no it bɜ?
MR. G: Ik just supoz'd it bɜ'd.
MR. B: Bɜ nqt du wedu du sɑm evriver?
MR. G: W4 nqn, it bɜ wqmer in som plɑsez Δnd kolder in uduz.

And so on.

In the second era of language invention (that of the simplified international language), for every upstanding, respected member of society who had a language plan (the chemist Wilhelm Ostwald, the mathematicians Louis Couturat and Giuseppe Peano, the linguist Otto Jespersen), there were two or three Shaftesburys leaving their impression on the public perception of language creation. People who had once reacted to the practice with interest, bemusement, or mild irritation began to react with revulsion. One prominent psychologist had his own, distinctly Freudian explanation for this reaction: the drive to create languages was traceable to "displaced anal affects (ultimately derived from the satisfaction gained by the production of faeces or flatus)." The language inventors were smearing it on the walls, and the public was getting disgusted.

Pretty soon anyone with prestige to protect stayed as far away as possible. The torch was passed to brave souls who were either too passionate about their missions to concern themselves with respectability or too out of touch with reality to care.

And so began the third era of language invention. It is less well-defined than the first two. There was no unifying theme or idea behind the languages, no particular problem the inventors were trying to address. There were only individuals, working on the fringes of society, each with a separate, lonely agenda. They came up with further iterations of regularized Latin or English, or Esperanto-type hybrids. Some created philosophical-type languages, believing they were the first to have thought of such a thing. However, a few found a completely new approach, one that hadn't been tried before because it was so obviously unworkable. Only someone on the outside, someone heedless to calls for common sense, would be crazy enough to try it—a pictorial symbol language. One of those who did, in an unlikely turn of events, found success. But it was not the type of success he hoped for. He spent the rest of his life sabotaging his success and any respect he had earned from it. In the process he nearly destroyed those who had helped him to gain the recognition he always wanted.

Hit by a
Personality Tornado

What if your mind was sound but your body gave you no way to let anyone else know that it was? What if you had wishes, desires, complaints, and opinions but no control of your voice to speak them, no control of your hands to write or gesture about them? What if you could understand what everyone around you was saying—that you were a vegetable, that you were retarded, that it didn't matter what they did to you because you couldn't tell the difference anyway—and you could not let them know that they were wrong?

In 2007, I met with Ann Running, a woman in her thirties with severe cerebral palsy, at a group home for the disabled in Toronto. This is how we communicated: I moved my hand over a laminated chart of about eight hundred words that was attached to a tray on her wheelchair. The words were arranged both thematically (food words, sports words, color words, and so on) and by grammatical function (pronouns in one section, prepositions in another). At each section I stopped and checked to see whether she rolled her eyes upward. If she didn't, I moved to the next section. If she did, I pointed to the top of the first column of words in that section and checked for the eye signal, pointing to each column in turn until she indicated I had reached the correct one. When I had the right column, I started down the column, pointing to each word in turn until she signaled. Then we started the process again, until Ann had said all the words she wanted to say.

It was an incredibly slow and frustrating way to have a conversation. Often, I missed her eye signal—a random jerk of her body could make me think she had signaled when she hadn't—and I had to back up and check that I had the right section or column. Also, she refused to let me finish a sentence for her, even when it was completely clear where she was headed. And Ann didn't take any shortcuts. Her sentences were complete and grammatically correct—when she wanted to say "told," she didn't just lead me to "tell," but to "tell" *and* to an entry indicating past tense. When she wanted a name or a word that wasn't on her chart, she directed me to a section that had the alphabet arranged on a grid, and she spelled the whole thing out, letter by letter, even when I guessed the word correctly. She made no concessions to convenience.

To my convenience, that is. Her whole life was inconvenience, and she was accustomed to it. She depended on others to feed her, to dress her, to put her to bed at night and get her out of bed in the morning. She had no control over anything having to do with her body. But she did have control over her mind, and in her use of language she could prove it. She was not going to leave it up to me, and my convenience, to guess at a good enough approximation of her intentions. She had the ability, as difficult and time-consuming as it was, to say what she wanted to say, in exactly the way she wanted to say it, an ability that most of us take for granted. Ann had known what it was like not to have that ability, and she was never going to take it for granted.

I had come to Toronto to find out more about Blissymbolics, a pictorial symbol language invented by Charles Bliss in the 1940s. I had found a copy of his 1949 book about his system in a used bookstore in Washington, D.C. It was full of rambling utopian philosophy and naive scientific theories (complete with references to *Reader's Digest* articles). I was delighted to add it to my collection of nutty universal language schemes that I considered myself to be single-handedly rescuing from obscurity. Upon further investigation, however, I found out that Blissymbolics was not as obscure as I thought it was. There was a school in Canada for children with cerebral palsy that was actually using it for communication. But what, exactly, were they doing with it? How could a language as crazy as this one be useful for anything?

Ann was a graduate of the program at the Ontario Crippled Children's Centre (now called Bloorview Kids Rehab) that had started using Blissymbolics in the 1970s. But like all the other program graduates I visited on that trip, she now interacted through English text. All of the students I met with talked about the way Blissymbols had changed their lives. Ann said Bliss had "opened a door to my mind." But none of them used the language anymore. Why, I wondered, hadn't they just started with English, a language they could hear and understand, rather than spend their time learning this bizarre symbol language? I thought about Stephen Hawking, who communicates in a manner similar to Ann's (his computer pages through the word choices for him, and he clicks a device with his hand when it arrives at the word he wants). He never had anything to do with Blissymbols and gets along just fine.

I mentioned this, delicately, to Shirley McNaughton, the teacher who had started the Blissymbol program. "Oh," she said, "but Stephen Hawking was an adult when he lost the ability to speak." He has ALS, a degenerative neurological disorder. "He already knew how to use English to express himself. He already knew how to read. Ann was five or six when we started with her. What good is English text to a child who can't read yet? And if a child can't speak and can't move, how do you teach them to read? How do you know what they know, what they understand?"

McNaughton didn't know anything about children with disabilities when she began teaching at the Ontario Crippled Children's Centre (OCCC) in 1968. On her first day, as she was touring the center, she saw a little girl drop one of her crutches, and, she says, "I was about to run over and help her, but they held me back. 'She has to learn how to get up,' they told me." After that McNaughton relied on the kids to tell her what to do—how to open leg braces, how to adjust a wheelchair—and she learned to focus on their capabilities and strengths.

But she wasn't sure what to do with the children who couldn't speak. "They had little boards with pictures on them—a picture of a toilet, a picture of some food, all needs-based pictures—I went through a year just asking them yes-or-no questions: 'Would you like to do this? Would you like to do that?' But they couldn't initiate anything themselves." They seemed to understand what was said to them, and, more important, they seemed to have something to say. "You could just tell with the twinkle in their eye or something."

McNaughton started talking with some of the staff about trying to introduce reading to these kids. She and Margrit Beesley, an occupational therapist, went to the administration to ask for a half day to work just with the nonspeaking kids. "The administration agreed, and we were given a laundry room in the basement to try our experiment." First, they needed to figure out what the kids knew and what they understood. They decided to try making up symbols that the kids could point to in order to express themselves (most of the kids, unlike Ann, were able to point), but it took them a long time to figure out how to symbolize more abstract concepts, so they decided to see whether someone already had a system of symbols they could use.

Their search led them to *Semantography*, Charles Bliss's eight-hundred-page book. He claimed that with the small number of basic symbols in his book, thousands of ideas could be expressed through combination. For example, this was how the words for emotions were expressed:

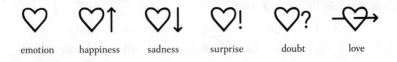

A noun could be made into a verb with the addition of an "action" symbol:

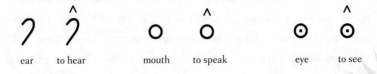

And adjectives could be made with the addition of an "evaluation" symbol:

man   manly   sun   sunny

Other words were derived from more complex types of combination:

beauty   smile   light   listener

This type of combinatorial system seemed promising. The children could only point to what they could reach from a seated position in their wheelchairs; they couldn't have a separate symbol for every word they might want to say. But if they could put two symbols together to create a third word, they could get more out of what fit in front of them.

Once McNaughton had taught the kids the meaning of a few symbols and showed them examples of how the symbols could be put together, she witnessed an explosion of self-expression. Kids whose communicative worlds had been defined by the options of pointing to a picture of a toilet, or waiting for someone to ask the right question, started talking about a car trip with a father, a brother's new bicycle, a pet cat's habit of hiding under the bed. Kids who were assumed to be severely retarded showed remarkable ingenuity in getting their messages across. When one little boy was asked what he wanted to be for Halloween, he pointed to the symbols "creature," "drink," "blood," "night"—he wanted to be Dracula. One particularly bright little girl named Kari took to this new means of expression with so much gusto that she could barely stand to be away from her symbols. When her father picked her up from school, she would cry through the whole car ride home, and could not be consoled until she was on the living room floor with her symbols, telling her family about the exciting events of the day.

McNaughton and the team of therapists she was working with took a picture of Kari, sitting in her wheelchair, surrounded by an array of symbols. Her eyes are sparkling, her smile is huge, and her dimples are adorable. When they finally tracked down Bliss in Australia, they sent him the picture. Before he received it, he later wrote, "I was resigned to my fate that I shall not see the fruits of my labours before I die. And then this picture, sent by Shirley, floated onto my desk. I can't describe the tumult of my thoughts. The heavens opened up and the golden sun broke through the darkened sky. I was delirious with joy."

He immediately mortgaged his house in order to make the long trip to Toronto. Everyone was excited. When he arrived, there were meetings and talks and parties. Bliss told jokes and played the mandolin and showered everyone he met with over-the-top compliments. The children loved him; he juggled and sang and shouted his love for them at the top of his voice. When he found out that the speech therapist had recently lost her husband to diabetes, he shed tears of deep sorrow, raged at the injustice of her misfortune, professed his undying love for her, and proposed marriage.

The staff didn't quite know what to make of that. It seemed kind of sweet and funny at the time. He was seventy-five years old. He was exotic, Old World, an Austrian Jew who had survived the war. He was effusive and emotional and not very Canadian. They stood back, amused but a little stunned. They had been hit by a personality tornado.

Near the end of his visit, Bliss gave McNaughton a copy of a book he had recently published, *The Invention and Discovery That Will Change Our Lives*. "We started to read it," she told me, "and we all had a private meeting and we said the administration should never see this book. It was really something—about how the nuclear bomb is all a myth, how the Soviets killed Kennedy, and how teachers are to blame for the problems of the world, and how they are all cowards and sex perverts—we thought that if the administration sees this, they'll never let him come back."

The staff's concern was for the children. They wanted to continue to develop the Blissymbols program, and they needed Bliss's help. He was a bit strange, but wasn't that often a mark of genius? They didn't need to subscribe to all his theories; they just needed his symbols. And he wanted to help. He was so glad to be there. He cared about the children so much. Surely he would do everything he could to make the program succeed. He was a wonderful man.

McNaughton had originally discovered Blissymbolics in a book called *Signs and Symbols Around the World*, where it was briefly mentioned. There was a reference to *Semantography*. Shirley and her team couldn't find the book anywhere. Eventually, they had the national library in Ottawa do a search across Canada, and one copy was found, at a university in Sudbury. They kept renewing the book as they searched for a copy they could buy. They wrote to the publisher but got no response. So they wrote to the book's distributor, who said, "We want nothing to do with that man. We dropped his stuff years ago." Their search led them to other distributors, who all said the same thing. At the time, Shirley was too preoccupied with finding the book to wonder about those comments. And in the whirlwind of Bliss's visit, she failed to make any connection between those comments and the man who inspired them.

FIFTEEN

Those Queer and Mysterious
Chinese Characters

Charles Bliss was born Karl Kasiel Blitz in 1897, in
Czernowitz, then part of the Austro-Hungarian Empire,
now part of Ukraine. His family was poor. "If you have seen the
musical 'Fiddler on the Roof,' " he wrote in one of his pamphlets,
"you will know the story of my parents." His father worked odd
jobs as an optician, a mechanic, an electrician, and a wood
turner, and as a boy Charles was fascinated by gadgets, circuits,
and chemistry. In 1908 he attended a lecture about the Austro-
Hungarian North Pole Expedition, and he was enraptured by
the tale of bravery in the face of extremes. He realized that
"life has been given to me to conquer hardship in the quest for
knowledge. I decided to become an engineer. I wanted to invent
things for a better life."

But he struggled in school. When he entered high school,

"suddenly I became an outcast to a group of fellow students. They went around with big books and talked big, very big and I couldn't understand what they said." Philosophy, logic, and especially grammar gave him trouble, and he often despaired that he was not intelligent enough to become the great thinker he wanted to be.

He fought as a foot soldier in World War I and then attended the Technical University of Vienna, where he graduated as a chemical engineer in 1922. He tried to get a job at the university, arguing that he should be awarded a professorship based on his invention of an education "machine" (questions written on one side of a page, answers on the other, and a separate sheet to cover up the answers during study), but he ended up working as a patent inspector in an electronics factory.

In 1938 the Germans marched into Austria, and Charles was sent to Dachau and then Buchenwald. His wife, Claire, who was a German Catholic twenty years his senior, worked tirelessly to get him released. Somehow, she helped secure him a British visa, and he was released on condition that he leave the country immediately. Claire had to stay behind. When the war broke out in 1939, she went to Czernowitz to stay with Charles's family, and when the war reached there, she fled through Greece, Turkey, Russia, and Siberia. Meanwhile, Charles traveled the other way around the world, through Canada, and on Christmas Eve 1940 they were finally reunited in Shanghai. Charles had worked at a factory in England, where co-workers told him he couldn't very well go around with a name like Blitz. So his name was now Charles Bliss.

The Blisses set up a photography and moviemaking business in Shanghai's bustling Jewish community. Over twenty thousand Jews who could not get visas for anywhere else had poured into Shanghai in the early years of the war, and they brought their

European way of life with them—filling the streets with cafés, concert halls, and Yiddish newspapers. But Charles, as he puts it, "went 'oriental.'" He became fascinated with "those queer and mysterious Chinese characters" when he saw them "at night in thousands of multi-coloured neon tubes filling the sky and making it a beautiful sight out of a fairy tale."

He hired a teacher and learned some characters, and he noticed, with astonishment, that when he recognized the characters on a shop sign or a newspaper headline, he read them off in his own language, not in Chinese. "Later on," he says, "the familiar words of my language disappeared and I could visualize directly the real things depicted by the signs." He thought he had discovered a potential universal language, a direct line to concepts. But the Chinese system was too complicated and arbitrary. Most of the symbols didn't look anything like the things they were supposed to represent, so it was too hard to learn. After a year of study, he gave up trying, and he started working on a new invention—a better, simpler system of pictorial symbols, "a logical writing for an illogical world."

Such a language, he thought, would not just enable people of different nations to communicate easily with each other, but it would also free their minds from the awful power of words. Bliss had seen how Hitler's slogans made people believe that lies were true. Propaganda—mere words—had instigated terrible acts. Such misuse of language would be impossible, he thought, in a "logical" system of symbols that represented the natural truth. One could not get away with malicious manipulation of words in such a system, because inconsistencies and falsehoods would be instantly exposed. Here was an invention, Bliss thought, that would benefit humanity more than any invention before it.

At the end of the war Charles and Claire immigrated to Australia, where they settled in the suburbs of Sydney. They were full of excitement about their future. "We felt that the scholars of the Western world would receive me and my work with open arms. We were sure that the University of Sydney would offer me a place to work out the primers and textbooks for this wonderful idea." But no one was interested.

Charles decided to work on his own, living off their savings, and write a book that would prove the value of his idea and convince the world to pay attention. For three years he worked feverishly, the words spilling out in such a torrent that he began typing directly onto wax stencils for printing—no editing. He finished the book in 1949, just as their money was running out. Claire sent six thousand letters to universities and government institutions all over the world announcing the publication of his fantastic new invention. They waited for the orders to start rolling in.

There was no response. Despite having lived through the horrors of the Nazis and the privations of refugee life in Shanghai, Charles would refer to the time after the publication of *Semantography* as their years of despair. He got a job as a spot welder in an automobile factory and worked on his symbols by night. His efforts to gain recognition became larger and more desperate. When he heard that a prominent American educator was coming to Sydney on a lecture tour, he went to the airport and managed to push his way into the man's taxi, where he spent the whole ride to the hotel firing off a sales pitch.

And when the philosopher Bertrand Russell came to town, Bliss somehow managed to wangle an audience with him. These kinds of actions did not endear Bliss to the public officials who sponsored lecture tours, but sometimes they did get him results.

Russell wrote him a polite letter of endorsement (which Bliss quoted, or reproduced in full, in everything he ever subsequently published), and Bliss got his name, and his system, into the local papers.

He struggled on, giving lectures on Semantography to any organization that would have him, until Claire died of a heart attack in 1961. Charles was devastated. He no longer wanted to go on living. But "after 3 years of desolation," he regained his "fighting spirit" and started working again, this time to vanquish the bureaucrats and university professors who, in his eyes, had murdered Claire with their apathy. He was also moved to action by the "tourist explosion." Governmental bodies started looking for ways to standardize and improve symbols on road signs and in airports, and "academic busy-bodies ran to scientific foundations and asked for millions of dollars for research." But they never mentioned Bliss's work in their papers. So Charles changed the name of his system to Blissymbolics, so the "would-be plagiarists could not take over."

Blissymbolics was in some ways a throwback to the seventeenth-century philosophical languages. Bliss broke down the world into essential elements of meaning and derived all other concepts through combination. But his symbols got their meaning not by referring back to a conceptual catalog (à la Wilkins) or a stanza and line of a memorized verse (à la Dalgarno) but by presenting a picture. Here are some of his basic symbol elements:

water   fire   earth   moon   star   pen

Bliss conveys more complex notions in a less direct manner— rain is not a drawing of rain, but a combination of "water" and "down":

rain

The basic symbol for water occurs in the symbols for all kinds of concepts having to do with liquid:

steam   river   spring   freezing   island   ink   spitting

The combinations are not strictly pictorial, but there is a connection between the meaning of the symbol and the way it looks. Because of this connection, Bliss claims, "the simple, almost self-explanatory picturegraphs of Semantography can be read in any language."

However, the further from the world of concrete objects Bliss gets, the more dubious this claim becomes. See if you can determine the meaning of the following combination:

♡↓⌒!

(⌒ = mind, — = negative)

Does it mean "depression," sad because of negative thoughts? Or maybe something like "forced optimism," when you feel unhappy and you mentally negate it? Or maybe it's some kind of bad emotion that happens when you have run out of ideas? Giving up?

According to Bliss's explanation, the meaning of the combination is "shame," the feeling you get when you are *"unhappy ♡↓ because your mind ⌒ thinks no ⁻! to what you have done."*

Well, sure. That's one way to create a picturable image for "shame." But it is not the only way. Another symbol-based language, aUI (the language of space), was developed by John Weilgart in the 1960s, at the same time Bliss was struggling to be heard. His word for "shame" was formed like this:

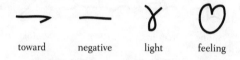

| toward | negative | light | feeling |

("negative light" is meant to be understood as "dark")

Weilgart's image for "shame" is "toward-dark-feeling" because "a boy ashamed flees 'into the dark' to hide." Both Bliss's and Weilgart's symbols for shame "look like" what they mean in some way, but there is nothing universal or self-explanatory about either one. The connection between form and meaning makes sense only *after* they have been explained (assuming a pretty broad reading of "makes sense"). There are many ways to symbolize an idea, and there are many ways to interpret the meaning of a symbol. Pictorial imagery, far from being a transparent, universal basis for communication, is a very, very unreliable way to get your message across.

Even the seventeenth-century language inventors understood this. Although they were developing "real" characters—symbols that would stand for ideas rather than words—they never considered making the characters *look like* the ideas they represented.

Such an approach was considered primitive, unsuitable for abstract, logical thought. They had the example of Egyptian hieroglyphics, which had not yet been deciphered, to discourage them. Hieroglyphics were assumed to stand for the objects they looked like. All other meaning had to be inferred through complicated chains of association. A serpent with a tail in its mouth meant "year" because a year returns into itself. A viper represented a child who plots against its mother because vipers are born by eating their way out of their mothers' bellies. A viper with a stag, however, represented a man who moves fast but without thinking—like the stag would move when trying to get away. All this reading into things was exciting for a good number of mystical-minded types who were swept up in the Egyptology craze of the Renaissance, but not for men of science, like Wilkins. Hieroglyphics could only portray fuzzy religious, spiritual, and magical meaning; they were distinctly unsuited to the needs of a clear, rational language.

Of course, the seventeenth-century understanding of hieroglyphics was wrong. It wasn't until the Rosetta stone was deciphered in 1822 that the nature of hieroglyphic writing was revealed. The figures did not represent vague, mystical concepts, but regular spoken words. The viper that showed up so often, and inspired all kinds of wrongheaded interpretations about the connotations of viperness, was nothing more than a symbol for the sound "f."

The sound glyphs combine with meaning glyphs to indicate words. In the symbol for "to cry"—

—the first two symbols represent the sounds "r" and "m," while the third symbol depicts an eye with lines coming down from it. Two pieces of partial information—the consonants in the word, and a pictorial approximation of its meaning—together indicate the full word, *rem*. There is no direct route from images to ideas here. Just a bunch of clues that converge on a word—not a concept, *a word*.

The Egyptian hieroglyphic system of writing died out, but what would have happened to it if it survived over many millennia? Probably this: The pronunciation of the spoken language would have changed, rendering the "sound" aspect of the glyphs harder to discern, and the imagery in the glyphs would have become more stylized and harder to recognize. The sound and meaning cues would have gotten weaker and less helpful. People would have had to resort more and more to just memorizing the glyphs. Imagine this scenario and what you end up with is Chinese writing.

Chinese writing does not operate on a pictographic principle, but Bliss, like a lot of people, became besotted with the idea that it did. He couldn't really be blamed for this impression. The teacher he hired probably started him off with the most iconic characters, as most teachers do:

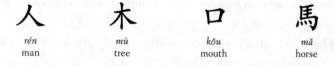

人	木	口	馬
rén	*mù*	*kǒu*	*mǎ*
man	tree	mouth	horse

Then Bliss would have learned about the poetic ways in which characters combine to make compound characters:

明

sun + moon
bright

好

woman + child
good

In this simple introduction to Chinese writing, Bliss would have found the primary elements that inspired his own system—pictographic symbols that represented concepts, and a method for combining them to make other concepts.

But he would then start learning a lot of characters that didn't look anything like what they meant, and a lot of compound characters that had no nice poetic explanation. So he would just have to memorize them, and the more characters he would learn, the harder they would be to remember. And so it makes sense that after a year of learning, he gave up.

But if he had been learning to *speak* Chinese as well as write it—if he hadn't been so impressed that he could read out the characters in his own language—perhaps he would have gotten further. Pronouncing the characters in Chinese, rather than in his own language, would help him to see why the character for "clamp," for example, is formed like this:

榪

It takes this form not because it has some conceptual thing to do with horses but because it is pronounced *mà*—just as the word "horse" is (but with a different tone). The tree part of the character provides a vague semantic clue that is open to interpretation (clamps are used on wood?), but the horse part is a much more reliable pointer to "clamp" because it doesn't take you on some roundabout journey of connotation to a *concept*. Instead, it sets you down on a nice straight path and gives you a little shove toward a *word*.

Unfortunately, the sound aspect of Chinese characters is not always so readily apparent. Thousands of years of language change coupled with a conservative writing tradition will do that. Look at English, after only a few hundred years of change, holding on to forms like "light" and "knee," when the pronunciations that gave rise to those spellings are no longer used. The situation in Chinese writing is much worse.

Still, most characters, more than 90 percent, give you some clue about the pronunciation of the word. You can't depend on those clues entirely, but it makes the task of learning and remembering thousands of characters a little bit easier. Chinese writing doesn't represent spoken language in the way that alphabetic writing does, but it still represents spoken language—just in a much more complicated way.

But what of the observation, marveled at since Westerners began reporting from the Far East in the sixteenth century, that character writing is understood throughout Asia? How can it be that people who speak completely different, non–mutually intelligible languages understand each other in character writing? The truth is, they don't. At least not in the way you would imagine from the ever popular "characters transcend language and go straight to concepts" account.

The Chinese writing system is based on Mandarin Chinese. Other languages spoken in China, like Cantonese, are different but historically related—about as similar as French and Italian are. So what happens when a Cantonese speaker picks up a Mandarin newspaper? Does he just read it off into his own language? No. Essentially, he reads it in Mandarin. In order to become literate, he has had to learn the Mandarin way of marking grammatical distinctions and the Mandarin way of putting sentences together. He may not have learned the Mandarin way of pronouncing every word, but many of the Cantonese pronunciations are similar (as are the French *jour* and the Italian *giorno*), so the sound clues in the characters are sometimes helpful. However, they are much less helpful, so he has had to do a lot more brute memorization. This is why it has taken him a couple of years longer than a Mandarin speaker to become literate.

As for a Japanese speaker, he does not understand the Mandarin newspaper at all. His spoken language is about as similar to Mandarin as Hungarian is to English. However, for historical reasons, Japanese is partially written with Chinese characters (along with other characters that stand for sounds). So when a Japanese speaker sees a Mandarin newspaper, he may indeed be able to recognize a number of the characters, but that doesn't mean he will be able to form anything more than a fuzzy guess at what it all means. The situation is comparable to a Hungarian speaker seeing the English sentence "I saw the information about the crime on television." Because Hungarian makes use of the international loanwords *informacio*, *krimi*, and *televizio*, a speaker will recognize "information . . . crime . . . television," and she might guess the meaning of the sentence correctly. However, she might make the same guess if the sentence says, "I took the *information* about the *crime* and hid it behind the *television*," and in that case her guess would be quite off the mark. And anyway, her interpretation of "crime" is probably wrong to begin with, since *krimi* means not "crime" but "crime story" or "detective novel" in Hungarian. The best a Japanese speaker can do with a Chinese text is pull out a big jumble of words. And a lot of them will mean something slightly—or even totally—different from what they mean in the Chinese version.

No, Chinese characters do not offer a magical ride to the land of pure ideas. Just a f@!*% hard slog to the city of words.

The Spacemen
Speak

After Bliss's first visit to Toronto things started to look up for Blissymbolics. He now had a real, practical success story to add to his dossier. He commenced an aggressive letter-writing campaign that got him some major international press, including an article in *Time* magazine. People from all over the world began to contact the center in Ontario, looking for more information about its program. McNaughton and her team began to develop educational materials and a teacher training protocol, so that others could take advantage of this new communication tool.

The more successful the program became, the more Bliss complained about the way the teachers at the center were doing things. They didn't draw the lines thick enough; the proportions were wrong; they used "fancy" terms like "nouns" and "verbs" (terms used by the evil grammar teachers, the torturers of his youth) to describe what he called "things" and "actions." Every time McNaughton sent him materials to look over, he wrote back lengthy tirades about all the ways they had gotten his system wrong. He was outraged that in one of their textbooks, they showed his symbol for vegetable, ♉, next to a picture of various vegetables, including tomatoes. They had totally misunderstood his system! This was the symbol for things you eat (mouth symbol) that grow underground! Tomatoes don't grow underground! The symbol for those kinds of vegetables is this: ♋!

Bliss failed to see that the ultimate goal of the program was to teach the children to express themselves in English. At first, the iconicity of the symbols was important. The children couldn't read yet, so they needed a way to recognize a word. The teachers would introduce a new symbol by pointing out how it resembled the object it stood for or, in the case of more abstract symbols, by explaining its motivation. Then the symbol would be added to each child's symbol board—a grid of squares, each containing a symbol, with the English word written underneath it. In interactions with others, the children would pick out a word by recognizing its symbol and pointing to it; the person they were talking to would understand it by reading the English below it. Over time, with the use and interaction by which we all come to understand the meaning of words, the imagery in the symbol would become less important, just a slight reminder of the word it stood for. The English word "vegetable" does cover tomatoes. And for the children using it, ♉ was just a nonalphabetic way to get to that word.

The teachers did the best they could to accommodate Bliss's criticisms. But his objectives were completely at odds with the practical problems they had to face. When the teachers encouraged the children to remember the symbol for "food," $\underline{\circ}$, by picturing it as a plate with a spoon under it, he was livid. It was crucial to his system that it be understood as the "mouth" above the "earth" because the true meaning (according to his "logical" system) was "all *food* which our *mouth* takes from *Mother Earth.*" When one of their newsletters showed a symbol sentence meaning "The Toronto Maple Leafs beat the Pittsburgh Penguins," he lamented, "All in spite of my condemnation of competitive sport in my book!" When they used the combination "food + out" to mean "picnic," he proclaimed, "FALSE!" It did not mean "picnic"; it meant "food out at a restaurant." When they wrote to him to request symbols for words they needed, he rarely responded. But he criticized without fail when they came up with something themselves.

He had created a "universal" language that nobody else could figure out how to use.

The staff's plan to keep Bliss away from the administration didn't last very long. He wrote to the principal, to the doctors, to the minister of health. He complained about the ways in which his symbols were being abused, and he started to demand some of the money he was convinced was pouring in from all sides.

He would come back to visit every spring, bearing gifts and kisses for everyone, and fervent apologies for those who had received some of his harsher letters. Then he would go back to Australia and start in again. Why hadn't anyone acknowledged his gifts? Didn't they realize how much he had spent on them? Didn't they realize he barely earned enough to afford the canned peas, mincemeat, and small pinch of beetroot he subsisted on day by day? Did they ever think about that while they collected the fat salaries they earned off the sweat of his life's work?

In fact, they were struggling to attract resources and support for their program. They needed to convince granting agencies and government officials of the value of this new and experimental teaching method. Shirley was on one side arguing against those who thought needs-based pictures (a toilet, a cup, a sandwich) were "good enough" and on the other side arguing against those who thought they should just start off by teaching the kids to spell. Meanwhile, Charles was traveling around Canada dismantling any progress they had made. He gave public lectures that were nothing more than point-by-point critiques of all their "mistakes." He badgered government officials to convince the OCCC teachers to stop damaging the children by using his system incorrectly (at one point he ambushed the Ontario minister of education outside his home). In Bliss's mind, he was helping the center to do a better job, and he expected them to be grateful.

So it was a surprise to him when, on his 1974 visit, the director of the OCCC called Bliss into his office and told him never to come back. They had had enough. In another room, on another floor, an Australian and Canadian film crew was setting up to record a scene for a documentary they were making about Bliss. Shirley went up to get him. He was shaken, coughing nervously, but he said nothing about what had just happened. He drank a glass of water and, in the time it took them to walk downstairs, transformed himself back into the jolly, hopping firecracker that he always seemed to be in front of an audience. He went ahead and performed for the camera and the children, grabbing a globe to demonstrate how far away Australia was. When I first watched the film, *Mr. Symbol Man*, I didn't notice anything different about him in the scene. But after hearing the story from Shirley, I went back and watched it again. After he puts down the globe, he sits off to the side as Kari dictates a letter to her teacher through her symbol board. He seems uncharacteristically subdued, and a little confused. His face is drained of animation and painfully vulnerable. A few scenes later he is back in Australia, sitting at his desk, smiling and throwing his hands up in dramatic exasperation. "People don't *listen* to me! They look right through me! What should I do? What should I do?" Then he turns away with a desperate, high-pitched laugh that's almost too much to bear.

At one point, Bliss was invited to give a lecture at a hospital in Sydney. Afterward, he fumed that only nurses had shown up. "Not one doctor!" he complained. He threatened to cancel an upcoming lecture at another hospital unless the organizers could guarantee that full, high-ranking medical doctors would be there. Instead, they canceled on him. Despite the documentary, the lecture invitations, the reporters knocking on his door, he felt ignored, disrespected. He was getting the attention of nurses, social workers, and teachers, when he wanted doctors, professors, and heads of state.

He was lucky to be getting any attention at all. Blissymbolics was not the only pictorial symbol language to emerge after World War II. There was Karl Janson's Picto (1957) and John Williams's Pikto (1959) and Andreas Eckardt's Safo (1962). No one was using those languages for anything.

Bliss had come to adulthood in interwar Austria, where a man was nothing without a title. He longed to inspire the same awed respect in others that he had felt when, as a poor, provincial nobody, he encountered the Herr Doktors, Herr Ingenieurs, and Herr Doktor Doktor Professors of Vienna. He thought people didn't listen to him because he lacked the right titles, and so he never ceased trying to get those titles. He wrote to every university in Australia, asking to be granted a professorship, or at least a Ph.D., on the basis of his success with the Toronto program, but none responded. (He did finally purchase a mail-order Ph.D., shortly before his death.)

The titles wouldn't have done him any good. While Bliss was traveling around giving interviews and lectures ("nurses'" lectures though they may have been), one Doktor Doktor Professor John Wolfgang Weilgart was unsuccessfully trying to get someone, anyone, to pay attention to *his* universal language.

Weilgart was a professor of psychology (at Luther College, in Iowa) with two Ph.D.'s when he first published his *aUI: The Language of Space*, in 1968. Weilgart was also from Austria, but had grown up in much more elevated circumstances than Bliss had. His grandfather was a Hungarian nobleman of some sort. His father, Hofrat Professor Doktor Doktor Arpad Weixlgärtner, was the director of the Kunsthistorisches Museum in Vienna. His uncle Richard Neutra was a famous architect. They lived in Schoenburg Palace for a time. They socialized with Freud and other luminaries of turn-of-the-century Vienna.

As a boy, Weilgart had visions of winged beings who came from the stars to deliver a message of peace. When he told his parents about his visions, they took him to a psychiatrist, who diagnosed nothing more than a high IQ but warned him that he should speak about such visions only as "dreams" or "poems." Since he seemed to be obsessed with words and sounds and meaning, his father encouraged him to get a degree in languages and philology, which he did, completing his dissertation a few months before the outbreak of World War II. He spent the war in the United States, teaching German, Spanish, Latin, and French at various schools and colleges in Oregon, California, and Louisiana. After the war, he returned to Europe and got another degree, in psychology.

He began teaching at Luther in 1964, where he completed his book on aUI. It begins with a poem about a boy who is visited by a kindly "Spaceman." The Spaceman wants to transmit the wisdom of his beings to the people of Earth, but cannot do it through the languages of Earth, because "if we learnt your millions of words, we would be infected by your warped way of thinking." So he teaches the boy the language of space.

In aUI, all concepts are derived from a set of thirty-three basic elements that have not only a motivated pictorial representation but a motivated sound representation.

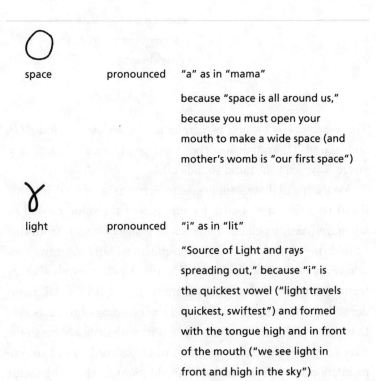

space   pronounced   "a" as in "mama"

because "space is all around us," because you must open your mouth to make a wide space (and mother's womb is "our first space")

light   pronounced   "i" as in "lit"

"Source of Light and rays spreading out," because "i" is the quickest vowel ("light travels quickest, swiftest") and formed with the tongue high and in front of the mouth ("we see light in front and high in the sky")

~

sound

| a sound wave | pronounced | "ee" as in a "shrieking police siren" because it is of the same quality as "i" ("light") but longer, "the sound we hear takes longer than the light we see" |

△

mind

| spirit trinity | pronounced | "oo" as in "true" because it is a high back vowel and "spirit soars high, but hides its mystery long" |

The word *aUI* is formed by combining "space" (*a*), "mind" (*U*), and "sound" (*I*) and means "the language of space" because language is "when your mind sounds off."

Weilgart's aUI was supposed to serve as a neutral international language, and a cure for diseases of the mind caused by language. Weilgart claimed it was a language of cosmic truth that could bring about peace, dissolve selfishness, and align the conscious and subconscious mind. He developed a psychotherapy technique where he had patients translate words into aUI, in order to help them better understand the meaning of the concepts that troubled them. He worked for a time with drug addicts in the navy's drug rehabilitation program, where, according to a recommendation letter from his boss, "meditations in these 'Elements of Meaning' superseded the desire for drug experience."

Despite his credentials, Weilgart could not get anyone to listen to him. His self-published books were full of bizarre line drawings, poems, and mystic philosophizing. Weilgart's bewildered colleagues at Luther tolerated him in their polite Lutheran way, while the administration pushed him to the margins as much as they could. He was asked not to peddle his books on campus, so some summers he left his family behind and toured across the country in a van, a prophet of the cosmos, stopping people on the street to tell them about aUI. He wrote to everyone he could think of, trying to drum up support for his project—Kurt Waldheim, B. F. Skinner, Pearl Buck, Albert Schweitzer, Noam Chomsky, the Shah of Iran. He asked Johnny Carson to make an announcement on his show. He asked Kurt Vonnegut to introduce aUI "in some of your stories . . . by letting e.g. a space-man speak in this language (I would be glad to translate any sentence into it)." In each case he molded his approach to what he thought the recipient might want to hear, often to embarrassing effect. He began his letter to Margaret Mead by appealing to her womanhood ("it takes a woman to teach the mother-tongue . . . I see you, dear Mrs. Mead, as prophetess of motherhood"), and his letter to Harry Belafonte describes aUI as a "language without prejudice" and dwells on the unfortunate sound associations of the word "niggardly."

He wrote to some of the same people Bliss did, and at some point one of them must have informed Bliss about Weilgart's project. Bliss wrote to him immediately, but kept it polite. After all, here was a Doktor Doktor Professor who didn't dismiss the idea of a universal symbol language but rather embraced it. Perhaps he could convince Herr Professor to support Blissymbolics instead. Weilgart wrote back an equally polite letter, expressing admiration for Bliss's ideals but not saying much about his project beyond that he thought it was "a most interesting endeavor." The rest of Weilgart's letter was a slyly aggressive description of his background—the illustrious relatives, the degrees he had received, his experience being diagnosed with an abnormally high IQ—every detail no doubt another knife twist in Bliss's fevered knot of insecurity.

Bliss received Weilgart's letter in April 1972, just before his first trip to Toronto. He was about to experience the peak of his career, and Weilgart, who wasn't being written about in *Time* magazine or anywhere else that Bliss knew of, soon seemed a much diminished threat. Bliss shifted his attention to other problems.

The Catastrophic Results of Her Ignorance

B oth Bliss and Weilgart claimed their languages expressed
the fundamental truth about things. They also claimed that
because they used "natural" symbolism—forms that looked like,
or sounded like, the things they referred to—their languages were
transparent, able to be universally understood. However, their
ideas of what was "true" and what was "natural" were completely
different.

For example, Bliss's symbol for water is Weilgart's symbol
for sound. For Weilgart, water is not a primitive but a complex
concept:

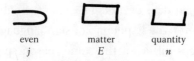

| even | matter | quantity |
| *j* | *E* | *n* |

The explanation is that water is the liquid (jE , matter that "stands even, when at rest") of greatest quantity.

For Bliss, sound is not a basic primitive but a complex concept, 2 —an ear on top of the earth—that "indicates a vibration of air molecules."

Weilgart's image of water refers to how it looks when it is level, and Bliss's refers to how it looks when it has waves in it. Bliss's image of sound refers to the organ that receives it, and Weilgart's refers to the "wave" physics of its transmission. Who has the truth? Whose representation is more "natural"?

If two men who come from the same place and speak the same language can't even agree with each other about the "true" representation of anything, how can either one of them stake a claim on universality? The act of understanding a sentence in either system is an act of figuring out one man's opinions, of guessing one man's intentions. These languages are about as opposite of universal as you can get. They require mind reading, a task considerably more difficult than, say, learning French.

Imagistic symbolism can transmit meaning, but in such a vague and open-ended way that it makes a terrible principle on which to build a language. This is why there are no languages, and no writing systems, that operate on such a principle.

This includes sign languages, which are assumed by many to be a sort of universal pantomime. In fact sign languages differ considerably from country to country, so much so that in the 1950s, the newly formed World Federation of the Deaf assigned a committee to look into the matter of developing an auxiliary sign standard that could be used at the federation's world congress and other international deaf events. The result, finally published in 1975, was Gestuno, the Esperanto of sign language.

Sign languages differ for the same reason spoken languages

differ—they evolved naturally, from communities of people interacting with one another. Wherever deaf people have come together in groups, whether because they lived in places with a high incidence of genetic deafness or because they were brought together in institutions or schools, they have spontaneously developed a sign language. These languages may have their origins in gestures of "acting things out"—a type of vague, *partial* communication—but over time set meanings developed, means of marking grammatical distinctions became fixed, and they turned into real languages, systems of *full* communication.

Signs mean what they mean by conventional agreement, and different communities of signers have different agreements. In American Sign Language (ASL), for example, the sign below means "hat," not because it looks like a hat being placed on the head, but because the community of users of ASL agree that it means "hat."

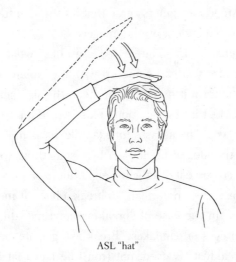

ASL "hat"

Users of Nepali Sign Language (NSL) have a different agreement: a sign that looks exactly the same means "well done."

NSL "well done"

Does this sign "look like" a pat on the head for a job well done or a hat being placed on the head? It doesn't really matter. What matters is that Nepalese signers agree that it's the sign for "well done" and American signers agree that it's the sign for "hat." The meaning isn't dependent on the imagery.

Many signs do, in some sense, "look like" what they mean, but just because you can come up with an explanation for why a sign has the form it has does not mean the sign gets its meaning by virtue of that explanation. This is true for spoken words as well. The word "breakfast," for example, has a motivated form, inspired by the idea of breaking a fast, something you do in the morning when you eat after going eight hours or so without food. But "breakfast" does not mean "to break a fast." It means "morning meal," or, in the case of "breakfast anytime" diners, a meal consisting of eggs or pancakes. "Breakfast" gets its meaning from the way "breakfast" is used, not from the fact that it was once formed from the words "break" and "fast." (Therefore it doesn't matter that the "break" in "breakfast" has come to be pronounced "brek." You don't need to recognize the motivation for the word in order to understand it.)

Likewise, the ASL sign for "girl," which traces a line on the cheek, gets its meaning through conventional usage, not from the fact that it was motivated by the image of a bonnet string. (Therefore it doesn't matter that girls no longer wear bonnets.)

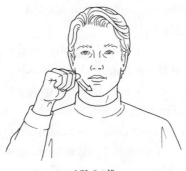

ASL "girl"

Gestuno, like most international language schemes, was a big flop. The committee had drawn from existing sign languages, trying to pick the most iconic signs, but without favoring any one country too much. Deaf people complained that the signs that had been chosen weren't easy enough to understand. Furthermore, Gestuno was only a lexicon, not a grammar, so there were no explicit guidelines for putting sentences together. At the 1979 World Deaf Congress in Bulgaria, the first congress to provide Gestuno interpretation of the presentations, the interpreters simply stuck Gestuno signs into (spoken) Bulgarian sentence structures (sign languages do not follow the same word order or grammar as their surrounding spoken languages). No one understood what was going on, and Gestuno never recovered from the fiasco.

Something else took its place—a spontaneous sort of pidgin

signing now called International Sign. It had actually been around long before Gestuno. Whenever deaf people of different sign language backgrounds get together at international events (like the Deaf Olympics, which began in the 1920s), they quickly find a way to communicate with one another. They sign more slowly, gesture, and repeat information in multiple ways, and pretty soon they come to a sort of miniature, incomplete, conventional agreement. They negotiate a standard, but one that is less reliable than any full sign language.

However, that standard, and a pretty good level of communication, is achieved far more quickly and easily than it ever could be between people who speak different *spoken* languages. That is because while the iconic imagery is not the primary principle on which sign languages depend, it is undeniably there, and it has the potential to be exploited. Spoken languages have this potential as well (something can last a "long" time or a "looooooooong" time) but a whole lot less of it.

Imagery, in signs or in symbols, isn't suitable for communication on its own. It must be interpreted, its meaning guessed at. But in a situation where the guesses can be constrained, where two people can use context and feedback from each other to put a limit on the possible interpretations, it is extremely useful. The teachers at the OCCC understood this, and what they did with the children was set up just such a situation. When a child wanted to say "dream" but did not have a symbol for it on her board, she pointed to "sleep + think." Her teacher guessed from the context that she meant "dream," and the child confirmed that guess. If a child tried a combination and the teacher guessed wrong, the teacher could take another guess, or the child could try a different approach. Communication had always been a guessing game for these children, but before Blissymbols they had no way to constrain the guesses. If a child had needs-based pictures to point to, he might have tried to say "dream" by pointing to a picture of a bed. Then the adult would ask, "Do you want to go to bed? Do you want to get your pillow? Is there a problem in your bedroom?" and the child would have no power to direct the line of questioning. When the children learned Blissymbols, and a method for representing abstract concepts through combination, they finally had a way to actively put limits on interpretation.

And this changed their lives tremendously. On my Toronto trip, I asked another of Shirley's former students how he used to communicate before he learned Blissymbolics. He typed out a one-word answer on his computer: "Kick."

Though Blissymbols was a huge improvement over what was available to the children before, it was still not good enough. The children could communicate about almost anything with their teachers, parents, and others who were familiar with the special mechanics of negotiated agreement that Blissymbols required, but they couldn't do this with just anyone. They had access to communication, but not full access. They had a very useful tool, but not a language.

So the OCCC staff modified and adapted Bliss's system in order to make it serve as a bridge to English. They added the alphabet to the symbol boards, so the kids, before they had fully learned to spell, could constrain a symbol by pointing to the first letter of the word they intended. Teachers using the symbols in other countries made adjustments in accordance with the requirements of their spoken languages: In Hungary, they changed the order of the symbols to reflect Hungarian word order and added symbols for grammatical markers as needed. In Israel, they wrote the symbols from right to left. All of these adjustments infuriated Bliss, because he thought he had invented a universal language.

After the OCCC administration told Bliss he was not welcome anymore, his level of interference increased tenfold, and he started threatening lawsuits. Twice, legal agreements were reached where he granted the center rights to use his symbols (under the terms of one agreement, the center was required to mark all symbols in its publications that he had not personally approved with a Ⓑ), but he always found an excuse to break the agreements and begin fresh attacks on its progress.

He sent an open letter to all institutions in Europe that worked with disabled children in order to "voice my flaming protest against the machinations and perversions of my work by an irresponsible and irrational woman, Mrs. Shirley McNaughton." He wrote a pamphlet called "My Terror of Toronto" and sent it to the government, the press, and anyone else he thought would listen. McNaughton started getting random "who do you think you are?" letters from strangers. At the same time, Bliss wrote her letters telling her how much he loved her and hoped they could "go on to a greater glory together." After he viewed the *Mr. Symbol Man* film, he sent her a telegram:

HAVE SEEN FILM EXTREME CLOSEUP OF YOU DEADLY TO HOLLYWOOD BEAUTIES BUT YOU CAME OUT MORE BEAUTIFUL THAN EVER HAVE FALLEN IN LOVE WHAT AGAIN YES AGAIN LOVE TO BOB KEVIN DAVID

Bliss was desperate for respect, but he was more desperate for love. He was genuinely shocked and hurt when people got angry at him, or cut him out of their lives, despite the fact that it was his own irrational behavior that drove them away. He saw himself as a charmer, an entertainer, a selfless lover of humanity. In his oft-repeated and unlikely account of his release from Buchenwald, he had melted the hearts of his Nazi prison guards with his mandolin playing. It was crucial to his view of himself that he believe in the magical power of his generous spirit.

So, often, when he sensed he had gone too far, he made an effort to win back love. But it never lasted very long. Sometimes the very next day after an apology, a flattery, a plea for pity and understanding, he would find himself fueled by a fresh wave of indignant anger, and the tirades would start up again. He couldn't help himself.

This was his holiday greeting the next year:

A MERRY CHRISTMAS TO YOU, PEACE ON EARTH AND GOOD WILL TO ALL MEN. Yes, Good Will to all Men, but not to a woman, Mrs. McNaughton. She's trying to kill me, make me drop dead so she can take over, but im not going to. Are you protecting your fair maiden, well she's not fair. She has black hair and a black mind.

At one point, Shirley almost resigned, but found she couldn't leave her students behind. Instead, she accepted dealing with Bliss as another part of her job. He still came back every spring, and she still greeted him warmly. Despite everything that had happened, she maintained respect and admiration for him, and really did want to please him. Her equanimity in the face of it all resulted in a workable but absurd situation, as captured in one of her letters to Bliss.

Dear Charles:

This is to acknowledge receipt of your July 19th letter, "Three Devastating Proofs That Shirley McNaughton Is Catastrophically Ignorant of My Logical Symbol System and the Catastrophic Results of Her Ignorance," and your more recent letter of July 21st. Prior to your second letter I discussed with [the administration] your request for $5,000. Please direct all future correspondence relating to your expenses to them.

Thank you for your speedy response to our cable regarding the thickness of the pointer, and for your July 21st letter expressing your desire to work on symbols in September.

We look forward to your involvement in developing more symbols in the fall.

Sincerely,

Shirley

Eventually, the workable could no longer coexist with the absurd. Bliss brought the lawyers back, and the center, desperate to make him go away, settled with him. In 1982, the OCCC got an exclusive, noncancelable, and perpetual license to use Blissymbolics, and he got $160,000. Easter Seals, the charitable foundation under whose auspices the program was now working, paid the settlement.

That's right. There's no other way to put it: Bliss, self-proclaimed savior of humanity, stole $160,000 from crippled children.

I found out about the details of the settlement when I met with Shirley in the sleepy Ontario town of Guelph, where she lives with her husband in a tidy retirement village. There are Blissymbols throughout their town house, on a mirror over the piano, on needlepoint cushions in the guest room. The kitchen backsplash is formed by a chain of painted tiles that say, in Blissymbols, "People helping people helping people helping people."

When she told me how much Bliss got in the settlement, I couldn't contain myself. I told her how selfish, how blind, how crazy I thought he was. "Yes, it was difficult," she said, "but it was all for the good of the kids who needed it in the end. Now I'm around the same age that he was when he first came to us, and I think I understand him better. I see that there's not a lot of time left, and that has made me less tolerant of some things."

Her biggest regret about Bliss's behavior is that it hurt the reputation of their program. The Blissymbol method is used in scattered, individual schools in Canada, Sweden, and a few other countries, but it never gained traction in the United States, Britain, or any of the places that tend to determine the types of technologies and teaching materials that will be made widely available. Other symbol systems are used today, but they are more picture-like, less abstract, and less flexible than the Blissymbols. They serve for communication, but not as a bridge to full language—at least not for kids with the types of disabilities Shirley has worked with. She sees the predominance of these other symbol systems as "a reflection of how society treats disability—'pictures are good enough.' There's no concern with enriching. They aren't worried about the dignity of full language."

On my last night in Toronto I had dinner with Paul Marshall—a former Bliss student of one of Shirley's colleagues—who now works on projects for the Blissymbol program. His cerebral palsy is relatively mild—his motions are jerky and unbalanced, but he can walk, and he can point and type with one finger. However, he cannot use his voice. He came to the Blissymbol program when he was twelve, able to recognize some written words, but mostly dependent on his mother's guessing. He was frustrated, angry, and depressed. By eighteen, he had made the transition to full English text. Today, he lives in his own apartment, about 120 miles north of Toronto, and works as a Webmaster. He told me, by spelling it out on a laminated alphabet grid, "Bliss is one of the greatest things ever to happen to me." After dinner he went to catch a bus back home. Later that night, a major snowstorm hit, and the highway he was on was shut down for five hours. He was able to ask his fellow passengers to call his mother and tell her not to worry. He used his own words and spoke his own mind. No vague interpretation, no guessing. He was only as stuck and frustrated as the rest of the people on that bus.

Bliss was fond of saying, "The greatest hindrance to Blissymbolics is the fact that I am still alive." Most of the time he meant this as an accusation against society and its inability to notice genius until it no longer walks among them. But sometimes he seemed to mean it as self-reproach, an admission that he was his own worst enemy. He angered and drove away almost everyone who could have done him any good.

And yet, in a few, he inspired a devoted kind of loyalty—partly based on his manic charisma, and partly based on pity. Shirley never expressed more than mild exasperation with him. On his last trip to Toronto, they spent their days together in a room full of administrators and lawyers, going through legal discovery for his case against her work. At night, she went to his seedy hotel room to help him put drops in his ears for a medical condition. When I asked her how that made any sense, she answered, "Well, he had no one else."

Bliss spent the money on a big publication run of his own Blissymbols teaching manual. It is the sharpest looking of all his publications—a bright red hard-vinyl cover over 564 high-quality card-stock pages held together in a two-ring binder. It is professionally illustrated, and all the symbols are drawn to his specifications. The content, however, is the same old classic Bliss—blustery and preposterous. Here is how he advises teaching the symbol for steam:

> Put a saucepan or a kettle on the stove and when the steam comes out
> let your handicapped child put its finger near the steam. Of course,
> it will get slightly burned, but it will be a lesson for life what steam
> really is and why it is the opposite of rain, which is usually rather cold
> or slightly warm.

Most of the books were destroyed in a fire after Bliss died in 1985. Douglas Everingham, a local Sydney doctor and politician, was named one of the executors of what was left. Everingham, himself interested in the international language cause, had been an early supporter of Bliss's work and had done what he could in the 1970s, during his term as national minister of health, to promote Blissymbolics (at great risk to his own reputation). Bliss, of course, thought Everingham didn't try hard enough and once showed up at a public rally where he was campaigning for reelection and heckled him, crying, "Down with Everingham!" and worse.

Everingham told me by e-mail that he still thought kindly of Bliss, and encouraged me to be charitable toward him as well. He reminded me that Bliss was a Holocaust survivor, a refugee, an immigrant; Bliss had seen terrible things, and he really did believe he had invented a solution, a way to ensure those things would never happen again.

But, in looking through Bliss's writings, I found that he did have his moments of doubt. Buried in one of his books, in a rant about psychologists and how they are always trying to read into things, is the following passage:

> Take Bliss, the author of this book. He thinks that his work is motivated
> by his conscience, that he slaves for humanity. But it may be only a
> craving for the limelight of public acclaim. He rises in defence of the

children of mankind (so he thinks) when he attacks the teachers. But it may be only envy and enmity and rage about their rejection of his work (which they didn't even bother to examine).

He thinks his invention will revolutionize the 21st century. The hell it will! The teachers will be adamant. So he cries, "To dream the impossible dream, to beat the unbeatable foe, etc., etc." feeling himself a pioneer and martyr rolled in one.

Well, what motivates him really?

He stops there.

JAMES COOKE BROWN AND THE LANGUAGE OF LOGIC

ei do cusku le do se skudji
You are obliged to say the desired-to-be-said thing.

i mi go'i i y ju'oru'e y i mi skudji le mi se cusku i ka'u la'e
di'u mintu
I am doing that last proposition just mentioned. I am the saying-desirer of the desired-to-be-said thing of me. I know culturally that the referent of the last utterance is the same thing.

na mintu
Not identical.

—*The Lojban* Alice's Adventures in Wonderland

"Then you should say what you mean," the March Hare went on.

"I do," Alice hastily replied; "at least—at least I mean what I say—that's the same thing, you know."

"Not the same thing a bit!" said the Hatter.

—*Lewis Carroll's* Alice's Adventures in Wonderland

1931	*Whorf begins studying linguistics*
1933	*Korzybski publishes* Science and Sanity
1938	*Chase publishes* Tyranny of Words
1949	*Orwell's Newspeak introduced*
1953	*Whorf conference*
1955	*Brown begins work on Loglan*
1960	*Brown publishes article in* Scientific American
1979	*Brown forms member-controlled corporation*
1984	*Elgin's Láadan*
1987	*Bob and Nora marry*
1988	*Lojban created*
1992	*Brown loses case*
2000	*Brown dies*

The Whorfian Hypothesis

B lissymbolics and aUI and the few other pictographic languages of the post-Esperanto era hardly constituted a *movement*, but they did reflect a widespread popular preoccupation with, as the title of one 1938 best seller called it, "the tyranny of words." Both Bliss and Weilgart advertised their projects not just as a way for people of different language backgrounds to communicate with each other but as a way to uncover the truths that our natural languages hid or distorted. They worked on the assumption that language warped the mind, and that assumption was not just some crazy outsider philosophy. It was very much a part of the general intellectual climate from the 1930s to the 1950s, when Bliss and Weilgart were developing their systems.

Of course, the Nazi and Soviet propaganda machines

provided dramatic evidence for the pernicious power of language, but the "tyranny of words" idea went beyond the claim that bad people sometimes used language to bad ends. It suggested that all of us, every day, were being misled, not by lies told by others, but by our own habits of thinking, as conditioned by the very structure of our languages.

This idea had become popular even before the war. In their influential book, *The Meaning of Meaning* (1923), C. K. Ogden and I. A. Richards blamed all sorts of confusion on "the superstition that words are in some way parts of things or always imply things corresponding to them"—the "Word Magic" problem that Ogden later proposed to solve with his Basic English. Ten years later Count Alfred Korzybski published his *Science and Sanity*, a dense, jargon-filled tome on the ways in which language "enslaves" us by conditioning our brains to perceive a false reality. More people probably claimed to have read it than actually did—even his followers called the azure-tinted volume "the blue peril"—but Korzybski's ideas, as interpreted by popularizers like Stuart Chase (of the previously mentioned *Tyranny of Words*) and S. I. Hayakawa (of the 1941 Book-of-the-Month Club selection *Language in Action*), rippled through the culture. For a time, any cocktail party guest with pretensions to erudition could pepper his conversation with a "general relativity" here, a "neurosemantic reaction" there, a melodious "Korzybski" or two to tie it all together, and he would be rewarded with some knowing, serious head nodding.

In the halls of mainstream academia, however, Korzybski's name got a different reaction. He was an independent scholar without professionally recognized expertise in any of the fields he drew on in creating his boastful, sprawling theory of everything. He published his books and ran his seminars under the rubric of his own Institute of General Semantics, where he promoted techniques for overcoming the thinking errors caused by language—beware of the verb "to be" ("Is-ness is insanity," he liked to say), mentally subscript the objects you talk about (to remind yourself that there is only pencil$_1$, pencil$_2$, pencil$_3$, and so on and no abstraction "pencil" that covers all cases), and frequently insert an "etc." (to remind yourself that there is always more to the story than your words would have you believe).

It didn't help that his seminars had the flavor of a tent revival, complete with emotional manipulation disguised as object lessons (he liked to bring a female student up to the stage and slap her face, then tell the audience that their horrified reaction was "unjustified, as what they have seen turned out to be merely a scientific demonstration of the mechanism of identification") and testimonials. People in various professions claimed that training in general semantics (as Korzybski's discipline came to be called) could solve an astonishing array of problems: businessmen said it saved their clients' money; psychiatrists said it cured alcoholism, homosexuality, frigidity, and nymphomania; teachers said it cured reading problems, stuttering, and stage fright; a dentist even said it helped keep fillings in place.

Many people were attracted to the idea that if you could control your language, you could control your mind and solve your problems. (The idea still has some popularity today, in the form of moneymaking self-help ventures like Neuro-Linguistic Programming, a descendant of general semantics.) And they took seriously the warnings about language and mind control coming from the new literature of dystopia. In Ayn Rand's *Anthem*, published in 1938, citizens of a futuristic collective society cannot conceive of their own individuality, because they lack the pronoun "I." In George Orwell's *1984* (first published in 1949), a totalitarian

state controls its subjects through the imposition of Newspeak—
people who are denied words for subversive thoughts are rendered
incapable of thinking those thoughts.

Poor language. People had always been blaming one thing or
another on it, but in the 1930s and 1940s it really took a beating. Before that, in the Esperanto era, language was accused of
turning people against each other. The problem was that it prevented mutual understanding, and the solution was to invent or
choose a language that everyone could understand. In the post-
Esperanto era, language was being accused of everything from
genocide to tooth decay. Now the problem with language was its
dangerous grip on thought. But what was the solution? Not to
invent a new language. No one took that idea seriously anymore.
Proposals like Blissymbolics were laughed right out of the arena.
(Bliss described a response he received from a prominent general
semanticist as "not nice at all.") This time, the solution was to
bring language into line with reality, to polish the grime and the
rust off the tools, teach people how to use them properly, and put
them into service for the truth.

But leaving aside the question of how the truth was to be determined, where exactly was this grime and rust? And how was
it to be removed? There were differences of opinion, of course.
Ogden had a problem with abstract words posing as truly meaningful words—"fictions" like "causation" and "political" mimicked
the behavior of good solid words like "chair" and "red." The key
was to stick to the good solid words. But for Korzybski "chair"
and "red" were just as big a part of the problem; the key was to
constantly remind ourselves that there was no such thing as a
chair (only $chair_1$, $chair_2$, $chair_3$, $chair_3$ as I experienced it in 1934,
$chair_3$ as I experience it now, and so on) and that red was only a
subjective individual experience of a certain wavelength of light.

For Orwell (as expressed in his 1946 essay "Politics and the English Language"), the villains were tired metaphors, long, fancy words, and passive verbs.

Though critics took issue with the various cures proposed for the language disease, no one really questioned the original diagnosis: language was a bad influence on thought. But in the 1950s scholars began to look more closely at that background assumption. Fields like psychology, anthropology, and sociology had picked up the machinery of the hard sciences—empirical observation, measurement, experiment—and were figuring out ways to apply it to the "soft" areas of human behavior: mind, meaning, culture. When it came to the matter of human thought, and what may or may not be influencing it, a modern social scientist had two choices: (1) reject all discussion of "thought" as unscientific, because it was impossible to observe directly (the stance of behavioral psychology, which was having a heyday); or (2) find a way to test your hypothesis using cold, hard data. Sitting in your armchair and musing about words and thought was no longer an acceptable option.

At the same time, the language/thought question was getting fresh attention in academic circles with the posthumous republication of the papers of Benjamin Whorf. Whorf had been a chemical engineer, working as an inspector at a fire insurance company, when he began studying linguistics as a hobby. He went on to work with the anthropologist and linguist Edward Sapir and to produce highly respected studies of Native American languages. Though Whorf's papers were published in the premier journals and he was granted an honorary fellowship at Yale, he was still something of an outsider. His primary employment remained at the insurance company, and he never completed an advanced degree. There was also a religious or spiritual angle to some of his linguistic investigations (he was a follower of the eccentric Theosophy movement) that made many of his academic contacts uncomfortable. His ideas about the influence of language on thought made them even more uncomfortable, as they seemed dangerously close to the fashionable language polemics about "the tyranny of words" floating around out there among the linguistically naive masses.

But Whorf (though perhaps naive in other ways) was not linguistically naive. His ideas about language and thought were informed by a highly technical and sophisticated understanding of the grammatical structure of languages that were very different from any European language. He saw what he called "the new, and for the most part probably misguided interest in semantics" as marred by the "parochial viewpoint to which 'language' means simply 'English,' " and he tried to dissociate himself from the "various popular bromides about the misleading nature of words."

He began to formulate his ideas about the relationship of thought to language when, after finally piecing together a grammatical description of Hopi (an Uto-Aztecan language spoken in Arizona), he realized that he knew how to form plurals but not how to use them. It was like knowing that the English plural is formed by *es* when a word ends in an "s" sound, but not knowing that it's inappropriate to refer to a pile of rice as "rices." He realized that "the category of plural in Hopi was not the same thing as in English, French or German. Certain things that were plural in these languages were singular in Hopi." For example, something like "day" could not be pluralized in Hopi, because days were experienced one at a time; they could not be assembled into an objective group that could be observed all at once—a Hopi criterion for pluralness. Whorf connected this observation to other features of the language that suggested the Hopi experience of time was not the same as it was for a speaker of an SAE (Standard Average European) language. Could it be that a different way of categorizing things in language reflected a different way of categorizing things in the world?

He never got a chance to fully explore the question. He died of cancer in 1941, at the age of forty-four. He left behind a number of papers on the topic—some published, some unpublished, some written for experts and some for lay audiences—that served as the basis for what came to be called the Whorfian hypothesis (or Sapir-Whorf hypothesis). The science-minded scholars of the 1950s reinterpreted Whorf's incomplete and complicated exploration of various issues having to do with language, thought, and culture as an empirically testable claim, hence the Whorfian "hypothesis."

The closest Whorf himself ever got to a hypothesis-style statement was a description of his "linguistic relativity principle," which held that "users of markedly different grammars are pointed by their grammars toward different types of observations and different evaluations of externally similar acts of observation, and hence are not equivalent as observers but must arrive at somewhat different views of the world." As to what exactly he meant by that, well, there are about as many interpretations as there are mentions of Whorf's name in print. In any case, this statement is a long way from saying that abstract nouns or passive verbs or words like "is" are conspiring to gang up on us and steal our good sense. Whorf's ideas were definitely fertilized by the language-fearing times in which he lived, but his formulation of the language/thought question was the most sensitive to the complicated way in which language actually works and the most attractive to the social scientists who decided to take up the question in the 1950s.

It proved very difficult to come up with a scientific test of the Whorfian hypothesis. Suppose you compared two groups of people who spoke different languages, and you found some kind of difference between the groups. How would you know it was the language that caused that difference? Perhaps it was from a difference in culture. Perhaps it was the culture that shaped the language, and not the other way around. Every language was attached to a culture, and there was no way to separate one thing from the other. This was one of the problematic issues that came up when a group of top linguists, psychologists, and philosophers got together for a conference on the Whorfian hypothesis in 1953. The papers from the conference were published in a book called *Language in Culture,* and soon every field that touched on language and human behavior was buzzing about it.

A sociologist named James Cooke Brown, who had just taken a position at the University of Florida in Gainesville, was paying close attention. In the winter of 1955, when classes let out for the holidays, he "sat down before a bright fire to commence what I hoped would be a short paper on the possibility of testing the social psychological implications of the Sapir-Whorf hypothesis." He wanted to show that "the construction of a tiny model language, with a grammar borrowed from the rules of modern logic, taught to subjects of different nationalities in a laboratory setting under conditions of control, would permit a decisive test." If the problem with the Whorfian hypothesis experiment was that *natural* languages couldn't be disentangled from the cultures in which they were spoken, then why not avoid the problem by using an *artificial* language? This "tiny model language" became Loglan (from *log*ical *lan*guage), a project that would occupy the rest of

Brown's life. It would grow large enough to be used for original poetry, translations of works like *Alice's Adventures in Wonderland*, and, in one case, a proposal of marriage. It would bring Brown fame and disappointment, admirers and enemies, and a trip to federal court over the question of who rightfully owns a language—the man who invented it or the people who use it?

A Formula
for Success

I n 1960, Brown published a sketch of Loglan in *Scientific
American*. This was an amazing coup for a language inventor.
In a post-utopian, postwar world, where no one even deigned to
laugh at new language projects anymore, it was incredible that
a major periodical would treat an invented language seriously
enough to devote ten pages to it.

Brown had found a way to make language invention
respectable by treating his creation with scientific detachment.
He didn't say his language would stop war and heal the world;
he presented it merely as an instrument for testing a specific
hypothesis. He didn't crow about how easy it was to learn; he
computed a "learnability score" for each word (based on how
many sounds in the word overlapped with the sounds for that
word in different natural languages) and proposed that the

correlation between learnability scores and actual learnability could be tested in the lab. He didn't make wild claims about the profound and life-altering effects his language would have on thought; he demurred that he was "by no means certain yet that Loglan is a thinkable language, let alone a thought-facilitating one." His approach, humble, rational, and unemotional, was nothing like the idealistic flights of foolishness that people had come to expect from language inventors. If you wanted to get any attention for your invented-language project in 1960, scientific detachment was definitely the way to go.

Another language called Interlingua tried to adopt a similar approach in the 1950s and 1960s, and got a little bit of success in return. Interlingua was created by a committee called the International Auxiliary Language Association (IALA), which had been founded by Alice Vanderbilt Morris in 1924. The original goal of the association was to promote intelligent and objective discussion of competing invented languages and to encourage scholarly research into the matter of determining both the best form for an auxiliary language and the best uses for it. It was a meeting ground for the high-prestige language inventors and other professionals who were interested in the international language idea (linguists such as Edward Sapir, Morris Swadesh, Roman Jakobson, and André Martinet). Activity fell off in the 1930s and was further disrupted by the war, but the organization survived and ultimately published its own committee-designed Interlingua in 1951.

The first Interlingua periodical was *Spectroscopia Molecular*, a monthly overview of international work in . . . molecular spectroscopy. (It involves shooting energy at something in order to see what does or doesn't bounce back—physicists, chemists, and astronomers do it.) Next came a newsletter, *Scientia International*, a digest of the latest goings-on in the world of science. Interlingua positioned itself as a way for scientists of different language backgrounds to keep up with their fields. They wouldn't even necessarily have to speak the language. As long as they understood it, it would fulfill its businesslike function. By attaching itself to science, and refraining from grand claims, Interlingua spread a little further than it otherwise might have. Some major medical congresses and journals published abstracts in Interlingua throughout the 1950s and 1960s. But it failed to sustain interest. Interlingua was another one of those Greco-Latin least common denominator languages, and if you were interested in those kinds of things, you were probably already doing Esperanto. Everyone else just wasn't interested in those kinds of things, science oriented or not.

Loglan, however, was doing a different kind of thing. Scientific detachment was only one part of the appeal of Loglan (the part that convinced people not to dismiss it immediately). What really got people interested was its new kind of design principle—the calibrated alignment of language with logic. Actually, the principle wasn't new at all. It stretched all the way back to Leibniz and Wilkins and the seventeenth-century idea that we could somehow speak in pure logic. It *was* new in that great strides had been made in the field of logic since then, so the idea of "speaking logic" now meant something a bit different.

In the early twentieth century, philosophers such as Gottlob Frege, Bertrand Russell, and Rudolf Carnap had developed a preliminary mathematics of language, but it was not a mathematics of concepts—no breaking down the concept dog into the basic elements that defined its dogness. It was instead a mathematics of statements. It was a method of breaking down propositions like "The dog bit the man" or "All dogs are blue" into logical formulas. These formulas were not expressed in terms of nouns, verbs, and adjectives. Instead, like mathematical formulas, they were expressed in terms of functions and arguments. Much like $x(x + 5)$ is a function waiting for you to tell it what the argument x is, $dog(x)$ is a function, "is a dog," waiting for you to tell it what particular x is a dog. $Blue(x)$ is a function, "is blue," waiting to find out "what" is blue. $Bite(x, y)$ is a function waiting for two arguments, the biter and the bitten. $Give(x, y, z)$ is a function waiting for three arguments—x gives y to z.

The power of such a notation, both the mathematical and the logical, is that you can do a whole lot without ever knowing what x is. The formula $x(x + 5)$ can itself become an argument in a larger formula; it can participate in the solving of equations and proofs. It may never return a specific number, but it can help you assess the general validity of the statements in which it plays a part. Logical formulas can do the same. "All dogs are blue" is represented by the logical statement $\forall x\ dog(x) \rightarrow blue(x)$. Translated back into English, this means, "For every x, if x is a dog, then x is blue." This logical breakdown can't tell you whether or not the statement is true out there in the real world (we know it's not true, but the logic doesn't), but it can tell you, more precisely than the original English can, *what conditions need to be met in order for it to be true.* This type of logical notation is even more abstract, and more powerful, than the most complex formulas of arithmetic. Not only do you not need to know what specific x's are dogs or are blue; you don't need to know exactly what "dog" and "blue" are, only that they are functions that take one argument (in logical terms, they are "one-place predicates"). This is very useful. It made whole new branches of theoretical mathematics possible, and it also gave rise to computer programming languages.

Brown's idea was to make logical forms speakable. Then he

could test whether this had a Whorfian effect on people who learned it. Would speaking in logic make people more logical? Would it facilitate thought? Of course logical forms already were speakable in the sense that you could give a long-winded paraphrase like "For every x, if x is a dog, then x is blue." But in Loglan the translation would be compact and independent of the grammar of English (or any other language).

radaku	da	kangu	u	da	blanu
all-x-that	x	dog	if-then	x	blue

"All dogs are blue."

Brown's article generated a great deal of excitement in the *Scientific American* audience. He received hundreds of letters asking for more information.

Brown was not the only one in the late 1950s working with the idea that the apparatus of formal logic could serve as a language. A Dutch mathematician named Hans Freudenthal sought to apply the idea to the problem of finding an adequate means for communicating with beings in outer space. In his 1960 book, *Lincos: Design of a Language for Cosmic Intercourse*, he proposed sending out, by means of varying radio wavelengths, messages that would begin with very simple statements of arithmetic and slowly introduce more and more complex types of statements in a way that would lead the space beings, one logical step at a time, to figure out how the Lincos symbols were related to meaning. They would start by deducing from examples that ">" represented "greater than" and progress to recognizing that this:

ᵇ⁰*Ha* Inq *Ba*ρ:

ᵇUsd.Apu *Ha·Ba* Movᵇ:

Hb Inq *Hc*·?*x*.t₁ t₂ Fit *x*⦂

Hc Inq *Hb*⦂ t₀ t₁ *Ha* Vul.PPN *Ba* Apu *Ha*˙

    Pau Pst.*Ha* Vul Etc⦂*Ba* Ani·Utr.PAN *Ha* Vul Etc˙

       t₁ Usq t₂·t₁ Loc *Ba*.Usd.t₁ Loc *Ha*·*Ba* Mov⁗

represented "whistling for one's dog."

Lincos was published by a highly respected international science publisher, and many academics found Freudenthal's idea interesting, but it never went anywhere. Freudenthal's dense, technical approach failed to attract a more general audience. A second planned volume was never completed.

The year after Brown published his *Scientific American* article, he expected to get a raise from the university, but the administration declined to give him one. He was insulted. He had brought scholarly recognition and money (in the form of a small government grant) to his department with his Loglan project, and he expected better treatment. Already bristling under the tension between his progressive politics and the conservative leadership of the university (at that time a Deep South university bracing itself against the growing civil rights movement), he wrote out a list of grievances and submitted it as his resignation. He didn't need the job anyway. He was making a fortune from the success of a board game he had invented that had been published by Parker Brothers a few years earlier.

The board game was called Careers. Brown, a lifelong socialist, objected to the single-minded focus on money in the game Monopoly. So he developed a game where success is defined not by money alone but by a combination of money, fame, and happiness. The players accumulate points in these three areas by moving around the board, entering different career tracks. They decide before the game what proportion of money, fame, and happiness makes up their personal "success formula." It does you no good to keep winning money if it is fame or happiness you are after. (Although if you land on the right square, you can buy a yacht to gain happiness points, or a statue of yourself to get fame points.) You win when you have fulfilled your own success formula.

In real life, Brown had spent his first forty years searching for the right track. He was born in 1921, in the Philippines, to Midwestern parents who had moved there to teach. When he was eight, his parents split up, and his mother took him back to the States. He was a bright student with a high IQ, and after serving as a combat navigator in England during the war, he majored and minored in various subjects at the University of Minnesota, including philosophy, mathematics, statistics, and sociology. He wrote a dissertation on "cooperative group formation," and formed a cooperative community of his own in Indiana, before moving to Mexico to write science fiction. But needing a better way to support his wife and two young children, he moved back to Minneapolis to work at an ad agency, a job he hated, and while he was there, he began working on Careers. His marriage broke up, and after some time in New York (working at the Institute for Motivational Research), and another short, troubled marriage, he found himself in Gainesville with a new wife, an exciting intellectual project, and a steadily growing income that meant he didn't have to work for anyone anymore. The money Brown earned from Careers allowed him to set up his own Loglan Institute in Gainesville and build a Frank Lloyd Wright–inspired modern home with a separate addition for institute activities. He was free now to devote himself to Loglan and to indulge in his passion for sailing and travel.

In 1962, Brown looked poised to fulfill his success formula and then some.

Suitable
Apologies

On a bright October day in 1987, Nora Tansky and Bob LeChevalier married in a small backyard ceremony at their home in Fairfax, Virginia. The soft rustling that accompanied the reading of their vows was not the sound of autumn leaves but the fluttering of sheets of white paper, each one printed with a copy of the vows and distributed among the guests so they would be able to follow along. Bob, a large, heavyset man with a wide smile, went first:

> *mi prami tu*
> "I love you"

> *.i mi djica lepo mi kansa tu*
> "I desire the state of being with you"

.i mi cuxna lepo mi speni tu
"I choose the state of being married to you"

Nora, petite and shy and unaccustomed to public speaking, was so nervous when it was her turn that she skipped a line without realizing it. After the ceremony, one of the guests, a student who had been taking the Loglan class that Bob and Nora held at their home, pointed out her mistake, and someone caught a photo of her reacting to the news with an embarrassed, happy laugh.

Loglan had brought Bob and Nora together. Nora was one of the few women who ordered a copy of Brown's Loglan book (which he finally published in 1975) after she saw an ad for it in *Scientific American*. A computer programmer who had enjoyed studying foreign languages in school, she had been working with her brother on making up her own invented language when she discovered Loglan and, deciding she liked the clarity of expression it offered, put her own project aside. She also ordered a subscription to the *Loglanist*, a journal edited by a philosophy professor in St. Louis, and was soon actively involved in the development of the language.

The *Loglanist* was a place where the correspondents that Brown had attracted could propose new words, hash out problems that came up in trying to use the language, and, as Brown particularly encouraged, build up a corpus of examples "to which the hungry learner of the language can sit down for his nightly repast." These Loglan texts, submitted by subscribers and vetted for accuracy by Brown himself, could be translations, such as the biblical story of Babel, of which the first line retranslates as "And point-all of the Earth was languaged by one something x and talked x" (And the whole earth was of one language and of one speech). Or they might be original compositions, such as this little dialogue about a tourist's visit to "Loglandia":

I uu no mi djano lepo ba sitfa be
"And I'm-sorry-that it-is-not-the-case-that I know the-event-of something-*x* being-the-location-of something-*y*."
(I'm afraid I don't know where anything is.)

Tu danza lepo gotso ie da
"You wish the-event-of going-to what *x*?"
(Where would you like to go?)

Mi cnida lepo sivdu la Tarc Kotl
"I need the-event-of location-discover the Star Hotel."
(I need to find the Star Hotel.)

Nora became the first paying member of the Loglan Institute when she sent a five-hundred-dollar donation of support to the institute in 1979. This gave Brown the idea to turn the Loglan Institute into a membership-supported organization. Some money was coming in from book orders and journal subscriptions, but not enough to hire the secretaries and programmers who were needed to move the project forward. Brown was still drawing income from Careers, but much less than before, and not enough for him to personally support Loglan development at the level he desired.

Nora's check arrived at a moment of financial crisis for the institute. Brown's third and last-chance proposal for a grant from the National Science Foundation (NSF) had just been rejected, an outcome that shocked and surprised him. He felt he had been treated unfairly by reviewers who showed "unmistakable signs of total ignorance of the project," and he asked that it be "done over again." His appeal, which included a point-by-point rebuttal of the reviewers' misgivings, burned his bridges to the science-funding academic establishment all the way to the top.

It also betrayed a damning lack of sophistication about how these things work. Brown had submitted almost two thousand pages of supporting documents with his proposal—grammar books, textbooks, dictionaries, and every copy of the *Loglanist* that had been printed so far—and was outraged that the reviewers had not made themselves intimately familiar with all this material. The terse, carefully worded reply that Brown received to his initial appeal emphasized that the scientific community cannot judge the value of a project by reading every single thing the author has to say about it. The usual yardstick by which merit is measured is a body of scientific results and reviews published in peer-reviewed journals (and journals published by the author himself generally do not count as such).

Because Brown had received an initial minor grant shortly after his first article on Loglan was published, he fully expected that the fifteen-plus years of work he had put into the language since that time would secure him a major grant. But when he left his job at the university, he also cut himself off from the normal channels through which a fundable reputation is established. Though he did seek advice and criticism as he worked on Loglan (he loved nothing better than a good, lively argument), he tended to surround himself with admirers. Those who could not submit to his powerful, stubborn temperament did not last very long in his circle. Those who excused the insults, the accusations, and the occasional angry blowup in order to remain in the orbit of this often intensely charming, always intellectually exciting man became his lifelong friends and collaborators.

After spending the early 1960s devoting his full attention to

Loglan, Brown put out some materials on microfilm, intending to make them available to the scientific community for review. He did receive one review in a top-tier linguistics journal, but it was not something he would have wanted to emphasize to the grant committee. Though the reviewer praised the project for its ambition and ingenuity, he threw serious doubt on its usefulness as any kind of scientific tool. The general verdict on Loglan was that it was an interesting, fascinating, and diligently executed . . . hobby.

Shortly after that, Brown left the country, losing contact with many of the people who were working on the language with him. He had divorced his third wife, a former student of his at the university who had done much of the work calculating the "learnability scores" for his Loglan vocabulary, and, in order to evade a custody dispute, took their toddler daughter to Europe and didn't return for a few years (his ex-wife wouldn't see their daughter again until she was a teenager). Loglan took a backseat to other projects—he wrote a utopian science fiction novel and worked on something he referred to as a "statistical study of interpersonal relationships." He got married again, this time to a woman who was one of his (openly acknowledged) mistresses during his previous marriage (his "progressive" politics carried over into the realm of sexual relationships, though in a rather one-sided way). When that marriage fell apart, he came back to the States and published a revised version of his Loglan grammar and dictionary, this time in book form, and purchased an advertisement for it in *Scientific American*.

The book stirred up interest again (many readers had been waiting for it since the 1960 article), and soon Brown had a group of followers who were willing to devote their time and skills to developing and promoting Loglan. Most of these volunteers were "computer guys" (Nora being the rare non-guy among them) who were excited about the possibility of the language serving as a human-computer interface. Brown also became excited about such a possibility and, after his first NSF grant proposal was rejected, put together "A Proposal for the Establishment of a Service/Support Relationship Between the Loglan Institute and the U.S. Computer Industry," in which he asked "the industry" to provide the institute with "approximately $275,000 per year." He expected them to fork over the money for the general good of the industry (surely, he emphasized, having a human-machine-interface system *made available* would benefit them all); exclusive rights to use any "proprietary information" would remain with the institute. Apparently, there were no takers.

So in 1979, Brown turned the institute into a "membership-controlled corporation," and most of the Loglan volunteers, around a hundred people, paid the fifty-dollar fee gladly. This would allow them to at least hire a permanent secretary while they worked on what Brown called "the Commercial Success Project," from which, he declared, all the members would eventually benefit.

There had never been any question among the Loglan volunteers that Brown was in charge. It was his language and he had the last word. But when they became paying members of his ostensibly membership-controlled corporation, they naturally expected more of a say in the development of the language. Under Brown's direction, they began an overhaul of the rules of Loglan word formation (something still referred to in Loglan lore as the Great Morphological Revolution) and developed their own opinions on the best way to proceed. However, Brown proved unable to relinquish any control, even going so far as to prohibit the members from discussing (in their newsletter) any issues he had not personally approved for discussion. In 1984 his mounting ledger of perceived slights and disloyalties drove him to make belittling personal attacks on the very members who had donated the most time to the Loglan cause. When the board objected, he fired the board, ordering them to have nothing to do with Loglan for one full year, after which time, if they made suitable apologies, they would be allowed back.

In the newsletter, a member named Birrell Walsh expressed sadness that Brown was "driving away ALL those who appreciate the magnificent thing he had built," and asked, "Do we owe it to Jim to give him a chance to wake up before he empties Loglandia?" His answer, like that of everyone else, was no. He concluded with a striking example of Loglan in action, an original poem:

> *le sitci fa nu kalhui ea nirve*
> *i lo nu gunti vu darli*
> *i la ganmre vi krakau*
> *va lo nortei troku*

> This city will be destroyed, empty;
> the people are far away;
> the king is a howling dog
> by the unlistening stones.

Most of the membership fell away, and the journal, the *Loglanist*, shuttered its doors for good.

In the midst of all this, Bob LeChevalier, Nora's future husband, sent in his check to become a member of the institute. He didn't know any of the other members, having been exposed to Loglan only through Brown himself, and he had no idea what was going on. Bob had been living in the San Diego area (where Brown—and the institute—were located in the late 1970s), and a friend of his, who was interested in Loglan, came to visit and decided to look Brown up in the phone book. Brown invited him over to talk, and Bob gave his friend a ride. "I knew nothing about language or linguistics and wasn't really interested, either," he told me. "I was just the transportation."

But he ended up enjoying the conversation that evening and kept in touch with Brown, visiting him occasionally to talk about Loglan or to assist him with other projects, such as testing out a new board game he was working on. Soon, he was a member of the institute and was assigned the task of putting together a digital dictionary.

Bob moved to the D.C. area to take a job as a computer systems engineer for a government contractor, and Brown moved back to Gainesville, but they had long talks on the phone, during which Bob tried to explain why he wasn't making much progress on the dictionary and Brown encouraged him to try harder. In 1986, Brown became ill with a life-threatening infection. "I called Jim in the hospital, and we talked about Loglan," Bob told me. "It seemed like he had had a taste of mortality, and he was worried about what would become of the project—like this might be the last chance." When he recovered, Brown invited Bob to Gainesville, and they spent a very intense weekend working on the language together. Bob was flattered; he felt like he was being treated as a full partner. Brown was preparing to sail across the Atlantic, and Bob left with the sense that he had been handed some sort of responsibility for the legacy of Loglan. He returned to D.C. full of renewed energy for the dictionary project, and a determination to do everything he could to please his mentor by helping Loglan succeed.

He decided to organize some local user groups where people who were interested in Loglan could get together and brainstorm, coordinate projects, and help each other learn the language. He began to contact people; Brown had given him a few names, and he found some others in old Loglan publications. Someone directed him to Nora, who was still an institute member (she had sent in a second five-hundred-dollar donation in 1984, so her membership was paid up for at least a decade) and lived not too far away in Philadelphia. They talked on the phone for hours, and a few weeks later she came down for a visit so they could work together on updating a Loglan flash-card program she had written. When Bob asked the former editor of the institute newsletter, which hadn't come out in about a year, for some addresses of other Loglanists, the editor sent him the entire mailing list. Bob used it to mail out an update on the work he and Nora were doing, and issued a rallying cry for other Loglanists who were near each other to establish their own working groups. From some of the members who were no longer active, he collected half-completed computer programs and bits of other work and started recruiting volunteers to revive these projects.

Over Labor Day weekend, Bob hosted the first annual Logfest at his house. About ten people showed up with sleeping bags, but not much sleeping went on, as they stayed up all night snacking on cold cuts, hashing out ideas, and trying to see how far they could go with live Loglan conversation (not very far, it turned out, but it was a start). They also did a detailed group review of a revised description of the language that Brown had asked one of them to have a look at. Bob put together a complete report of everything that had been accomplished over the summer, more than a hundred pages of comments and materials, and, with a rush of exhilarated pride, mailed it to Brown, who was due back any day from his sailing adventure.

When Brown did get back, about a week later, he exploded

in fury, yelling at Bob over the phone, accusing him of stealing the mailing list, of making a power grab. "I told you to work on the dictionary! I didn't tell you to contact anyone! I didn't tell you to review that draft." He accused Bob of consorting with "enemies" and "fomenting a revolt." Bob, flattened with bewildered disappointment, struggled to explain that he was only trying to be helpful, and spent the next four hours apologizing. At the end of their discussion, he was back in Brown's good graces, but very tenuously so.

And not for long. When Bob and Nora finished the flash-card program (they had been spending more and more time together), they told Brown they were planning to distribute it as shareware on a computer bulletin board so that other Loglanists could take advantage of it. Brown informed them they would do no such thing. Loglan was the property of the institute. He would consider letting them distribute the program only if they signed a statement of acknowledgment that the institute owned the copyrights to the language and agreed to pay the institute royalties.

Bob wasn't so sure *anyone* owned the rights to the language, or what that would mean in practical terms, and his own research into copyright law indicated that if he tested Brown's claims legally, they wouldn't hold up. He didn't want to have to test them, he explained in a series of letters, but he wouldn't sign any agreement. Through the first few months of 1987 the conflict escalated, with Brown demanding that Bob resign from the project ("Sorry it hasn't worked out for you, Bud") and Bob refusing ("If I can't find a way to work around our dispute, I will take up the gauntlet you have thrown down, Don Q. But I'm not a windmill and neither are you"). Though Bob had initially agreed that some type of legal protection for Loglan was necessary in order to give the language a chance to stabilize (he just thought the members who were working on it should be given more freedom with it), as the argument grew more heated, he transformed into a sort of Loglan public-domain crusader. In his view, the only way to advance the language was to give it to the users and let them run with it. His position slowly crystallized into a mission: he would bring this creation to life, even if it meant going against the will of the creator himself.

In March, Bob proposed to Nora in Loglan and she accepted. In April, when Bob ordered some Loglan materials for the class he was teaching, Brown sent his check back. Orders would only be filled for those who signed an "Aficionado Agreement" with a "non-disclosure" clause. When Bob explained to his students what had happened, one of them asked whether they could get around the copyright problem by just making up their own words and substituting them into Loglan sentences. Could they? It was worth a try.

On Memorial Day weekend Bob drove to Philadelphia to help Nora pack up her things and move her into his house in Fairfax, where two of his Loglan-interested friends were visiting. The four of them spent the rest of the weekend laying out a system for creating the new vocabulary, and Bob and Nora then spent their first summer together generating great heaps of paper in their "relexification" of Loglan, which they called Loglan-88. In August they hosted the second Logfest, where the attendees voted on whether it was worth splitting up this already small community in order to have the freedom to do what they wanted. They decided it was, 18–0.

Still, the split was not complete. Bob considered himself to be working on Loglan—Brown's language—and he still held out hope for the possibility of reconciliation. In October, Bob and Nora married. On their honeymoon in Colonial Williamsburg, in a demonstration of their commitment both to Loglan and to each other, they sustained a two-hour Loglan conversation. Most of it was spent trying to establish that each had understood what the other one said, as good a foundation for a marriage as any.

Upon their return, Bob redoubled his efforts toward his mission. He announced Loglan-88 at a science fiction convention, collected new recruits, and started putting out his own newsletter. A few weeks into 1988, "Jim had fifty Aficionados, and I had a mailing list of three hundred." In March, he received a letter from Jim, notifying him that he was in violation of Loglan's trademark (to be registered shortly) and that, should he not cease such violation, he risked being sued "for the recovery of profits, damages and costs, with, as you may know, the possibility of treble damages and attorney's fees."

With that letter, the gauntlet had been irretrievably thrown. Loglan-88 was officially renamed Lojban (from the new words *logji*, "logic," and *bangu*, "language"), and the Lojbanists incorporated their own, competing (nonprofit) organization, the Logical Language Group (LLG). A year later, the LLG challenged the Loglan trademark. After almost two years of motions and countermotions, the Trademark Trial and Appeal Board ruled that the trademark should be canceled. A few months later, Brown filed an appeal, and the case went to trial before the federal circuit court. Bob hadn't seen Brown for six years, and hadn't had any direct communication with him for five, when they finally came together in a courtroom in 1992. But no words would be exchanged, not even a glance. "I'd never been snubbed so completely," Bob told me. "He refused to look at me, like I didn't exist." Brown lost the appeal.

Can a person own a language? The law is still not really clear on that. The Loglan case did not settle the matter; it said only that the word "Loglan" could not be trademarked because at the time the trademark was filed (over thirty years after Brown had coined the word) it was already in general use as a "common descriptive term." (The Loglan case would later be cited in a judgment against Harley-Davidson when the motorcycle company claimed that another company's use of "hog" to mean "motorcycle" was trademark infringement.) The Lojbanists were free to use the word "Loglan" to describe their project (though they continued to call it Lojban).

There is much more to a language, of course, than its name. At the beginning of the dispute (but not in court), Brown claimed he owned the rights to the *vocabulary* of Loglan. Did he? Brown did have copyrights on his books, including the dictionary. But copyright does not extend to each individual word in a copyrighted work, only to the particular configuration of the words. Would it have been possible for him to copyright each Loglan word separately? Perhaps, but he didn't; to do so would have been too costly and time-consuming (and useless, since the Lojbanists had already made their own words). In any case, such a strategy for language ownership has never been attempted, and it is not clear what the law would have to say about it if challenged in court.

There is yet more to a language than its words. Language is also a system, a set of rules for creating sentences and deriving other words. These rules were very explicit in Loglan, and they were the part of the language that had involved the most effort to develop. Can the rules of a language be owned? Probably not. You can patent a machine that uses a certain mathematical formula, but not the formula itself. You can own an implementation of an algorithm, but not the algorithm. There is, however, some blur in this area within the murky world of software patents, so given the right lawyer and the right judge, who knows?

There is one invented language that is essentially owned by a private company, though the terms of ownership have not been tested in court: Klingon is protected by a trademark held by Paramount Pictures. Without proper license, you cannot use the name "Klingon" to describe, say, a book of your own original Klingon poetry. But could you sell the same poems if you didn't explicitly call them "Klingon" poems? It's probably not worth it to you to find out, unless the sales of your poetry have somehow provided you with the resources to fight off a bottomless barrel of lawyers. As a practical matter, Paramount owns whatever aspects of the language they say they own. As a legal matter? Unless someone comes up with a *very* compelling reason to bring on the lawyers, we'll never know.

In his original *Scientific American* article, Brown set himself apart from the mad language inventors, with their utopian missions and blindly confident claims, by presenting himself as the cool, impartial scientist. Clearly, he was anything but cool and impartial.

In the final few pages of the final chapter of his final book on Loglan, the revised grammar he published in 1989, we get a brief, illuminating glimpse of his unguarded ambitions when he launches into a breathless description of what might happen if the experiments showed that Loglan did indeed have a "mind-expanding, thought-facilitating" effect:

> Wouldn't the entire experimental program, in fact, now be seen as a successful assessment of a proposed new educational experience, one that was available to everyone? It might even be seen as a treatment of a disease we didn't know we had! LLL, the disease of "logical language limitation," or UNM of "unnecessarily narrowed

minds" . . . And wouldn't Loglan itself then be seen as the gentle new cure for that ancient human malady? . . . An antidote for the bigotry with which even "civilized people" tend to view their neighbors in the global village? . . . This is what is very likely to happen given what the journalists will call a "positive" outcome of our Whorfian experiment . . . Backed up by such a result, Loglan would probably be seen as ideal in the role of that international auxiliary, for example: the first language to be taught to the world's school children, the one slated to become everybody's second tongue . . . our engineered new second-language would be seen as the mind-expander, the instrument of thought, reason, invention, and exposition . . . and perhaps also the medium of intercultural mediation, a culture-spanning bridge to a more tolerant and peaceful world.

You can almost see the film reel unrolling behind his starry eyes— the international news conferences, the front-page headlines, the Nobel Prize ceremony. His hopes for Loglan, and for himself, were much grander than he let on. Beneath the detached scientific demeanor lay the passionate soul of a language inventor.

"When he lost the case, Jim couldn't believe it," his widow, Evelyn Anderson, told me. "Both he and his lawyer thought they had it for sure. But within a few months he wasn't talking about it anymore. He just moved on." He put his energy into other projects— a paper on his theory of the origin of language, a book about his utopian economic plan, called *The Job Market of the Future*. He continued to work with a small group of loyal Loglanists, one of whom told me he thought "the split did soften his attitude toward suggestions and criticism from those who stuck with him."

Brown was seventy-one when he lost the case and had been working on Loglan for over thirty years. It hadn't brought him money or fame, but it did yield some happiness points. "He considered it pure joy when he was working on it," Ms. Anderson told me. "Right until the end he was working out something that he found totally fascinating, and he was not put off by the fact that it had not achieved what he had . . ." She paused for a moment, then continued. "He went to his death thinking it was the greatest thing that he had published."

Though Brown would never publicly make peace with or accept Lojban, one of the friends who stuck with him in the split told me that "he acknowledged privately that he considered Lojban to be one of his intellectual children, albeit an illegitimate child, that he was still pleased to see succeeding." Perhaps one day, he thought, after he was gone, the rift would be repaired. But even then, it would still have to be on his terms—they were written into his will. The institute could only accept rapprochement if Bob LeChevalier was no longer involved.

Brown died of a heart attack in 2000 while on a cruise off the coast of the southernmost tip of Argentina, and he was buried there. For about a week after that there was some discussion of reunification on the Lojban message boards—how the vocabularies might merge and so forth—but it faded away quickly. All the action was in Lojban anyway. And that's where it stayed.

Meaning
Quicksand

To all the language curmudgeons out there who insist that
people ought to speak more *logically,* I say, be careful what
you wish for. You go on about the "logical" mismatch between
"everyone" and "their" in perfectly normal-sounding sentences
like "Everyone clapped their hands." You argue that phrases
like "very unique" and "sufficiently enough" don't make logical
sense. You harp on "hopefully" and "literally" and "the reason is
because," all the while calling logic to your side to defend your
righteous anger.

Before you judge me as some kind of "anything goes"
language heathen, let me just say that I'm not against usage
standards. I don't violate them when I want to sound like an
educated person, for the same reason I don't wear a bikini to a
funeral when I want to look like a respectful person. There are

social conventions for the way we do lots of things, and it is to everyone's benefit to be familiar with them. But logic ain't got nothin' to do with it.

And oh, how grateful I am. Do you know how good we have it, how much easier our speaking lives are made by the fact that language and logic part ways? Consider the word "and." Why, you barely have to know what you mean when you say it! When you say you "like ham and eggs," do you have to specify whether you like each of those things as evaluated on its own merits separately or whether you like them served together as an entrée? No. You just lazily throw out your "and" and let context do the rest of the work for you. When you say you "woke up and ate breakfast," do you mean that you woke up first and then ate breakfast? Or did you do the two things simultaneously? Or maybe your breakfast was asleep, so you woke it up and then ate it. Pshaw, you say. You know what I mean. Perhaps I do, says the Lojbanist. Perhaps I don't.

There are many ways to say "and" in Lojban. If you use the word .*e* in the following sentence (the . stands for a slight pause):

> la djan. .e la .alis. pu bevri le pipno
> "John and Alice carried the piano."

you assert two propositions: "John carried the piano" and "Alice carried the piano." Maybe they took turns. Maybe one of them did it in 1963 and the other one did it yesterday. But this sentence does not apply to the situation where John and Alice carried the piano together. For that you would use *joi*:

> la djan. joi la .alis. pu bevri le pipno
> "John and Alice (as mass entity) carried the piano."

You would be wrong to use *joi,* however, if you wanted to say, "John and Alice are friends." For that situation you must use *jo'u:*

la djan. jo'u la .alis. pendo
"John and Alice (considered jointly) are friends."

If you used *joi* here, you would have said John and Alice massed together form some kind of friend entity. If you used *.e,* you would have said that John is a friend (of someone) and Alice is a friend (of someone), and maybe they don't even know each other.

There are at least twenty ways to say "and" in Lojban. But that's nothing compared with what happens when you get into "or" and "if." Even if you master the many, many rules pertaining to those little words, you've still barely begun to scratch the surface of the tip of the iceberg that is Lojban.

Frankly, the thought of trying to capture Lojban in a nutshell for you—something I have tried to do with the languages I've discussed in previous chapters—fills me with despair. There is just so much. The language is specified to within an inch of its life. The reference grammar comes to over six hundred pages. This doesn't even include a dictionary.

I read the whole thing—I swear I did. And I'll tell you, not only did I still not speak Lojban, but I started to lose my ability to comprehend English.

"How many Lojbanists does it take to change a broken lightbulb?" goes the old Lojban joke. "Two: one to decide what to change it into and one to decide what kind of bulb emits broken light." The further I waded into Lojban, the more everything I heard seemed to be filtered through the sensibilities of a bratty, literal-minded eight-year-old—"You love birthday cake? Well, why don't you *marry* it?" "Can you use the bathroom? I don't know, *can* you?"—with the difference that while the eight-year-old knows what you really mean, my lapses of understanding were genuine. One day during my weeklong immersion in the Lojban grammar, I was watching an Elmo video with my son when a friendly puppet character popped up to ask, "What are the two numbers that come after the number 6?" I had no idea what this puppet was getting at. "What the hell does she mean?" I wondered. "There are an infinite number of numbers that come after the number 6." I honestly did not know what the answer was supposed to be until the video told me (it's 7 and 8, by the way).

Was this some kind of Whorfian effect? Well, no. It was more of a Freudian effect—like when you read a little Freud and suddenly everything starts to look like a penis. If someone keeps calling your attention to hidden meanings, or distinctions in meanings, you may start to see them. Your view of the world can be shaped by lots of things, but the Whorfian hypothesis wants only to know which parts are shaped by the language you speak. And I did not speak Lojban. In fact, after reading the grammar, I was pretty sure it was impossible for anyone to speak it.

But people *do* speak it. Well, they sort of do. I saw this for myself when I attended Logfest (*jbonunsla* in Lojban), a gathering of about twelve computer guys (plus Nora) that took place in 2006. Bob and Nora had stopped hosting Logfest at their home a few years before, not because they were unwilling, but because, as Bob told me, "I think the newer members wanted something a little more formal than the accommodations we provided. They wanted to stay in a hotel, eat at restaurants, more of an official conference-type thing." The Logfest I attended was held at Philcon, "the [Philadelphia] region's premiere conference of Science Fiction and Fantasy." We got bumped out of one and then another room we had been promised when it turned out that an author signing or panel discussion had already been scheduled for that space, and so we ended up crowded around a coffee table in the eighth-floor, end-of-hall suite that a few of the participants were sharing. This made it hard for interested newcomers to drop in and hear the presentations designed to entice them into joining the cause, so talks like "What Is Lojban?" and "Introductory Lojban Class" ended up being preached to the choir.

I was scheduled to give a talk on the history of invented languages (when I registered, the organizer discovered through my Web page that I was writing a book and invited me to give a presentation about it). I came armed with my own Lojban translation of Borges's quotation about the futility of classifying the universe, the one I had translated into Wilkins's language: "It is clear that there is no classification of the universe not being arbitrary and full of conjectures. The reason for this is very simple: we do not know what thing the universe is." Studying Lojban had given me the same unsettling feeling that I had experienced deep within the thickets of Wilkins's tables—the sensation of being sucked into meaning quicksand, where the struggle for greater precision was not a lunge toward solid ground but a hopeless kicking and flailing that only pulled me in deeper.

But in Lojban it was worse. Not only did I have to pin down which translation I should use for content words like "clear," "arbitrary," and "reason" (is the best I can do for "arbitrary" really *cunso*—"x is random/fortuitous/unpredictable under conditions y, with probability distribution z"?); I also had to grapple with little function words like "the," "and," "of," and "no"—words for which Wilkins had supplied straightforward substitutes.

Then I had to deal with syntax. Until Loglan, invented languages had never been very explicit about how sentences should be put together. In philosophical languages like Wilkins's, or symbol languages like Blissymbolics, once you had done the hard work of finding the appropriate concept words, you just arranged them in an English-Latin-type hybrid grammar. There was never a well-defined "correct" syntax for these languages. Esperanto developed a better-defined standard of proper sentence structure, but it came naturally through usage, and not because the inventor laid down the rules from the beginning. You don't learn the rules of Esperanto; you intuit them from examples. When speaking Esperanto, I could draw on my general familiarity with European languages and wing it pretty successfully.

There is no winging it in Lojban. The language has an exhaustively defined syntax, and it is completely unambiguous. One must clearly specify the structure of the sentence as a whole, using various markers that serve, in effect, as spoken parentheses. There can be no confusion, for example, between an "ancient (history teacher)" and an "(ancient history) teacher" in Lojban. When you say "I saw the man with the binoculars" in Lojban, you can leave no doubt as to whether you had the binoculars or the man did. Lojban sentences have only one structural parse.

So you have to make sure it's the one you really want. Composing a sentence in Lojban is like writing a line of computer code. Choose the wrong function, drop a variable, forget to close a parenthesis, and it doesn't work. But how do you know it doesn't work? At least when you write a computer program, you have a way to determine whether you've made a mistake: you hit enter, and the program doesn't do what you wanted it to do. How do you sit down with a six-hundred-page book of grammatical rules and determine whether you've followed them correctly?

Fortunately, you can visit *jboski*, the online Lojban-to-English translator, and at least see if your Lojban sentence parses. If you've made any major errors, or left out a crucial structural element, you'll get an error message. If you managed to create a valid Lojban sentence, you will get something like this, the product of my first (after several tries) successfully parsed translation of "It is clear that there is no classification of the universe not being arbitrary and full of conjectures":

li'a ro da poi se ciste le munje fi'e zo'e cu cunso gi'e culno so'i
smadi

li'a {clearly . . .} [₁(₂*cunso1 (random thing(s))* , *culno1 (full thing(s)):]* (₃(₄ro every (of) da X)₄ <₅poi which [₆«₇se ciste being system structure(s)»₇ (₈*cistel (system(s)):]* le the **munje** universe(s))₈ (₉fi'e created by zo'e unspecif it)₉]₆>₅)₃)₂ cu is/does «₁₀cunso being random»₁₀ gi'e and «₁₁culno being full»₁₁ (₁₂*culno2 (filler) :]* so'i many **smadi** guess thing(s))₁₂]₁

I got a little thrill when my sentence returned this parse. It was the same thrill I would get during grad school, when, after a long night of beating my head against the keyboard trying to write a data-crunching program, a beautiful stream of output would finally pour down the screen like a light-dappled waterfall of celebratory champagne.

But was this parse cause for celebration? I wasn't so sure. I knew that I had composed a grammatical Lojban sentence, but I couldn't be certain it meant what I wanted it to mean. When I presented it to the Lojbanists at Logfest, I discovered that it didn't. I had actually said that all classifications of the universe were random and full of people who guess. *Smadi* means "*x* guesses *y* is true about subject *z*." According to the syntax of my sentence, I was making a statement about the *x* argument—the guesser. What I wanted was the *y* argument—the guess. I should have used *sesmadi* instead.

I didn't feel too bad, though. Lojbanists are always making this kind of mistake. They are always making all kinds of mistakes. I know this because on the message boards where Lojban is used, hardly a sentence goes by that is not questioned or corrected—often by the very person who wrote the sentence. In fact, the main topic of Lojban conversation is Lojban itself. When one heated exchange (in English) led a commenter to write "Go fuck yourself!" in Lojban, it turned into a lengthy discussion of why he hadn't said what he meant to say, and what the proper Lojban expression for the sentiment might be.

I didn't see much live conversation at Logfest, but I did see a little. It goes very, very slowly. It's like watching people do long division in their heads. Of course, the types of people who are attracted to Lojban are precisely the types who are good at doing long division in their heads. Almost everyone there had some kind of engineering or math background (except for one enthusiast who, being fifteen years old, couldn't properly be said to even *have* a background). For dedicated Lojbanists, only part of the difficulty of speaking Lojban comes from the mental effort involved in keeping track of functions and variables. The rest of the difficulty comes from having to hyper-vigilantly guard their Lojban against the influence of English.

The temptation is there, for example, to use the word *gunka* (work) in a sentence like "This phone doesn't work." But *gunka* means "*x* labors/works on *y* with goal/objective *z*." It doesn't cover the English sense of "work" meaning "to function." It would likewise be inappropriate to use *dizlo* (low) to say you're feeling low, because *dizlo* only means low "as compared with baseline/standard height z." The metaphorical extension of lowness to emotions doesn't hold in Lojban. There is a Lojban word for these kinds of mistakes—*malglico* (damned English!). *Malglico* is what happens when you let the assumptions of English creep into your Lojban.

And this must be avoided in Lojban, because to remain valid in a test of the Whorfian hypothesis, it must remain culturally neutral. In terms of vocabulary, this means that definitions should be unclouded by connotations and metaphorical extensions that may not be shared from culture to culture. In terms of grammar, this means that it should have the resources to express the range of distinctions that languages express, including distinctions that English might not have. For example, English does not make the grammatical distinction between alienable and inalienable possession, but other languages do. In the Austronesian language Mekeo, you express possession one way if the possessed thing could potentially be transferred to someone else (*e?u ngaanga*: "my canoe") and a different way if it cannot (*aki-u*: literally "brother-my," so "my brother"). If it is true that the difference in the grammatical treatment of possession between English and Mekeo gives rise to some difference in worldview between the two cultures, Lojban doesn't want to force Mekeo speakers to blur the distinction, thereby forcing them to take on the English view of possession. In Lojban you can make the distinction, but you are not required to (because that would be forcing the Mekeo worldview on English speakers). However, if the English speaker chooses to use the neutral form, he should be aware that if he introduces someone as *le mi bruna* (the-somehow-associated-with-me brother), he has said only that that person is a brother (maybe his own, maybe someone else's) who has some connection with him. If he assumes he has said "my brother" in the commonly understood English sense, he is being rather *malglico*.

Lojban wants to be both *everything*, a language that accommodates all worldviews, and *nothing*, a language committed to no particular worldview. At the same time, it wants to be a specific *something*—a language that trains your mind in the rules of formal logic. It's hard work keeping on top of all these goals at once.

And somewhat futile. Not only do we "not know what thing the universe is," but we don't know what assumptions we make about it. We cannot see our own worldview any more than we can see our own eyes. We don't think about the difference between alienable and inalienable possession until we chance upon a language that makes the distinction. Lojbanists have done an admirable job of incorporating these types of distinctions into the grammar when they discover them, but they can never be sure they have discovered them all.

They are aware of this. No Lojbanist today will go so far as to claim that Lojban is free from what they call "metaphysical assumptions." They will only say that they are doing their best to make the language as culturally neutral as they can. Lojbanists are nothing if not conscientious analyzers of their own hidden metaphysical assumptions. And when someone comes across an especially exotic type of meaning (or distinction in meaning) encoded in another language, they will all pitch in, with great excitement, to see whether it can somehow be accommodated. The size of Lojban grew rapidly, after the split, from a frenzied burst of just this type of activity. In one case inspiration came from an unlikely source: another invented language, also created for the purpose of conducting a Whorfian experiment. It was a language designed not to avoid committing to a worldview but to express one that the inventor felt no language adequately expressed: a woman's point of view.

To Menstruate
Joyfully

Suzette Haden Elgin, as her Web site biography states, "was born in Missouri in 1936. All sorts of things happened, and in the late 60s she found herself widowed, re-married, mother of five, and a graduate student in the Linguistics Department of the University of California San Diego." In order to earn some extra money, she started writing science fiction, and in 1970 she published her first novel. A few years after that she finished a dissertation on Navajo syntax and then worked as a linguistics professor until 1980, when she retired and moved back to her native Ozarks.

A year later, she was invited to speak as a guest of honor at a feminist science fiction convention. She planned to address the topic of why the fictional worlds of women writers tended to be based on the idea of matriarchy—where women are superior to men—or androgyny—where women are the same as men—but not a third alternative, where women are entirely different from men. Perhaps, as she explains in the introduction to her grammar of Láadan, the language she eventually created, it was because "the only language available to women *excluded* the third reality . . . the lack of lexical resources literally made it impossible to *imagine* such a reality."

She had recently become aware, through a book she had been asked to review, of the "feminist hypothesis that existing human languages are inadequate to express the perceptions of women," and she began thinking about what a language that did adequately express those perceptions might look like. And if there were such a language, how might it change the people who spoke it? How might it change society?

She wanted to explore these questions further, but wasn't quite sure how to go about it. "A scientific experiment and a scholarly monograph would have been nice," she wrote, "but I knew what the prospects of funding would be for an investigation of these matters." So she took her questions to the laboratory of fiction, beginning her work on *Native Tongue*, a futuristic novel in which a marginalized class of women linguists create a language for themselves.

Elgin wanted to know, as a linguist, exactly how her fictional language worked, so she set about creating it, going far beyond the rough description and smattering of vocabulary of other fictional thought-experiment languages, such as Newspeak. She put her language to the test by translating various texts into it, in the process refining and expanding it, and by the end of 1982 Láadan had a well-defined syntax and a vocabulary of over a thousand words. Elgin began to see the possibility for a real-world experiment as well. If women really did feel that existing languages were inadequate to their perceptions, what would happen when they were offered a woman's language? Either "they would welcome and nurture it, or it would at minimum motivate them to replace it with a better women's language of their own construction." Láadan was released to the world when *Native Tongue* was published in 1984, and Elgin decided to wait ten years to see how it fared out there. She would declare the experiment a success or a failure by 1994.

Early on, Láadan was embraced by a small group of women science fiction readers who formed the Láadan Network. One of them put together a zine of contributions from the network—letters, comments, Láadan poetry, suggestions for new words. In 1988, the Society for the Furtherance & Study of Fantasy & Science Fiction, the group that organized the WisCon convention, published a grammar and dictionary of the language that included lessons and exercises.

Láadan establishes itself as a "woman's language" through some rather obvious devices. It has the only language textbook I know of that gives the word for "menstruate" in Lesson 1. But the approach has a level of sophistication that far exceeds non-gendered pronouns or "womyn's herstory"–type coinages. The language is meant to convey a female perspective in the way it carves up the world of experience into linguistic forms. The experience of menstruation, for example, is carved up the following way:

oshdána	to menstruate
áshdána	to menstruate joyfully
elashdána	to menstruate for the first time
hushdána	to menstruate painfully
deshdána	to menstruate early
weshdána	to menstruate late

Pregnancy is also covered by a range of vocabulary items:

lawida	to be pregnant
lalewida	to be pregnant joyfully
lewidan	to be pregnant for the first time
lóda	to be pregnant wearily
widazhad	to be pregnant late in term and eager for the end

As is menopause:

zháadin	to menopause
azháadin	to menopause uneventfully
elazháadin	to menopause when it's welcome

The effort to capture the perspective of women in words is not limited to the particularities of the female body. Other words cover a range of situations that could conceivably be experienced by men, but that are nonetheless designed to make you want to nod your head and go, "Uh-huh. Tell it, sister."

> *radíidin:* non-holiday, a time allegedly a holiday but actu-
> ally so much a burden because of work and preparations
> that it is a dreaded occasion; especially when there are
> too many guests and none of them help

rathom: non-pillow, one who lures another to trust and rely on him or her but has no intention of following through, a "lean on me so I can step aside and let you fall" person

rathóo: nonguest, someone who comes to visit knowing perfectly well that he or she is intruding and causing difficulty

ramimelh: to refrain from asking, with evil intent; especially when it is clear that someone badly wants the other to ask

thehena: joy despite negative circumstances

bala: anger with reason, with someone to blame, which is futile

bina: anger with no reason, with no one to blame, which is not futile

áayáa: mysterious love, not yet known to be welcome or unwelcome

áazh: love for one sexually desired at one time, but not now

ab: love for one liked but not respected

am: love for one related by blood

The lexicon is shot through with fine distinctions in emotion, attitude, reason, and intention, presumably because these are aspects of experience that are important to women. The fact that English vocabulary doesn't make such distinctions does not mean they are impossible to talk about in English, but, as Elgin stresses, it does mean they are more "cumbersome and inconvenient" to talk about, so that women are often accused of "going on and on" when they try to express their perspective on things.

The idea of female perspective is also carried by aspects of linguistic structure outside the word. Elgin, noting that women are often "vulnerable to hostile language followed by the ancient 'But all I said was . . .' excuse," built into the syntax a requirement that speakers make clear what they *intend* when they speak. Every sentence begins with a word indicating the speech act being performed (statement, question, command, request, promise, warning) modified by an ending that marks whether that act is performed neutrally, in anger, in pain, in love, in celebration, in fear, in jest, in narrative, or in teaching. In Láadan the "It wasn't what you said, it was how you said it" objection can't be so easily dismissed. If a person uses the marker for a neutral speech act and then tries to claim, "Hey, I was just kidding!" the responsibility is on the speaker for not being clear, and not on the hearer for taking it the wrong way.

Láadan speakers also have to take responsibility for the validity of what they say. Every sentence ends with an "evidence morpheme" in which the speakers make clear on what grounds they base their statements:

Bíi	*mehada*	*ben*	*wa*
Statement	laugh-plural	they	I know because I perceived it myself
			wi I know because it's obvious to everyone
			we I know because I perceived it in a dream

wáa
I assume it's true
because I trust the
source

waá
I assume it's false
because I don't
trust the source

wo
I imagine it, it's
hypothetical

wóo
I have a total lack
of knowledge as to
whether it's true or
not

"They laugh"

I'm not exactly sure what aspect of women's perspective the evidence morphemes are supposed to make accessible (Elgin mentions that it makes exchanges like "I'm cold . . ." "Oh, you ARE not" impossible), but they are a neat thing to have in a language. In fact, markers like this (called "evidentials" in the linguistics literature) actually exist in many languages. When Elgin was constructing Láadan, she drew on aspects of natural languages she thought were "valuable and appropriate" to the job of expressing a woman's perspective, but I suspect in many cases she incorporated features simply because they appealed to her. As she says, she created the "pejorative" marker *lh* (it helps turn *bini*, "gift," into *rabinilh*, "a gift with strings attached") after a similar marker in Navajo, because it "is something so very handy that I have always wished it existed in English." She sounds less like a woman who has discovered a way to better express women's perceptions than a linguist who has discovered another juicy tidbit on the ever-fascinating banquet table of natural languages. While her appropriation of the Navajo pejorative marker is justified by her overall goal of making attitudes usually conveyed by body language or tone of voice more explicit, when she lovingly picks it up and places it into her own language, she seems motivated less by scientific mission than by artistic vision. It is not a female thing to have in a language; it is an interesting thing to have.

Láadan never really took off. Small "working groups" formed here and there, but they dissolved as people got busy with other things. There was also a negative reaction to Láadan from a segment of the lesbian academic community who accused Elgin of being biased against lesbianism because she hadn't included anything about it in the language. "The whole altercation," she told me in an e-mail, "caused me great distress and sorrow. The absence of lesbian vocabulary and content was simply an accident of my personal circumstances. I was living way out in the country in rural Arkansas, totally isolated from the academic world and academic feminism. I was totally 'ignorant' about lesbianism and couldn't have written about it even if I'd thought of it." She offered to include vocabulary relevant to lesbianism in any future editions of the dictionary and solicited suggestions from her critics, but no further editions were published (the new vocabulary does appear in the online dictionary).

After ten years passed, and women had still not embraced Láadan or come up with another language to replace it, Elgin declared the experiment a failure, noting, with some bitterness, that

Klingon (a hyper-male "warrior" language) was thriving. Still, she had found the challenge interesting and "well worth the effort."

Bob LeChevalier, who discovered Láadan through his contacts in the science fiction community, found certain aspects of the language so interesting that he was inspired to adapt them for Lojban. After checking with Elgin to make sure she didn't mind (she didn't), the Lojbanists developed their own system of evidential markers, as well as a set of special indicators that greatly expanded the range of speaker emotions, attitudes, and intentions that could be expressed. Of course, they ran with it in the usual Lojban way and ended up with a system capable of distinguishing among hundreds, maybe thousands of feelings. Along with .*ui* ([happiness] Yay!), .*u'u* ([repentance] I feel guilty), .*ii* ([fear] Eek!), and .*o'u* ([relaxation] Phew!), there are compound indicators ranging from .*uecu'i* ([surprise][neutral] ho hum), to .*o'unairo'a* ([relaxation][opposite][social] I feel social discomfort), to .*uiro'obe'unai* ([happiness][physical][lack/need][opposite] Yay![physical] Enough!), something you might say after enjoying a big meal. As the Lojban grammar states, "We have tried to err on the side of overkill. There are distinctions possible in this system that no one may care to make in any culture."

Strictly speaking, these indicators fall outside the realm of formal logic: their validity cannot be evaluated; there are no truth tables that can account for them. But the Lojbanists love them, and they have a lot of fun playing with them. So much fun that one of them proposed a new language called Cinban (from *cinmo bangu*, "emotion language"), which would just be English with the attitudinal indicators thrown in, something the Lojbanists had been doing casually for a long time. He set up a new Web forum in which "to practice .*o'o* [patience] using Cinban until I'm fully fluent .*a'o* [hopefully] in it. Anyone's welcome .*e'uro'a* [suggestion, social] to join me, of course *.uenaidai* [expectation, empathy]." Using the indicators often, and in a creative way, is a hallmark of Lojbanness—which is to say, something Lojban culture values highly.

Lojban culture? A language, of course, once it gets off the drawing board and into the hands of people who use it, can never be culture-free. Loglan, and Lojban after it, were bound to develop a culture of their own. They attracted a self-selecting group of people who already shared many of the same interests and thought about things in similar ways. As one of them put it in an early issue of the *Loglanist*, Loglan speakers "have a prior weirdness that ruins any whorf-test." To become a Loglanist, you had to, in a certain sense, already think like a Loglanist. James Cooke Brown did not see this as too much of a problem, though, because the experimental tests that were expected to eventually occur would be performed not on the Loglanists who had developed the language but on "normal" subjects, who would learn Loglan in the (culturally) sterile environment of the laboratory. Some Lojbanists still dream of the day when the laboratory tests will finally be implemented, but it is unclear whether even they themselves are capable of learning Lojban to a level of basic proficiency, much less any "normal" people.

Though Brown put an enormous amount of detailed engineering into his experimental tool, he never had more than a vague and unrealistic plan for how any actual experiments would be conducted. The experiments never took place, and it looks like they never will. While Brown and his followers toiled away on Loglan, the Whorfian hypothesis endured a long half century of being proven, disproven, defended, demolished, revived, mocked, and revived again. Over time, researchers brave enough to get near the Whorfian question have devised increasingly refined experiments designed to look for very specific effects under strict conditions of control. In this context, the idea that you could do something as broad as teach someone an entire made-up language (so many confounding factors!) and look for some kind of effect on thought (measured how?) looks downright amateur.

But the experiments are beside the point now. The Lojbanists are living out their own personal Whorfian tests. They report that learning Lojban makes them more clear in their use of English; it makes them better at drawing correct logical inferences; it makes them more aware of their metaphysical assumptions, causing them to reexamine their views of the world. They find it mind opening, and these results, anecdotal and unscientific as they may be, are satisfying in their own way. As one Logfest participant told me, "I like how it messes with my head."

Somewhat accidentally, the Lojbanists have come to follow Whorf's own intended program more closely than did any of the researchers who interpreted his work as a hypothesis that needed to be tested. Whorf took his linguistic relativity principle as a given: different types of grammars "point" people toward different views of the world. The job for the researcher was not to see whether this was true but to explore how it was true. If we were to do this right, we had to be made conscious of our own hidden, language-conditioned thought habits. And the best way to become conscious of them was "through an exotic language, for in its study we are at long last pushed willy-nilly out of our own ruts. Then we find that the exotic language is a mirror held up to our own."

Loglan did not become the sober, scientific instrument it was intended to be. It will never prove or disprove anything about the Whorfian hypothesis. However, as it evolved into the Lojban of today by committing itself to its contradictory goals of becoming a language of everything, nothing, and something, it transformed into a different kind of instrument—an enormous, minutely faceted fun-house mirror that, if it doesn't freak you out too much, will definitely push you out of some of those ruts Whorf was talking about. It's not science, but it just might be art.

THE KLINGONS, THE CONLANGERS, AND THE ART OF LANGUAGE

taH pagh taHbe' . DaH mu'tlheghvam vIqelnIS.
quv'a', yabDaq San vaQ cha, pu' je SIQDI'?
pagh, Seng bIQ'a'Hey SuvmeH nuHmey SuqDI',
'ej, Suvmo', rInmoHDI'?

One either continues or doesn't continue.
    Now, I must consider this sentence.
Is it honorable, when, inside the mind,
    one endures the torpedoes and phasers of aggressive fate?
Or, when one obtains weapons to fight a seeming ocean of
    troubles,
And, by fighting, one finishes them?

—*The Klingon* Hamlet

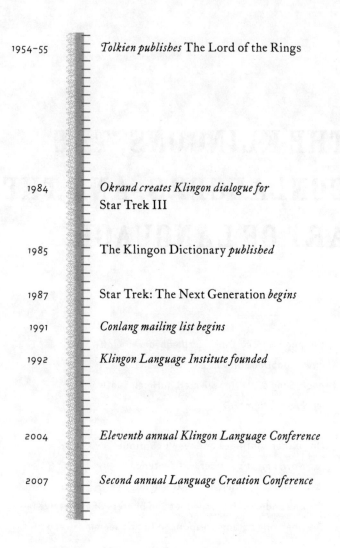

1954–55   *Tolkien publishes* The Lord of the Rings

1984   *Okrand creates Klingon dialogue for*
Star Trek III

1985   The Klingon Dictionary *published*

1987   Star Trek: The Next Generation *begins*

1991   *Conlang mailing list begins*

1992   *Klingon Language Institute founded*

2004   *Eleventh annual Klingon Language Conference*

2007   *Second annual Language Creation Conference*

Flaws or Features?

The story of invented languages has not been entirely a story of failure. While Wilkins's project did not become a universal language of truth, he produced an extraordinary document, a snapshot of linguistic meaning in his culture and era—and paved the way for the thesaurus. Esperanto did not become an auxiliary language for the whole world, but it did become a real, living language, and in the small sphere of people who use it, it does seem to promote a general atmosphere of international understanding and respect. Blissymbolics found a way to be useful, despite the wishes and actions of its creator, and Loglan lives on today, despite not having fulfilled its scientific mission.

One could argue that the "success" of these languages is only accidental, and makes their inventors no less naive, or misguided, or presumptuous. Just because they produced some-thing that turned out to have some value for someone doesn't mean they deserve to be admired. We *should* admire them, how-ever, for their raw diligence, not because hard work is a virtue in itself, but because they took their ideas about language as far as they could go and really put them to the test. Who hasn't at one time or another casually suggested that we would be better off if words had more exact meanings, or if people paid more attention to logic when they talked? How many have unthinkingly swooned at the "magic" of Chinese symbols or blamed acrimony between nations on language differences? We don't take responsibility for these fleeting assumptions, and consequently we don't suffer for them. The language inventors do, and consequently they did. If we pay attention to the successes and failures of the language in-ventors, we can learn their hard-earned lessons for free.

We can also gain a deeper appreciation for natural language and the messy qualities that give it so much flexibility and power, and that make it so much more than a simple communication device. The ambiguity and lack of precision allow it to serve as an instrument of thought *formulation*, of experimentation and discovery. We don't have to know exactly what we mean before we speak; we can figure it out as we go along. Or not. We can talk just to talk, to be social, to feel connected, to participate. At the same time natural language still works as an instrument of thought transmission, one that can be *made* extremely precise and reliable when we need it to be, or left loose and sloppy when we can't spare the time or effort. OR CHOOSE TO OBFUSCATE ?

When it is important that misunderstandings be avoided, we have access to the same mechanism that allowed Shirley McNaughton's students to make use of the vague and imprecise Blissymbols, or that allows deaf people to improvise an international sign language—negotiation. We can ask questions, check for signs of confusion, repeat ourselves in multiple ways. More important, we have access to something that language inventors have typically disregarded or even disdained—"mere" conventional agreement, a shared culture in which definitions have been established by habit. It is convention that allows us to approach a Loglan level of precision in academic and scientific papers or legal documents. Of course to benefit from the precision, you must be "in on" the conventional agreements on which those modes of communication depend. That's why when specialists want to communicate with a general or lay audience—those who don't know the conventions—they have to move back toward the techniques of negotiation: slowing down, answering questions, explaining terms, illustrating with examples. Convention is a faster, more efficient instrument of meaning transmission, but it comes with a cost. You have to learn the conventions. In the extreme cases this means a few years of graduate training or law school. In general it means getting experience with the way other speakers—of English, Spanish, Greenlandic Eskimo, or whatever language you're interested in learning—use their words and phrases.

When language inventors try to bypass convention—to make a language that is "self-explanatory" or "universal"—they either make a less efficient communication tool, one that shifts too much of the burden to negotiation, like Blissymbolics, or take away too much flexibility by over-determining meaning, like Wilkins's system did. When they try to take away culture, the place where linguistic conventions are made, they have to substitute something else—like the six-hundred-page book of rules that define Lojban, and that, to date, no human has been able to learn well enough to comfortably engage in the type of conversation that any second-semester language class should be able to handle.

There are types of communication, such as the "language" of music, that may allow us to access some kind of universal meaning or emotion, but give us no way to say, "I left my purse in the car." There are unambiguous systems, such as computer programming languages, that allow us to instruct a machine to perform a certain task, but we must be so explicit about meanings we can normally trust to inference or common sense that it can take hours or days of programming work to achieve even the simplest results. Natural languages may be less universal than music and less precise than programming languages, but they are far more versatile, and useful in our everyday lives, than either.

Ambiguity, or fuzziness of meaning, is not a *flaw* of natural language but a *feature* that gives it flexibility and that, for whatever reason, suits our minds and the way we think. Likewise, the fact that languages depend on arbitrary convention or cultural habit is not a flaw but a feature that allows us to rein in the fuzziness by establishing agreed-upon meanings at different levels of precision. Language needs its "flaws" in order to do the enormous range of things we use it for.

But what about irregularity? All those exceptions to the rules? Does language really need that? Probably not. But it comes about as a natural by-product of convention. Languages like Esperanto have an advantage in that they are built from preexisting conventions—the general language habits of speakers of European languages. Esperanto itself does particularly well because it developed its own culture and community, and therefore has better-defined conventions for what words mean and how they should be used. But at the same time, it has sacrificed some of the perfect regularity that it was intended to have. For example, the accusative -*n* ending used to mark the object of a verb is in the process of being lost. Speakers often leave it out—and joke about what a pain it is to remember to use it—and one study found that even native speakers don't use it all that consistently, even when the language of their home country has an accusative marker. But they always use it when they say *saluton*, "hello," or *dankon*, "thanks." Those words were originally formed as the objects of verbs (as in "I wish you greetings" or "I give you thanks"); now they are just set phrases that happen to have an *-n* ending. But they are used so often, and their forms are so established by habit, or convention, that they are immune from the erosion of the grammatical marker they express.

Some of the irregularities in natural languages came about in a similar way. At one stage in the history of English, the past tenses of verbs were marked by a regular vowel change process; instead of "help/helped," we had "help/holp." Over time, *-ed* became the preferred way to mark the past tense, and eventually the past tense of most verbs was formed by adding *-ed*. But the old pattern was preserved in verbs like "eat/ate," "give/gave," "take/took," "get/got"—verbs that are used very often, and so are more entrenched as a linguistic habit (the *very* frequently used "was/were" is a holdover from an even older pattern). They became irregular because the world changed around them.

Nobody means for words to become irregular. Some things are well reinforced by the habits of the language users, and other things give way to change. One day someone comes along and asks, "Hey, why doesn't this one fit the pattern?" and the answer has to be, "Well, 'cause that's the way we say it." One day, newcomers to Esperanto may ask the same thing about *saluton* and *dankon*. They will also probably want to know why people say *stas* for "is" (a shortened pronunciation that many young Esperanto speakers use today) instead of *estas*, or *ĝis* for "goodbye" (the colloquial rendering of *ĝis la revido*, "until we see each other again").

They already have to just learn the idiomatic meanings of certain expressions like *ne jukas min* (it doesn't itch me—"I don't care") and *jam temp' esta'* (a reference to a line of an old Zamenhof poem that modern speakers use—instead of the proper *jam la tempo estas*—to mean "the time has come"), and many other phrases you can't figure out with a dictionary or list of affixes alone. Esperanto is still pretty regular, and still pretty easy to learn, but it's governed by the way people use it—not by some perfect mathematical system or universal standard of meaning. Our languages have inconsistencies and irregularities because they are run by us, and not by some perfect rule book or grand philosophy. I don't know about you, but the story of invented languages only convinces me that I wouldn't have it any other way.

The transmission of customs and conventions, linguistic or otherwise, from one generation to the next is never perfect. Over multiple generations, any sign, symbol, or picture that once conveyed meaning may become completely unrecognizable. This is a problem that was addressed by the semiotician Thomas Sebeok when, in the early 1980s, he was asked by the Office of Nuclear Waste Isolation to prepare a report on how best to encode a warning message on sites where nuclear waste had been buried. To ensure the safety of future generations, the message had to be interpretable for ten thousand years. He recommended extreme redundancy of encoding: the message should be printed in all known languages; there should be pictures, icons, and other relevant symbols; repositories around the world should store technical messages written in mathematical formulas (or perhaps, he suggests, in something like Lincos, Freudenthal's self-teaching logical language). But even all of this redundancy, he noted, might prove worthless in ten thousand years.

The best way to make sure the message would get through to

the future, he proposed, was to include a second "metamessage," with a "plea and a warning" that every 250 years or so the information (including the "metamessage" itself) be re-encoded into whatever languages, symbols, and unknown-as-of-yet communicative devices were current at that time. Still the possibility would exist that the people of the future would ignore the plea, or forget to comply, so as added insurance he suggests the creation of a sort of folklore, perpetuated through rituals and legends, that would promote the development of a superstition or taboo about the dangerous sites. An "atomic priesthood," a group of scientists entrusted with the true reasons for the danger, "would be charged with the added responsibility of seeing to it that our behest, as embodied in the cumulative sequence of metamessages, is to be heeded . . . with perhaps the veiled threat that to ignore the mandate would be tantamount to inviting some sort of supernatural retribution." Even if the "priesthood" should forget the original reason for its existence, it is hoped that whatever kind of entity it should evolve into would maintain some sort of authority and sense of responsibility toward passing on the folklore.

According to Sebeok's analysis, the best chance for transmitting meaning ten thousand years into the future was not to find some optimal, stable, universal way to encode that meaning, because there is none. Meaning resides not in the symbol or the image or the language in which it is encoded but in the society that interprets it. New generations are born, societies change, and, with them, the interpretation of meaning. The best shot we had at getting our message across was to try to influence the *society* of the future—either by entreating it to adapt the encoding of the message to its times or by planting an aura of danger in a broad social tradition.

Though language inventors may have set their sights on issues a little more immediate than the ten-thousand-year communication problem, too many of them have made the mistake of believing that if they just worked hard enough, they could come up with a language that would transcend society. But it is society that creates meaning, and therefore language. The best hope a language inventor has for the survival of his or her project is to find a group of people who will use it, and then hand it over and let them ruin its perfection.

Though there have been successes in the story of invented languages, they have been qualified ones. Some languages have gotten attention or praise or even communities of speakers, but none of them have fulfilled their original missions. We still don't have a worldwide international auxiliary language or a proven cure for all the supposed inadequacies of language. And so ambitious inventor types are still working on it. Every year still sees a few more proposals for a new world language, an improved Esperanto, or a perfect system of mathematical concept formation. I recently purchased a book, self-published by John Yench in 2003, on Idirl, "a universal language for all mankind, with none of the inconsistencies and awkward irregularities of existing natural languages, a self-consistent language where a word's sequence of sounds alone tell you its meaning, without needing a dictionary." Mr. Yench is a bit behind the times in his method of spreading the word about his language. These days, language inventors no longer scrape together their savings in order to print books and mail them out to the libraries and government offices of the world. Instead, they set up Web sites. The language inventors, like most everyone else, have taken their ideas and their products to the Internet.

And, like most everyone else, they are able to find *some* kind of audience this way. Well-established languages like Esperanto and Lojban, by providing forums where people can use and learn the languages without having to travel or wait for feedback, have attracted a good number of converts every year, and even old projects like Volapük, Ido, and Interlingua have picked up some new life online. But so much easy access to information about so many projects makes the competition that much fiercer. As many languages as there are on the Web, there are more angry flame wars and long manifestos about why *this* language is more logical, more systematic, more international, more likely to be adopted by the UN, less biased toward Europeans, less difficult to learn, less ambiguous, less likely to be abused by politicians . . .

All this fighting stems from the illusion that people choose to learn a language for rational reasons, that they are looking for the language that has the most useful features, the best agenda. But no one is out there comparison shopping for an artificial language. They find what they like, and there's no accounting for taste. There are Esperanto types, and there are Lojban types, and there are even a few proudly defiant Volapük types.

As it turns out, it is possible for an invented language to succeed even if it has no useful features at all. One of the most successful languages of the current era is neither free from irregularities nor easy to learn. It has no mission: it wasn't intended to unite mankind or improve the mind or even be spoken by people in the real world. But it suited the personal taste of a certain group of people so well that as soon as they saw it, they fell in love, clamored for more, and formed a community that brought it to life.

And so we come back to the story of Klingon.

The Go-To Linguist

When the Klingons first appeared on the original *Star Trek* television show, which ended in 1969, they were little more than grunting belligerents in greasepaint. They developed their trademark ridged foreheads for the first *Star Trek* movie in 1979, but it wasn't until the second incarnation of the television series, *Star Trek: The Next Generation*, which began in 1987, that Klingons were portrayed as complex members of a richly articulated alien culture.

In that series and subsequent *Star Trek* movies, audiences learned that Klingons are rough, crude, loyal, violent, and honorable—a sort of Viking-Spartan-samurai motorcycle gang. They eat *qagh* (live serpent worms), drink strong alcohol, and sleep on hard surfaces. They have a rite of passage (a youth is ceremoniously beaten with something called a *painstik*) and a creation myth (the first Klingon and his mate destroyed the gods who created them and burned down the heavens). Cursing is an esteemed art form, one of the most offensive insults being "*Hab SoSlI' Quch*" (Your mother has a smooth forehead). Their mating practices involve the hurling of heavy objects and often result in injury. They are fond of reciting their numerous proverbs, which express their values: "*quv Hutlh HoHbogh tlhIngan 'ach qabDaj 'angbe'bogh*" (The Klingon who kills without showing his face has no honor); "*Dubotchugh yIpummoH*" (If it is in your way, knock it down); "*bIjatlh 'e'yImev, yItlhutlh*" (Stop talking and drink!); and my personal favorite, "*bortaS nIvqu' 'oH bortaS'e'*" (Revenge is the best revenge).

Klingon is indeed difficult to pronounce, but at least it uses phonetic spelling—once you know what sound each letter represents, you can pronounce any Klingon word. The vowels are easy—*a* as in "father," *e* as in "ten," *I* as in "give," *o* as in "phone," *u* as in "tune." The consonants are more difficult. The *H* is pronounced as the "ch" sound in Yiddish words like "chutzpah" or the German exclamation *ach!* The Klingon *D* is pronounced as someone from India might pronounce a *d*—place the tip of your tongue at the middle of the roof of your mouth rather than the ridge behind your teeth. The *S* is similar to the English "sh," but also with the tongue tip at the roof of the mouth. If you say the word *SoD* (flood) properly, it will feel bunched up and sluggish in your mouth. The *q* is pronounced like a *k* but farther back in the throat, as if you are choking. The *Q* is pronounced like the *q*, but more forcefully. If you're the adventurous type, try saying the word for the verb "to mutiny"—*qIQ*. If some saliva flies out, great job. If your lunch flies out, try again later.

The other Klingon spellings requiring explanation are *ng* (the same as in English, but it can also occur at the beginning of a word, as in *ngav*—"writer's cramp"), *gh* (the same sound as Klingon *H,* but with the vocal cords vibrating, as if you were gargling), *tlh* (begins like *t,* but leave the tip of your tongue in position while you lower the sides to let the air through), *j* (the *j* of "job," not of "hallelujah"), and finally, the glottal stop *',* indicating a complete closure of the glottis, as performed before "oh" in the phrase "uh-oh." Now go back to the previous page and try a proverb, if you dare.

The phonological system of the language is by design harsh, guttural, and alien, like Klingons, but it also makes a certain kind of linguistic sense. The language doesn't include barks, growls, or other sounds not used in human languages. And the sounds it does use are not even that exotic as far as real languages go: no clicks, trills, ingressives, or voiceless vowels.

"The goal was for the language to be as unlike human language as possible while at the same time still pronounceable by actors," I was told by Marc Okrand, the inventor of the Klingon language. "The alien character of Klingon doesn't stem so much from the sounds it uses as from the way that it violates the rules of commonly co-occurring sounds. There's nothing extraordinary about the sounds from a linguistic standpoint. You just wouldn't expect to find them all in the same language."

Okrand, who has a Ph.D. in linguistics, came to be the creator of Klingon through a happy accident involving the 1982 Academy Awards. At the time, he was working for the National Captioning Institute (where he still works), developing methods for the production of real-time closed-captioning for live television. That year's Oscars presentation, the year of *Chariots of Fire* and *On Golden Pond,* was the first major live closed-captioned event. "I arrived in Hollywood a week before the broadcast, and they weren't ready for me yet. I had nothing to do, so I called an old friend, who happened to work for Paramount. While we were having lunch there at the commissary, a secretary for the associate producer of *Star Trek II* came by, and my friend introduced me, mentioning that I was a linguist. The secretary said they happened to be looking for a linguist. They needed a few lines of dialogue in Vulcan [the language of Mr. Spock] for the movie, and I think an arrangement with another linguist had just fallen through. I thought it sounded like fun, so I asked when did they need it? End of the week."

Despite his other obligations Okrand came through on time and skillfully—the scene, between Leonard Nimoy and Kirstie Alley, had been filmed in English, and he had to create lines that could be dubbed over their mouth movements in a believable way—so two years later, when the production team of *Star Trek III* wanted some scenes in Klingon, Okrand was their go-to linguist. This time he was not constrained by preexisting mouth movements—the actors would be filmed speaking Klingon—but there were two other preexisting conditions he had to take into account. The first was the existence of a few words of Klingon already invented by James Doohan (the actor who played Scotty) for a short scene in the first *Star Trek* movie. He had to incorporate those lines of Klingon into his own language. Second, he knew the language was supposed to be tough sounding, befitting a warrior race—which he achieved through the preponderance of back-of-the-throat sounds and the intentional absence of small-talk greetings such as "Hello." (The closest translation in Klingon is *nuqneH*—"What do you want?")

Okrand did not just make up a list of words. Knowing that fans would be watching closely, he worked out a full grammar with great attention to detail. Klingon both flouts and follows known linguistic principles, and its real sophistication lies in the balance between the two tendencies. It gets its alien quality from the aspects that set it apart from natural languages: its phonological inventory of sounds that don't normally occur together, its extremely rare basic word order of OVS (object-verb-subject). Yet at the same time it has the feel of a natural language. A linguist doing field research among Klingon speakers would be able to work out the system and describe it with the same tools he would use in describing a remote Amazon language.

He would quickly deduce, for example, that Klingon is an agglutinating language. Such languages, like Hungarian and Finnish, build words by affixing units that have grammatical meanings to roots, one after the other. In these languages, entire phrases can be expressed in single words. This is how the Klingon proverb "If it is in your way, knock it down" can be expressed in only two words: "*Dubotchugh yIpummoH.*" The words are composed of smaller meaningful units:

Du	-bot	-chugh	yI	-pum	-moH
it-you	block	if	imperative	fall	cause

"If it blocks you, cause it to fall!"

Klingon has twenty-six noun suffixes, twenty-nine pronominal prefixes, thirty-six verb suffixes, two number suffixes, a phrasal topicalizing suffix, and an interrogative suffix. Words have the potential to be very long. The Klingon Language Institute publishes a journal called *HolQeD* (Language Science, or Linguistics), which held a contest asking readers to come up with the longest possible three-word Klingon sentence. The winning entry, from David Barron:

nobwI''a'pu'qoqvam'e'
nuHegh'eghrupqa'moHlaHbe'law'lI'neS
SeH'eghtaHghach'a'na'chajmo'

"The so-called great benefactors are seemingly unable to cause us to prepare to resume honorable suicide (in progress) due to their definite great self-control."

The sentence contains three roots (give, kill, control) and twenty-three affixes. Here is the breakdown:

nob	-wI'	-'a'		-pu'	-qoq	-vam	-'e'
give	-er	augmentative	plural	so-called	these	topic

"As for these so-called great benefactors,"

nu-	Hegh	-'egh	-rup	-qa'	-moH
them-us	kill	self	ready	resume	cause

-laH	-be'	-law'	-lI'		-neS
can	not	apparently	in-progress		honorific

"they are apparently unable to cause us to prepare to resume honorable suicide (in progress)"

SeH	-'egh	-taH	-ghach
control	self	continue	nominalizer

-'a'	-na'	-chaj	-mo'
augmentative	definite	their	due-to

"due to their definite great self-control."

The functions of these affixes are common, from a linguistic point of view. The representation of causation (*-moH*) or verbal aspects such as "in progress" (*-lI'*) by verbal suffixes is routine in the language world. The use of an augmentative suffix (*-'a'*) to convey literal or figurative largeness of the root to which it attaches occurs in languages as familiar as Italian, where the augmentative *-one* makes *padre* (father) into *padrone* (boss, master, big daddy). The -*law'* ending in the second word belongs to a class of suffixes called evidentials, used in languages such as Turkish, which qualify statements according to how strongly the speaker can attest to their validity. Honorifics (-*neS*), used to recognize superior social status in the person being spoken to or about, are a part of Korean and Japanese.

The *nu-* that attaches before the verb "to kill" in the second word is part of a complex verb-agreement system that uses prefixes to show who did what to whom. Most people are familiar with a system that uses word endings that indicate who is doing the verb. For example, in Spanish, the -*o* ending on a verb like *hablar* (to speak) indicates a first-person-singular subject (*hablo*— "I speak"), while the -*amos* ending indicates a first-person-plural subject (*hablamos*—"we speak"). Klingon has such affixes, but they attach before rather than after the verb root, and instead of having six or seven of them, like most Romance languages, it has twenty-nine. The prefixes proliferate because they indicate person and number not only of the subject (who is doing) but also of the object (who is being done to). For example, *qalegh* means "I see you," and *vIlegh* means "I see them"; *cholegh* means "you see me," and *Dalegh* means "you see them." This type of system is unusual in the realm of languages that people typically study, but not as a general possibility for language.

Subject and object agreement by prefix is quite common, for example, in the Native languages of North America. However, it is not a feature of Mutsun, a West Coast language of the Utian family and the subject of Okrand's dissertation. Many have speculated that Klingon is based on the Native languages that Okrand studied as a linguist. "I used some features from other West Coast languages, like the 'tlh' sound, for example," said Okrand, "but my basic strategy was to switch sources whenever it started becoming too much like any one language in particular." This strategy explains my reaction, as a linguist, to Klingon: it is completely believable as a language, but somehow very, very odd.

And very, very difficult for the average English speaker to learn. But neither the mind-bending complexity of putting Klingon sentences together nor the uvula-twisting chore of articulating Klingon words prevents the Klingonists from studying, speaking, and writing the language. In fact, the challenge is part of the attraction, maybe the main one. Learning the Klingon language, though mocked as the most absurd thing a person could do, is what makes Klingon speakers feel above the usual *Star Trek* fandom. Lawrence Schoen, the head of the KLI, recalls how after an article about the Klingon language appeared on the front page of the lifestyle section of the *Chicago Tribune*, "memberships poured in from people who thought this was all about playing Klingon. You know, the foreheads, the costumes. But when they found out what we really did, they couldn't hack it. It was too much work." Those who can hack it feel a haughty pride in their linguistic accomplishments, despite the fact that no one who hasn't attempted to hack it can understand what they have to be proud of. The difficulty of the language keeps it from being just another part of the costume. The ones who end up sticking with it are in it for the language—and the cachet, the respect, that comes (from however small a group) with showing that you can master it. Anyone can wear a rubber forehead, but the language certification pins must be earned.

When I arrived at the Klingon conference in Arizona, I didn't know a thing about *Star Trek*. I hadn't seen any of the movies. I couldn't name one Klingon character from the show. But I knew one thing for sure: I wanted one of those pins.

What Are
They Doing?

I n 1999, the satirical paper the *Onion* ran a story under
the headline "Klingon Speakers Now Outnumber Navajo
Speakers." This is absolutely not true, but it would have been
true had they picked nearly any other Native American language.
How many speakers are there? It depends on your definition of
"speaker." *The Klingon Dictionary*, written by Okrand and licensed
by Paramount, has sold more than 300,000 copies of its two
editions. But a dictionary buyer does not a speaker make. There
are probably more than two thousand people who have learned
to use Klingon in some way. Many of them have learned a word
or two. Others have composed poems, stories, or wedding vows
in Klingon without regard to the grammar, simply by popping
dictionary words into English sentences. They haven't done the
work. They count only as dabblers, not speakers. At least a few

hundred, however, have done the work and are pretty good at written Klingon.

But what about speakers in the sense of people who can carry on a spontaneous live conversation in Klingon? How many of them are there? I would say, oh, twenty or so. Maybe thirty.

This estimate doesn't sound very exciting, but considering the difficulty of the grammar, and the relatively small vocabulary size, it's amazing that spontaneous conversations happen at all. The annual *qep'a'* is one of the few places where such conversations occur.

On the first afternoon of the conference, I stepped timidly into the over-air-conditioned lobby of the hotel with Mark Shoulson. He and I had spent the long flight to Phoenix going over the finer points of Klingon colloquialisms, but I wasn't sure I was ready to put them to use. I saw a small group gathered around a table, PalmPilots in hand. They were conversing in Klingon, haltingly, and with much use of their PalmPilot dictionaries, but nonetheless getting their points across. No one was in costume. Mark introduced me to the group, and I smiled and waved weakly, not sure what to say or how to say it. I sat and listened for a while. I was privately pleased when I understood my first spoken Klingon sentence: *"Ha'DIbaH vISopbe'"* (Animal I-it-eat-not)—"I'm a vegetarian." Not a very Klingon sentiment.

I wasn't impressed with the fluency level of the conversation. It seemed that nearly every sentence was repeated two or three times to the request of *"nuq?"* (What?). But because people were out of practice and the group was of mixed skill level, this particular conversation wasn't the best display of Klingon-speaking potential. I saw that later, as we walked over radiating sidewalks to a Mexican restaurant for the opening banquet, when I witnessed Captain Krankor and his girlfriend holding hands and chatting in Klingon, sans PalmPilots.

Captain Krankor (also known as Qanqor) is a software engineer and musician from Massachusetts known as Rich when he's in regular clothes. When he wears his Klingon costume, he is Krankor, and he only speaks Klingon. In both of his personas he is round and compact, with a large, appreciative laugh that shows off his dimples. His costume includes a travel guitar, on which he might strum a few bars of his translations of the Beatles or the Stones, or lead the group in the Klingon anthem "taHjaj wo'" (May the Empire Continue), a stirring and complex round of his own composition. He is known for being the first speaker of Klingon, and he speaks as smoothly as one could speak a language with so many glottal stops—especially when he speaks with his incredibly fluent girlfriend, Agnieszka, a delicate, shy linguist from Poland.

But no matter how well one speaks Klingon, he admits, it isn't easy to "take the vow," as the Klingonists call it when they make the commitment to speak only Klingon. None of the conference goers took a vow that lasted for the *entire* weekend. Some, like Krankor, attached the vow to the costume, and wore the costume only for certain events. Daniel, a newspaper deliveryman from Colorado, told me a little sheepishly that he was postponing putting on his costume, because then he couldn't participate as much in the general socializing, which takes place in English. Others, like Scott, a magician from Florida who, before he discovered the language, "couldn't give a shit about *Star Trek*," didn't have a costume and simply declared they were taking the vow for a particular day.

Scott and I were the early risers of the group, and the first morning we chatted at breakfast (in English). He answered some questions I had about vocabulary, which he was well qualified to do as the current Beginner's Grammarian, an official title at the

KLI for the person who responds to newcomers' questions on the e-mail lists. Having such a title is a mark of distinction and an endorsement of language skill. He said he was having a great time so far, and he was really hoping Marc Okrand would make an appearance, as he sometimes does at the *qep'a*'s. "I'm starstruck," he said with a wide smile. "I brought a new copy of *The Klingon Dictionary* for him to sign."

The second morning, when I greeted Scott by the coffee machine, he would only speak to me in Klingon, having taken the vow for that day. Luckily, someone had beamed me a PalmPilot dictionary at lunch the previous day, so I had the means to understand him in a painfully pause-filled kind of way. As the rest of the group came down from their rooms, he gained more game conversational partners and I gained some interpreters, the most skilled of whom was my guide, Mark, who through the rest of the weekend made it a point to keep me included with unobtrusive simultaneous translation in a low, gentle voice.

Mark's translation was also for the benefit of Louise, another beginner who became my study partner. Louise, a French-Canadian ad copywriter in her late forties, had been to three previous *qep'a*'s and had failed the first certification exam each time. She was going to try again. Unlike most of the other attendees, she didn't seem to be into computers, games, science fiction, or even language. She went for a run every morning and then smoked a cigarette. She had short hair and tomboy clothes, but she traveled with a pile of stuffed animals, and when I saw them on the chair in her hotel room, all propped upright like a matinee audience, I asked her, a little embarrassed on her behalf, "Are they animals you've collected since your childhood?" "No," she answered, not embarrassed in the least, "well, you might say my extended childhood."

I still don't fully understand why she wanted to learn Klingon, and I asked her more than a few times, trying to make sense of her response: "When I saw *Star Trek VI: The Undiscovered Country*, I saw those boots, yeah? In the Klingon costume? And I said, 'Wow! I want to make those boots.' I thought maybe Japanese Klingon speakers would love to buy them. So I started to learn Klingon." As far as I know, there are no Japanese Klingon speakers, but she didn't seem worried about this. As for the boot-making part of her plan, she had apprenticed herself to a cobbler in Montreal.

Enigma though she was, Louise was relaxed and likable, and the only other person at the conference besides me who would have a drink at meals. We almost always sat next to each other, so Mark could translate for us and so we could study together.

And I was studying constantly, feverishly. Until I arrived at the *qep'a'*, I thought I was done studying. I had scored perfectly on my postal-course lessons. I was confident, bigheaded even. After all, I was a *linguist* (and we don't get many opportunities to feel superior). I was already familiar with the grammatical concepts. I memorized the affixes and about forty words of core vocabulary. I leaned back and crossed my arms over my puffed-up chest.

The language has a lexicon of about three thousand words, and there's no way anyone knows all of them without peeking, or so I thought. The words are totally arbitrary and must simply be memorized one by one. You don't get any help from cognates (for example, German *Milch* for English "milk") or international words (for example, *informazione*), and you must deal with words for such things as dilithium crystal (*cha'pujqut*) and transporter ionizer unit (*jolvoy'*). How could anyone be expected to remember all of them? I assumed that for the first test, the smattering of words in the postal-course exercises would be sufficient.

Soon after I arrived in Phoenix, I found out that the first test was "beginner's" level because you were expected to know "only 500 words." I frantically made five hundred flash cards on tiny slips of paper, and carried them around with me to every activity and every meal, cramming and cramming.

If you have a sharp eye and an active imagination, Okrand does offer a narrow foothold into the lexicon. The word for "fish," for example, is *ghotI'*. If you get the reference to the George Bernard Shaw anecdote about the absurdity of English spelling ("gh" as in "tough," "o" as in "women," "ti" as in "nation" = "fish"), you remember this word. The word for "guitar" is *leSpal* (parsed Les Paul). Other associations are simpler, but just as memorable. The word for "pain" is *'oy'*. "Hangover" is *'uH*. This wink-wink tendency in the vocabulary, however, is no more than a faint undercurrent and can't be relied upon as a study aid.

Unless, like me, you never met a mnemonic you didn't like. In order to memorize five hundred words in three days, I spun my mind into a frenzy of associative madness: *waq*—"shoe," shoes are for walking; *Qob*—"danger," cobras are dangerous; *wIgh*— "genius," Einstein's hair looked like a wig; *rur*—"resemble," the first letter resembles the last letter; *ngeD*—"easy," ironic because "ng" and "D" are some of the harder sounds to pronounce. But careful not to get it mixed up with *Qatlh*—"difficult" (not ironic) because "Q" and "tlh" are the most difficult to pronounce.

Flip, flip, flip. The flash cards flashed. In my room at night, while everyone else hung out at the pool, I sorted them into piles of ten, only moving on to the next pile when I had one fully memorized. In the lobby, after the sing-along and before Klingon Pictionary, I had people quiz me. At the Old Spaghetti Factory, while we waited for a table for eighteen, I badgered Louise, who, frankly, didn't seem to be studying hard enough, into reciting my intra-Klingon word associations with me (*"wIv, tIv, yIv"*—"choose, enjoy, chew"—I *choose* to *enjoy* to *chew*).

By the afternoon of the test, I was feeling burned-out. My head was swimming with what were essentially useless nonsense words. And some of the Klingons were getting on my nerves. Did they have to be *so* weird? Did they have to be so weird *in public*? At a small Thai restaurant that we practically took over during the lunch rush, I shrank in my seat as an exceptionally polite waitress patiently guessed at what my costumed tablemates were pointing to when they insisted on giving their orders in Klingon. I wanted to meet her gaze and apologize with my eyes, but she was too rattled by the experience to look my way. Later, as the group made its rubber-foreheaded, vinyl-gloved, wool-caped, guttural-Klingon-speaking way toward the door (with me ineffectively hiding behind my hair), I saw a table of cute teenage girls mouthing a silent chorus of "Oh . . . my . . . God!" I have to say, it stung.

Marc Okrand didn't make it to the *qep'a'* that year. Scott wouldn't get his dictionary signed. But the greater disappointment was that no new words would be handed down. At previous *qep'a*'s Okrand had come through with new vocabulary. Some words he created in response to lists of requests. ("You can't ask for anything impolite," my guide, Mark Shoulson, told me, "but one year we did get the word for 'snot.'") Others were created on the spot—one year during the Klingon "Hokey Pokey," when it came to Okrand's turn, he said, "You put your *Sa'Hut* in . . ." Everyone stopped for a mental dictionary scan, thinking, "Do I know this word?" Finally they looked to Okrand, and he turned and stuck his backside in. And that's how Klingon got the word for "tush" (*Sa'Hut*, incidentally, is *tuchis* backward).

Klingonists are strict about language authority. They have been especially strict since the early 1990s, when arguments about the KLI's translation projects for *Hamlet* (since completed) and the Bible (still ongoing) led to the formation of a splinter group called the ILS (Interstellar Language School, no longer active). No one but Okrand can introduce new vocabulary. And no dispute about grammar or usage is considered settled until Okrand has spoken. He handles this responsibility cleverly, especially in light of the fact that he himself is not a very good speaker of his own language. The conceit he uses is that he has sole access to a native Klingon speaker, a prisoner named Maltz (and let's just be clear that everyone realizes it's a conceit). When questions arise about the correct way to tell time in Klingon, or the proper use of prefixes to indicate indirect objects, Okrand can claim that the matter requires further research. Sometimes he will publish an answer (on Internet newsgroups or in the journal *HolQeD*), but he has the luxury of waiting to do so until the expert Klingonists have fully debated the possibilities. "I have to be careful what I say, because if I make a mistake it *will* be noticed," Okrand told me. He made a big mistake when for the instructional audiotape *Power Klingon* (published by Simon & Schuster), he put the subject before, rather than after, the verb in the toast "May your blood scream" (*'IwlIj jachjaj*—"blood-your scream-may-it"). He later explained that in the formalized domain of toast giving, the word-order rule is object-subject-verb rather than object-verb-subject. This modification rings true; it is often the case that ceremonial domains bend the rules in natural languages. (When but in toasts do we begin English sentences with "May your . . ."?) Okrand is a skilled back-fitter.

Part of what allows him to deal with accidental inconsistencies in such a natural way is that a realistic amount of wiggle room was built into the language from the beginning. In the introduction to the first edition of his dictionary, he discusses some "dialect differences" in Klingon vocabulary and pronunciation. (The notion of dialect difference has been important, he told me, "considering the difficulty in getting the actors on the show to say things right.") He also allows for exceptions to the grammatical rules. For example, as stated in the chapter on nouns, the plural suffix -*mey* "cannot be used with body parts. It should be noted, however, that Klingon poets often violate this grammatical rule in order to evoke particular moods in their poetry. Thus, forms such as **tlhonmey** *nostrils scattered all about* do occur." The language is just messy enough to be credible, and this messiness, built into the design from the very beginning, sets Klingon apart in the history of language invention. Klingon has no bone to pick with natural language; it is rather a respectful homage to the strange and interesting things that languages can do.

Another quality that makes Klingon stand out from the vast graveyard (for the most part) of previous inventions is that it has no purpose. It is interesting to note that in terms of the attraction of real, live speakers, Klingon is second only to the invented language with perhaps the most purpose—Esperanto. Esperantists are motivated by the goal of fostering peace by bridging language barriers. While they enjoy their language, and indeed often revel in it, the language itself is considered secondary to this goal. Learning a language takes work. It doesn't make sense to do the work if you have no reason to do it. After I attended the *qep'a'*, I talked with a prominent Esperantist about my experiences among the Klingon speakers. He shook his head with confused dismay and asked me, "But what are they *doing*? Really, what are they *doing*?"

My Esperantist friend poses a good question. What *are* they doing? If Klingon has no purpose, and you get nothing but a withering dose of ridicule from the entire world in return for the time you put into it, why ever would you bother?

Klingon is a type of puzzle that appeals to a type of person. It is difficult, but not impossible, formed from the stuff of real languages, just strange enough, just believable enough, small enough that you can know every word, the entire canon, but flexible enough to lend itself to the challenge of translation. The boundaries are set and the game is on. "How far can we take this?" is the collective call of the Klingon community. Could we translate *Hamlet*, under the given constraints? They could and they did, and what the translation lacks in elegance, it makes up for in the fact of its existing at all. Does Klingon have a poetic potential of its own? Let's see! (A phrase that came up in the improvisation game I witnessed: *"QI'lop lopmo' qI'Qo' qoH"*—"The fool won't sign the treaty, because he is celebrating warrior day.") Are there puns, holorimes, palindromes to be discovered? You bet! (The winner of the *HolQeD* palindrome contest: *"tlhab 'oS 'Iw HoHwI' So' batlh"*—"Blood represents freedom; honor hides the killer.") What are Klingon speakers doing? They are engaging in intellectually stimulating language play. They are enjoying themselves. They are doing language for language's sake, art for art's sake. And like all committed artists, they will do their thing, critics be damned.

*The
Secret Vice*

K lingon is the solution to an artistic problem, not a linguistic
one. Okrand set out to create a believable language for
a fictional culture, a language about which fans could say, "If
Klingons existed, there is no question that this is what they would
speak," a language with the mysterious quality of having just the
right feel.

And that urge, to create a language that captures an artistic
vision, is the motivation for a new generation of language
inventors. Their languages are designed for creativity's sake, not
to shape thought or change the world, or even to be spoken by
anyone, but to satisfy the urge that J. R. R. Tolkien called his
"secret vice." For his *Lord of the Rings* trilogy, Tolkien crafted an
entire family of languages, along with a realistic and extremely
detailed explanation of the "historical" derivation processes

through which the languages were related. Actually, it is more accurate to say that he crafted *The Lord of the Rings* for his languages. By the time the books were published in the mid-1950s, he had been working on his languages for over forty years. The creation of these languages consumed him almost against his will. At twenty-four years old he wrote of his obsession, "I often long to work at it and don't let myself 'cause though I love it so it does seem such a mad hobby!" He later claimed that he wrote *The Lord of the Rings* to legitimize his madness: "Nobody believes me when I say that my long book is an attempt to create a world in which a form of language agreeable to my personal aesthetic might seem real. But it is true."

As a boy, Tolkien had become enchanted with the Welsh words he saw printed on the freight cars that stopped at the train station behind his home. He loved the way the words looked and later, when he began to study the language, found he loved their sound even more. He explained his feeling for Welsh in the following way: "Most English-speaking people, for instance, will admit that *cellar door* is 'beautiful,' especially if dissociated from its sense (and its spelling). More beautiful than, say, *sky*, and far more beautiful than *beautiful*. Well then, in Welsh for me *cellar doors* are extraordinarily frequent."

When he discovered Finnish as a student at Oxford, he said, "It was like discovering a wine-cellar filled with bottles of amazing wine of a kind and flavour never tasted before. It quite intoxicated me." He began to construct his own language around the aspects of Finnish that inspired him, and as he worked on it, he began to develop a history and mythology for the language as well. His method of language construction was less a process of premeditated invention than a discovery. He would try out sounds and words until they seemed "right," and to know what was right, he felt the need to know something about the hypothetical people who spoke the language. His Finnish-inspired language would later evolve into Quenya, one of the languages of the Elves in *The Lord of the Rings*. Part of his construction of the history for the language involved the back-engineering of an ancestor language from which it could realistically have been derived. That ancestor language became "Primitive Quendian," from which a "contemporary" of Quenya, the Welsh-inspired Sindarin, spoken by a different community of Elves, was also derived. On the way to Sindarin (or rather the various dialects of Sindarin), Tolkien worked out aspects of Old Sindarin, Middle Sindarin, and a variety of other stages in the life of the language.

Plenty of other authors throughout history have provided fictional languages for their imagined lands. The citizens in Sir Thomas More's *Utopia* (1516) have a Utopian language that looks very much like Latin. The inhabitants of the moon in Francis Godwin's *Man in the Moone* (1638) speak a musical language. The people in *Terre australe connue* (1676) by Gabriel de Foigny speak a philosophical language like that designed by Wilkins and his contemporaries. From the strange cries of Swift's Lilliputians in *Gulliver's Travels* to Orwell's Newspeak to the street slang of Burgess's ruffians in *A Clockwork Orange* to the x- and z-filled jabber of countless works of science fiction, language creation has always been practiced for artistic purposes. However, these creations usually aren't languages so much as they are ideas, a bit of vocabulary, a few phrases. They don't invite further examination. They serve the story, never the other way around.

For Tolkien, language creation was an art all its own, enhanced and enriched by the stories, but still valuable even without them. He knew that others practiced the art as well. Once, while his attention wandered during a dreary presentation when he was in army training, he heard a fellow soldier suddenly say to himself, "Yes, I think I shall express the accusative case by a prefix!" He later recalled how, as these words were spoken,

> the little man's smile was full of a great delight, as of a poet or painter seeing suddenly the solution of a hitherto clumsy passage. Yet he proved as close as an oyster. I never gathered any further details of his secret grammar; and military arrangements soon separated us never to meet again (up to now at any rate). But I gathered that this queer creature—ever afterwards a little bashful after inadvertently revealing his secret—cheered and comforted himself in the tedium and squalors of "training under canvas" by composing a language, a personal system and symphony that no else was to study or to hear.

Tolkien told this story during a speech given in the early 1930s (before the publication of his fiction), which he introduced as being on the subject of "nothing less embarrassing than the *unveiling* in public of a secret vice." After issuing a sort of apologia and explanation for what he was up to, he presented some examples of poetry in his own languages, thereby opening his secret to scrutiny in the name of the advancement of the art form whose "development to perfection must . . . certainly be prevented by its solitariness, the lack of interchange, open rivalry, study or imitation of others' technique."

Things are different now. In an increasing number of online "artlang" or "conlang" (constructed language) forums, the formerly closeted (this is the word they use) practitioners of the no-longer-secret vice share the details of their languages with each other looking only for feedback and appreciation, and for the satisfaction of giving concrete linguistic shape to their personal aesthetic. The creator of P@x'áãokxáã incorporated influences from

Mohawk, Swahili, and Japanese in creating a language with "an emphasis on emotion, touch, and action" in order to reflect his "philosophical views (existentialism, idealism, absurdism, etc.)." Toki Pona, a language of simple syllables that uses only positive words, is intended to promote positive thinking, to be "fun and cute . . . one could almost imagine a race of little cartoon creatures speaking in Toki Pona." Brithenig was designed as "the language of an alternate history, being the Romance language that might have evolved if Latin speakers had displaced Celtic speakers in Britain." Nunihongo is an "attempt to answer what Japanese might look like if half its vocabulary were derived from English." The Azak language was inspired by the inventor's "discovery of agglutinative languages and ergativity" (grammatical types common in the world's languages, but exotic with respect to English) and is meant to "take those features and push them to their limits."

The urge to push features to their limits is also found in languages like Aeo, which uses only vowels, and (the self-describing) AllNoun. Other projects push the idea of language itself to its limits. Ilish is the language of a hypothetical sea creature that communicates by electrical shocks representing points in a Cartesian coordinate system. Meaning is completely carried by pronouns, which contain information about "attitude (beneficial, threatening, neutral), location (x, y, and z coordinates) and context (seen at that location now, expected to be at that location now, at that location in the past)." Rikchik is the language of octopus-like aliens that use seven tentacles to form combinations of shapes to make utterances.

In this atmosphere of lively exchange and discussion, some critical standards have emerged. Languages that are too Englishy are frowned upon, as are "kitchen sink" languages or "Frankenlangs," which just throw together every cool feature the author can think of but don't make sense as a whole. First timers often make the mistake of excitedly trumpeting a great new idea for marking pronouns, or negating sentences, or indicating tense, only to be patiently referred to the hundreds of natural languages that already do it that way. It is much harder to come up with something original than one might think. And while originality is appreciated, it must be backed up by complexity and depth. The most respected languages in the conlang community often have years of work behind them, and may even be attached to whole "conworlds" or "concultures" that help give them coherence and a model "literature."

It is clear that the upper-echelon active conlangers have a lot of knowledge about a wide range of natural languages. Many critiques of proposed conlang features branch off into lengthy discussions about exotic Australian languages or the sound-change rules of ancient Greek. In the summer of 2007, I attended the second annual Language Creation Conference in Berkeley, where about forty conlangers gathered to give presentations, participate in workshops, and socialize. The technical level of the discussions was sometimes incredibly high; people really knew their stuff. When one presenter began by playing some sound files and asking the audience to guess which languages they were, someone guessed right every time—Breton, Finnish, Navajo.

For these language inventors, language was not an enemy to be tamed or reformed but a muse. And they bowed down before her. Jeff Burke, a tall man who seemed nervous and shy at the podium, explained how he had been inspired to build his own family of "Central Mountain" languages by the incredible beauty he found in Mohawk when he took a course on it in college. He said the language "did something to me," and he began to dig into the history of the language, becoming a self-taught expert in the development of Mohawk from Proto-Iroquoian. He was also fascinated by Cheyenne and wanted to capture "the spirit of its sounds," so he studied the development of the language from Proto-Algonquian. His talk didn't focus so much on his own creation as on the real languages that inspired it. He wanted us to understand where his artistic vision had come from. As he went over the complicated details of the Mohawk pronominal system, he spoke softly, but with such love and wonder in his voice that I thought he might burst into tears.

I was energized by the proceedings, reminded of the reason I had gone into linguistics in the first place—my own heart-fluttering fascination with languages. Over the years that visceral feeling had been somewhat dampened by the intellectual focus that an academic track demands. All linguists begin with that spark of love for language, but they sometimes end up so involved in supporting a theory or gathering evidence against someone else's theory that they forget it. Languages become cold bundles of data that they pick through for what they need. There is value in this kind of activity, and sometimes excitement as well, but it rarely inspires delight.

And there was plenty of delight at the conlang conference. One of the most popular presentations was by Don Boozer, a librarian at the Cleveland Public Library. His language, Dritok, was born when he began to wonder if it was possible to make a language out of chipmunk noises. He started constructing a voiceless language, carried solely by clicking, popping, and hissing sounds. The loudest sound in the language (used for pejoratives) is a sort of forceful pig snort. The examples he gave sent waves of glee through the audience—they sounded so strange, so inhuman, but there was a detectable structure or system that gave Dritok a scent of "languageness." He had also worked out aspects of a cultural context that would help the language make sense. Dritok is the language of the Drushek, long-tailed beings with large ears and no vocal cords who value solitude and quiet. They also use gestures for some syntactic functions. People immediately started asking questions: "How do they yell?" "Do they make art?" "Can they use whistling?" "Can they throw objects to get someone's attention?" "Do they have thick skin?" Boozer hadn't yet worked things out that far, but it was clear that if he wanted to, he had the blessings of the conlang community. They were clamoring for more.

Watching the presentations at the conlang conference got me thinking that I might like to make a language of my own. I came up with lots of ideas: a pan-conlang hybrid, formed from the features of various other invented languages; a language that used English words, but with different functions and meanings from those they have in English; a language whose phonemes were physical objects that had to be juggled in distinct patterns to make words; a language where every word is defined by its relationship to one specific concept; a language where the mesage has to be physically eaten and digested to be understood—immediacy of communication could not be a factor in that culture. I realized as I came up with these ideas that they were too "clever." I had no desire to sit down and fill out the details of how any of them would work. I was moved not by the muse but by a desire to impress, to be seen as creative or original. I wanted to inspire that feeling of delight, to get the admiration and the respect that I had seen expressed for certain conlang projects, but I didn't want to do the work. I was that guy who wants to play guitar in order to get the girls, that woman who wants to write a novel so she can go to fancy New York cocktail parties. I wasn't driven by a need to practice the art, to satisfy a personal vision; I just thought it would be cool for other people to think my language was cool.

I guess I don't have it in me. I'm not a language creation artist. But I *can* still be a language creation art appreciator, which itself takes a certain amount of work and background knowledge. The more you know about language and linguistics in general, the better you can enjoy the truly elegant or complex idea, and the better you can tell the good stuff from the lazy stuff, the mature solutions from the beginners' mistakes. One of the presenters, John Quijada (whose own language, Ithkuil, has been thirty years in the making and claims as its influences the "consonantal phonology and verbal morphology of Ubykh and Abkhaz, certain Amerindian verbal moods, Niger-Kordofanian aspectual systems, Basque and Dagestanian nominal case systems, Wakashan enclitic systems, the Tzeltal and Guugu Yimidhirr positional orientation systems, the Semitic triliteral root morphology, the evidential and possessive categories of Suzette Elgin's Láadan, and the schematic word-formation principles of Wilkins' Analytical Language and Sudre's Solresol"), compared the activities of the conlangers at the conference to a convention of biologists getting together to create an animal. "*They* would know and appreciate what they were doing, but it might be hard to explain to nonbiologists why some choices were praised as brilliant, some got a laugh, and others got a groan."

At a very basic level, language invention is an expression of the creativity that is latent in all of us. Children like to draw pictures, playact scenes, and make up little tunes, and many of them also go through a phase where they experiment with sounds and invent their own words. When my son was two years old, he started saying, "*Goaji, goaji, goaji,*" with a strange Hindi sort of intonation, to represent "talking going on." (He would say it when he heard a foreign language—though he never heard Hindi—or when people were talking around him without paying attention to him.) I don't know why he settled on *goaji* except that it just felt right to him. This doesn't mean he is any more likely to grow up to be a language inventor than he is to continue his passion for coloring into adulthood, but the raw urge to create is there, as it is in everyone. As with painting, or music, or acting, only in some does that urge take root and blossom into a lifelong passion.

The language inventors of previous eras spent a lot of energy trying to convince others of the practical justifications for doing what they did. They had rational reasons for making their languages. But the artistic drive has always been there. In a recent book on Hildegard von Bingen's twelfth-century language, the medievalist Sarah Higley (herself an accomplished conlanger and science fiction author working under the pen name Sally Caves) argues that the purpose of Hildegard's language was personal expression, that she "looked upon her invention as a purer way than even Latin, Greek, or Hebrew to dignify and describe her world." It wasn't, as some scholars have argued, a secret code for her nuns to use or the spontaneous product of a religious trance. It was the first published conlang.

You can see the art in the way John Weilgart, the creator of aUI, felt so sure that "ah" was the sound of space and "j" was the sound of evenness. Or in the way Johann Schleyer stubbornly clung to his beloved umlaut when the Volapük reformers argued that it hurt their international chances. It was there for Wilkins in his quest to make sense of the universe and order it accordingly, and for Suzette Elgin when she filled Láadan with her favorite natural-language features. It is even there in Esperanto, which Tolkien once praised for intuitively capturing the right balance between engineering and aesthetics. He criticized one of its competitors for looking too much like a "factory product," for seeming "made of spare parts" and being without the "gleam of the individuality, coherence and beauty, which appear in the great natural idioms, and which do appear to a considerable degree (probably as high a degree as is possible in an artificial idiom) in Esperanto—a proof of the genius of the original author."

The artistry is obvious to the Esperantists, who tell stories, write poetry, and make jokes in what only they can fully appreciate as a quintessentially Esperanto way. It is there for the Lojbanists, one-upping each other by composing tongue twisters, riddles, and plays on words that work only in Lojban. It is there for the Klingon speakers, who put up with an awful lot of abuse in order to do what they love.

I finally ran out of time to study for my Klingon test. I went into the test feeling confident but weary. I was ready to go home. I needed to get back into the world and reassert my coolness.

First I had to endure the institute's business meeting, where at least thirty minutes was devoted to a discussion of whether the journal *HolQeD* should continue to be published in a print version in addition to the electronic version. (Pros: "It's neat to be archived at the Library of Congress." "There's one on display at the Museum of Peace in Uzbekistan." Cons: "It costs too much." "It's redundant.") "Who cares?" I grumbled under my breath from the back of the room, where I was flipping through my flash cards one last time.

Finally, the room cleared, leaving me, Louise, and a couple of other, more advanced test-takers. I dug in as soon as the test was laid in front of me, knowing my fragile web of mnemonics wouldn't last very long. I filled it out quickly. I couldn't remember the word for "sergeant" (*bu'*) or the translation for *ngu'* (identify), but otherwise I breezed through. I handed it in and went out to wait in the lobby with the rest of the *qep'a'* attendees while it was being graded.

I got a score of 93 points, well above passing. Everyone congratulated me and remarked on how well I did. My mood lifted. I felt proud. I looked around and saw, near the reception desk, a group of glossy-toothed "mundanes" checking in to the hotel. They appeared to be in town for a sales meeting, or maybe just the wedding of an old fraternity brother. They looked at us, immediately noticing, of course, a costumed member of our group. One of these so-called normal people walked right up to him and, without asking for permission, took out his cell phone to take a picture, saying to no one in particular, and certainly not to the Klingon in question, "If I don't get a picture of this, no one will believe me." The Klingon stood up tall and posed like a true warrior. At that moment, I knew whose side I was on. The world of Klingon may be based in fiction, but living in it takes real guts.

Louise didn't pass the test. "Oh, well," she said with a shrug and a smile. "I will try again next year." And I was there the next year, at a highway hotel outside of Philadelphia, when she did pass the test. I bought her a drink, and we toasted to perseverance.

The List of
Languages

What follows is a list of five hundred invented languages in chronological order. Why five hundred? Why not all of them? For one thing, no one knows how many there are. Any claim to completeness in a list would surely be undone by the discovery of yet another self-published book or pamphlet in a library storage room somewhere. Another problem is determining what should count as an invented language. Should a few lines of made-up gibberish in a novel earn a place on the list? What about a sketch of an idea with none of the detail filled in?

When I started assembling this list, I had the ambitious intention to be as complete as possible, to include every project that anyone anywhere had any evidence for, but this soon proved impractical. The story I was trying to tell got lost in a swamp of data. I wanted the list to be big enough to impress, to make you exclaim, "I had no idea there were so many!" But I also wanted it to be manageable enough to serve as a sort of mini-history, where just by looking at the dates and the names of the languages, you could spot some general trends and get a sense of the connections between the ideas and the times.

I culled my list from the more than nine hundred languages covered in Aleksandr Dulichenko's *Mezhdunarodnye vspomogatel'nye iazyki* (International Auxiliary Languages, 1990). This massive piece of research includes all of the projects covered by previous overviews, such as *Histoire de la langue universelle* by Louis Couturat and Léopold Leau (1903), *Bibliografio de internacia lingvo* by Petr Stojan (1929), *Historio de la mondolingvo* by Ernest Drezen (1931), and *Précis d'interlinguistique générale et spéciale* by Marcel Monnerot-Dumaine (1960), in addition to others mentioned in various sources. Dulichenko's work is about as complete as you can get. It's in Russian, and it's not easy to get ahold of, but you can find it at some major universities and the Library of Congress.

In deciding what to include in my own list, I didn't set any strict criteria. I just used my judgment and aimed for a list that would tell the story without distorting the facts. I left out a lot of works titled *Pasigraphie*, but put in enough to show that pasigraphies (universal writing systems) were big in the early nineteenth century, and still popped up occasionally after that. Although many languages from the early twentieth century got left out on account of having boring names (how many variations on "Lingua International" do you need to get the picture?), there are enough in there, proportionally, to highlight the explosion in the number of projects during this era. Languages with strange or interesting names got in, as did those whose authors exposed their desire for personal glory by naming their projects after themselves (see, for example, Isly's Linguum Islianum of 1901, Ostaszewski's Ost of 1926, and Anderson's Ande of 1960). I left out quite a few projects that were just reforms or improvements of other projects, but put in enough to show how widespread the "reform and improve" disease is among language inventors.

I included any work that I myself had seen in a library but had not seen in anyone else's list of invented languages (for example, *A Universal Language* by James Ruggles [1829] and Walter Cuthbertson's *Standard World Language for International Use* [1919]). I avoided works that involved too much uncertainty about dating or authorship—unless there was something intriguing about them (who was this Prince Immanuel of Jerusalem, the creator of Universal [1914?]?). Languages with weird names got in, as did languages from underrepresented countries such as Ghana (El-Afrihili, 1970), India (Koine Romai, 1973; Om, 1925; Sputnik, 1964), Iran (City-Language, 1959), Nigeria (Guosa, 1981), and Vietnam (Frater, 1957).

If an inventor had multiple languages, I sometimes admitted only one—Weferling's Intal (1956) made it in, but not his Intal II (1964) or III (1968)—but for especially prolific inventors I might include the whole bunch. (Hats off to Petr Stojan, who gave us, over the years from 1911 to 1926, Spiranta, Aryana, Ariana, Amiana, Liana, Unita, Espo, and Eo.)

Dulichenko's list goes only as far as 1973. Past 1973, I simply included languages I had heard of or seen myself in libraries. The criteria for dating a language require some explanation. Generally, the year given for a project represents the initial date of publication in an article or a book. I date Tolkien's languages, for example, as 1955, even though he had already been working on them for forty years by that point, because that is when he first published information about them (in the appendix to the third book of *The Lord of the Rings*).

The dating of languages in the Internet age gets even more complicated. The years given for most of the languages I list from 1990 on represent (approximately) the first posting about the language on the Web, in a newsgroup, or on a site dedicated to the language. The "conlangs" or "artlangs" I have listed here amount to a vanishingly tiny portion of the number that are out there. Sites like Langmaker.com list hundreds of them. On forums like the "zompist" bulletin board (www.spinnoff.com/zbb), new languages are born every day. I have listed only the projects that I mention in the text, along with a few other especially noteworthy or well-developed ones—languages that most of the highly regarded conlangers will have heard of.

Samples of various languages are given in appendix B. You can sort this list by language name or author, and see further information about some of the languages and their inventors at inthelandofinventedlanguages.com.

	Language	Author	Date
1	Lingua Ignota	Hildegard von Bingen	c. 1150
2	Balaibalan	Muhyî-i Gülşenî	c. 1500
3	Common Writing	F. Lodwick	1647
4	Lingua Universallis	P. Labbé	1650
5	Arithmeticus Nomenclator	P. Bermudo	1653
6	Logopandecteision	T. Urquhart	1653
7	Universal Character	C. Beck	1657
8	Clavis Conveniente Linguarum	J. Becher	1661
9	Ars Signorum	G. Dalgarno	1661
10	Universal Language	I. Newton	c. 1661

	Language	Author	Date
11	Pasigraphie	Earl of Worcester	1663
12	Polygraphia	A. Kircher	1663
13	Panglottie	J. Komenský (Comenius)	1665
14	Arte Combinatoria	G. Leibniz	1666
15	Ruski Jezik	J. Križanić	1666
16	Philosophical Language	J. Wilkins	1668
17	Pasigraphie	F. Besnier	1674
18	Langue Universelle pour Negotiants	de Bermonville	1687
19	Allgemeine Schrift	D. Solbrig	1726
20	Scriptura Oecumenica	Carpophorophilus	1732
21	Langue Nouvelle	J. Faiguet	1765
22	Universal Philosophical Language	R. Jones	1769
23	Lingua Philosophica	G. Kalmár	1772
24	Lingua Universale	F. Soave	1772
25	Allgemeine Rede und Schrift-Sprache	C. G. Berger	1779
26	Opšteslovenski Jezik	B. Kumerdej	1793
27	Langue Universelle	C. Delormel	1795
28	Pasigraphie	C. H. Wolke	1797
29	Pasigraphie	J. Maimieux	1797
30	Noématopasigraphilalie	F. Dumont de Bonneville	1799
31	Polygraphie	Z. Hourwitz	1801
32	Pasigraphie	J. Z. Näther	1805
33	Pangraphie	H. Burmann	1807
34	Pasilalie	A. Burja	1808
35	Sinnensprache	A. Riem	1809
36	Lingua Filosofica Universale	M. Gigli	1818
37	Universalis Nyelvnek (Steganographia)	I. Gáti	1820
38	Lingua Universalis	A. Réthy	1821

APPENDIX A

	Language	Author	Date
39	Lingua Slavica Universalis	J. Herkel	1826
40	A Universal Language	J. Ruggles	1829
41	Genigrafia Italiana	G. Matraya	1831
42	Vilagnyelv	J. Bolyai	1832
43	Langue Universelle	A. Grosselin	1836
44	Communicationssprache	J. Schipfer	1839
45	Phonarithmon	W. H. Henslowe	1840
46	Lugar	S. Herpain	1843
47	Langue Universelle et Analytique	E. T. Vidal	1844
48	Orbidáie	J. Bazin	1844
49	Pangraphie	S. Ivičević	1848
50	Lengua Universal	P. L. Martinez	1852
51	Lengua Universal y Filosofica	B. Sotos Ochando	1852
52	Universal Language	G. Edmonds	1855
53	Monopanglosse	P. Gagne	1858
54	Pantos-Dîmou-Glossa	L. de Rudelle	1858
55	Nouvelle Numératon Parlée	Dr. Verdu	1859
56	Pasigraphie	M. Paić	1859
57	Alevato	S. P. Andrews	1862
58	Mundographie (Gablenzographia)	M. H. von Gablenz	1864
59	Uzajmeni Slavjanski Jezik	M. Majar	1865
60	Solresol	J. F. Sudre	1866
61	Langue Universelle	A. Caumont	1867
62	Pasigraphie	A. Bachmaier	1868
63	Universalglot	J. Pirro	1868
64	Universal Dolmetscher Sprache	A. F. Staffler	1869
65	New Universal Cipher Language	C. Stewart	1874
66	Lingua Lumina	J. W. Dyer	1875
67	Langue Internationale Étymologique	F. Reimann	1877
68	Ixessoire	L. and R. Poincaré	1879

	Language	Author	Date
69	Volapük	J. M. Schleyer	1879
70	Weltsprache	A. Volk and R. Fuchs	1883
71	Blaia Zimondal	C. Meriggi	1884
72	Néo-Latine	E. Courtonne	1884
73	Neulatein	A. Sturmhöfel	1884
74	Pasilingua	P. Steiner	1885
75	Chabé-Aban (Langue Naturelle)	E. Maldant	1886
76	Sprachwissenschaftliche Kombinatorik	J. Bauer	1886
77	Langue Universelle	C. Menet	1886
78	Langue Universelle	C. L. A. Letellier	1886
79	Nal Bino	S. Verheggen	1886
80	Pasigraphia	J. Bobula	1886
81	Rosentalographia	Rosenthal	1886
82	Balta	E. Dormoy	1887
83	Bopal	M. Streiff (S. de Max)	1887
84	Esperanto	L. L. Zamenhof	1887
85	Kokographie	F. Friedrich	1887
86	Nuvo-Volapük	A. Kerchoffs	1887
87	Pasilingua Hebraica	F. Lenz	1887
88	Visona	Dr. Sivartha	1887
89	Weltsprache	N. Eichhorn	1887
90	American Language	E. Molee	1888
91	Kosmos	E. A. Lauda	1888
92	Lengua Universal	T. Escriche y Mieg	1888
93	Lingua Franca Nova	S. Bernhard	1888
94	Mundolinco	J. Braakmann	1888
95	Spelin	J. Bauer	1888
96	Verkehrssprache	J. Lott	1888
97	Anglo-Franca	G. J. Henderson	1889
98	Compromiss-Sprache	J. Lott	1889
99	Lengua Universal	E. G. Ugarte	1889
100	Myrana	J. Stempfl	1889

APPENDIX A

	Language	Author	Date
101	Oidapa	Chancerel	1889
102	Panglossie	Le Dantec (pseud.)	1889
103	Sermo	A. Browne	1889
104	Lengua Catolica	A. Liptay	1890
105	Lingua Internazional	J. Lott	1890
106	Mundolingue	J. Lott	1890
107	Nov Latin	D. Rosa	1890
108	Pure Saxon English	E. Molee	1890
109	Zilengo	A. Oka	1890
110	Idiome Universel	H. Marini	1891
111	Anti-Volapük	F. Mill	1893
112	Dil	Fieweger (pseud. Dr. Gül)	1893
113	Francezin	A. Lyakide	1893
114	Luftlandana	G. A. Larsson	1893
115	Orba	J. Guardiola	1893
116	Universala	E. H. Heintzeler	1893
117	Casuela	S. Voirol	1894
118	Communia	J. Stempfl	1894
119	Novilatiin	E. Beermann	1895
120	Adjuvanto	L. Beaufront	1896
121	Linguo Moderna	A. Grabowski	1896
122	Veltparl	W. von Arnim	1896
123	Lasonebr	A. Nilson	1897
124	Nuove-Roman	J. E. Puchner	1897
125	Dey Daynd	A. J. Guerero	1898
126	Dilpok	A. Marchand	1898
127	Patoiglob	P. B. Bohin	1898
128	Prometej-Prosvetitelj	E. Gurin (pseud. Dr. Novodum)	1898
129	Bolak (Langue Bleue)	L. Bollack	1899
130	Dialect Centralia	A. Nilson	1899
131	Lingue International	J. Lott	1899
132	Langage Humain	Umano	1900

	Language	Author	Date
133	Lingua Komun	F. Kürschner	1900
134	Linguum Islianum	F. Isly	1901
135	Zahlensprache	F. Hilbe	1901
136	Idiom Neutral	W. K. Rosenberger	1902
137	Neu-Latein (Universal-Latein)	E. Frandsen	1902
138	Reform-Latein	K. Frölich	1902
139	Tutonish	E. Molee	1902
140	Universal-Latein	W. Möser	1902
141	Völkerverkehrssprache	C. Dietrich	1902
142	Ziffern-Grammatik	W. Riegler	1902
143	Adam-Man Tongue	E. Shaftesbury	1903
144	Latino sine Flexione	G. Peano	1903
145	Panroman	H. Molenaar	1903
146	Tal	A. Hoessrich	1903
147	Mundelingva	J. von Hummler	1904
148	Perio	M. Talundberg	1904
149	Spokil	A. Nicolas	1904
150	Lingua Internacional	A. Zakrzewski	1905
151	Glanik (Glan-ik)	E. Ware	1906
152	Mondlingvo	H. Trischen	1906
153	Niu Teutonish	E. Molee	1906
154	Pan-Kel	M. Wald	1906
155	Ulla	F. Greenwood	1906
156	Antido I	R. de Saussure	1907
157	Apolëma	R. de la Grasserie	1907
158	Idiom Neutral Reformed	J. B. Plinth	1907
159	Idiom Neutral Reformed	W. K. Rosenberger	1907
160	Ido	L. de Beaufront and	1907
		L. Couturat	
161	Lingua European	B. Bijlevelt	1907
162	Master Language	S. C. Houghton	1907
163	Neuslawisch	I. Hošek	1907
164	Novilatin	E. Beermann	1907

	Language	Author	Date
165	Parla	C. Spitzer	1907
166	Corintic	A. Miller	1908
167	Ilo	C. Lemaire	1908
168	Interprète International	V. Hély	1908
169	Mez-Voio	J. Jamin	1908
170	Ro	E. P. Foster	1908
171	Auli	E. Wahl	1909
172	Dutalingue	A. Duthil	1909
173	Esperanto Reformita	R. Brandt	1909
174	Idiom Neutral Modifiket	J. Meysmans	1909
175	Ile	A. Seidel	1909
176	Ilo	H. Ziemer	1909
177	Ispirantu	A. Seidel	1909
178	Italico	R. Triola	1909
179	Median	A. Huart	1909
180	Nummer	N. Jekel	1909
181	Perfektsprache	A. Hartl	1909
182	Salvador	F. Gavidia	1909
183	Unial	J. Weisbart	1909
184	Antido II	R. de Saussure	1910
185	Eulalia	S. Škrabec	1910
186	Langue Universelle Sémantique	J. E. Croegaert	1910
187	Latino Internationale	U. Basso	1910
188	Linguo Romane Universale	J. Słonimski	1910
189	Mondea	J. Scheefer	1910
190	Mondlingu	S. E. Bond	1910
191	Perfektigo de Esperanto	Z. Romański	1910
192	Reform Esperanto	P. D. Hugon	1910
193	Reform-Esperanto	P. Rodet	1910
194	Semilatin	W. Moeser (pseud. Austriacus)	1910
195	Veltlang	F. Braendle	1910
196	Altutonish	E. Molee	1911

	Language	Author	Date
197	Internacionu Sientu Lingua	A. Kovalyev	1911
198	Medio	O. Nachtigall	1911
199	Molog	H. de Sarranton	1911
200	Simplo	Ferranti	1911
201	Spiranta	P. Stojan (pseud. P. Radovich)	1911
202	Adelfeal Lingw	A. Kovalyev	1912
203	Aryana	P. Stojan	1912
204	Europal	J. Weisbart	1912
205	Lingvo Kosmopolita	R. de Saussure	1912
206	Manbab	A. Beuthner	1912
207	Omnez	S. E. Bond	1912
208	Reform-Neutral	W. K. Rosenberger	1912
209	Slavina	J. Konečný	1912
210	Tersboca	M. Rotter	1912
211	Altayko (Esk)	M. Sondahl	1913
212	Nepo	V. Tscheschichin	1913
213	Slovanština	E. Kolkop	1913
214	Telekaba	K. Pirquet	1913
215	Uropa	W. Donisthorpe	1913
216	Viva	N. Nesmeyanov	1913
217	Ariana	P. Stojan	1914
218	Europeo	C. A. Bravo del Barrio	1914
219	Universal	Prince Immanuel of Jerusalem	1914?
220	Alteutonik	E. Molee	1915
221	Wede (Weltdeutsch)	A. Baumann	1915
222	Filosofskiy Jezik	J. Linzbach	1916
223	Geoglot	T. J. Donoghue	1916
224	Weltdeutsch	W. Ostwald	1916
225	Weltdeutsch, das Verbesserte Wede	A. Baumann	1916
226	Etem	N. Yushmanov	1917

	Language	Author	Date
227	Glot	V. Petracevitch (pseud. V. Pevich)	1917
228	Ujlatin	A. Koleszár	1917
229	Nov Latin Logui	K. Pompiati	1918
230	Parlamento	G. Perrier (pseud. G. Ferry)	1918
231	Universalspråket	K. Keyser	1918
232	Esperantida	R. de Saussure	1919
233	Latinulus	V. Martellotta	1919
234	Lips-Kith	J. Scarisbrick	1919
235	Standard World Language	W. J. Cuthbertson	1919
236	Verbessertes Esperanto	P. Völz	1919
237	Ao	V. Gordin	1920
238	Ariadna Lingvo	V. Shmurlo (pseud. Vlasha)	1920
239	Slavski Jezik	B. Holý	1920
240	Dynamic Language	E. Molee	1921
241	Hom-Idyomo	C. Cárdenas	1921
242	Nove-Latina	J. van Diemen	1921
243	Optoez	S. E. Bond	1921
244	QJ	S. Kukel-Krajevsky	1921
245	Timerio	Thiemer	1921
246	Transcendent Algebra	J. Linzbach	1921
247	Amiana	P. Stojan	1922
248	Interlingua Systematic	J. Rossello-Ordines	1922
249	Medial	J. Weisbart	1922
250	Mundolingua (Menimo)	D. Starrenburg	1922
251	Occidental (Interlingue)	E. von de Wahl	1922
252	Qôsmianî	W. M. L. Beatty	1922
253	Babilonska Uganka	A. Ertl	1923
254	Espido	M. Pesch	1923
255	Federal	J. Barral	1923

Language	Author	Date
256 Liana	P. Stojan (pseud. P. Radovich)	1923
257 Lingvo Kommona	KJL	1923
258 Neolatine	G. Semprini	1923
259 Toito Spike	E. Molee	1923
260 Unesal Interlingu	E. Weferling	1923
261 Unilingue	A. Lavagnini	1923
262 Unita	P. Stojan (pseud. P. Radovich)	1923
263 Uniti Langue	F. Riedel and O. Scheffers	1923
264 Esperanta	J. Železný	1924
265 Latuna	G. du Bois	1924
266 World English (Cosmo-English)	J. W. Hamilton	1924
267 Arulo (Gloro)	M. Talmey	1925
268 Esperido	H. E. Raymond	1925
269 Europan	J. Weisbart	1925
270 Ido Avancit	R. Harding	1925
271 Latinesco	H. J. Macmillan	1925
272 Monario I	A. Lavagnini	1925
273 Nov-Esperanto	R. de Saussure	1925
274 Om	L. Vulda	1925
275 Universal	G. Muravkiy	1925
276 Eo	P. Stojan (pseud. Ribaulb)	1926
277 Espo	P. Stojan (pseud. Ribaulb)	1926
278 Meso	S. E. Bond	1926
279 Neoromani (Neoromano)	J. Słonimiski	1926
280 Omo	V. Vyengyerov	1926
281 Ost	A. Ostaszewski	1926
282 Una	F. Buckel	1926
283 Weltpitshn	A. Baumann	1926
284 Anglido	H. E. Raymond	1927
285 Cosman	H. Milner	1927

APPENDIX A

	Language	Author	Date
286	Cosmolingvia	S. Horowitz	1927
287	Ideala Lingvo	T. Jung	1927
288	Loqa	G. Nield	1927
289	Mond-Lingvo	J. Weisbart	1927
290	Obshchyechyelovyeskiy Jezik	K. Tsiolkovskiy	1927
291	Panedo	M. Pisaryenko	1927
292	IDO (Idiom di Omni)	G. Meazzini	1928
293	Neolatino	P. Lundström	1928
294	Novam	G. Touflet	1928
295	Novial	O. Jespersen	1928
296	Oiropa Pitshn	A. Baumann	1928
297	Serve	O. T. Kunstovný	1928
298	Uniala	P. J. Troost	1928
299	Monario II	A. Lavagnini	1929
300	Mondialo	R. de Saussure	1929
301	Mondik	J. Jousten	1929
302	Aliq	R. P. G. Vallaeys	1930
303	Anglic	R. E. Zachrisson	1930
304	Basic English	C. K. Ogden	1930
305	Esperilo	H. E. Raymond	1930
306	Evoluto	S. E. Bond	1930
307	Mundi Latin	J. Weisbart	1930
308	Mundial	F. V. Lorenz	1930
309	Neoglyfy	A. S. Batěk	1930
310	Sintesal	N. Rubinin	1930
311	Susal	A. Levanzin and L. Maxwell	1930
312	Mondi-Lingue	T. Martineau	1931
313	Mu-Nba-B	A. Beuthner	1931
314	Scinterlingua	G. Viveros	1931
315	Simplificat Italian	A. Faccioli	1931
316	Mondyal	G. Durant	1932
317	Oz	C. Elam	1932

	Language	Author	Date
318	Sabir	P. Moralda	1932
319	Fitusa	B. Rosenblum	1935
320	Internasional	P. Mitrović	1935
321	Mundal	J. Eylenbosch	1935
322	Sona	K. Searight	1935
323	Synthetic English	A. P. Draper	1935
324	Universal-Esperanto	R. de Saussure	1935
325	Ofat	O. Farnstad	1936
326	Panamane	M. E. Amador	1936
327	Amxrikai Spek	R. O. Foulk	1937
328	Esperanto II	R. de Saussure	1937
329	Mondilingwo I	A. Lavagnini	1937
330	Neo	A. Alfandari	1937
331	Mondilingwo II	A. Lavagnini	1938
332	Panlingua	L. Weber	1938
333	Mondilinguo	A. Lavagnini	1939
334	Nature's Mother Tongue	B. E. Lyster	1939
335	Neolatinus	A. da Monte Rosso	1939
336	Latino Hodierno	W. Doran	1940
337	Sveslav	C. Djurdjević	1940
338	Latini	C. G. Cline	1941
339	Relingua	J. Tempest	1941
340	Tal	A. H. Talano	1941
341	Monling	K. Littlewood	c. 1942
342	Interglossa	L. Hogben	1943
343	Mondial	H. Heimer	1943
344	Olingo	R. S. Jaque	1944
345	Leno Gi-Nasu	M. A. de la Cruz	1945
346	Code Ari	F. Kovarik	1946
347	Komun	F. Musil	1946
348	Maryala	B. Máriás	1946
349	Auxilia	G. Morin	1947
350	Hoykoy	G. Ottander	1947

APPENDIX A

	Language	Author	Date
351	Inter-sistemal	P. Mitrović	1947
352	Ling	A. Olson	1947
353	Neolatino	A. Schild	1947
354	Romanés	W. D. Hinde	1947
355	Auxil	A. Belie	1948
356	Merican	R. O. Rouek	1948
357	Munda Linguo	F. Weber	1948
358	Universel	A. J. Decormis	1948
359	Kosmo	G. Schröder	1949
360	Semantography	C. K. Bliss	1949
361	Antibabele	G. Magli	1950
362	Antro	N. Andreev	1950
363	Peace Language	F. Sosdy	1950
364	Uni-Spik	G. de Biran	1950
365	Altuta	C. Ternest	1951
366	Esperantuisho	J. Železný	1951
367	Interlingua	A. Gode/IALA	1951
368	Mundion	H. Weinrich	1951
369	Concorde	S. F. Hall	1952
370	Universal-Latein	K. Pötzl-Pecelius	1952
371	Eur(op)ean	R. Jego	1955
372	Mondi Lingua	A. Lavagnini	1955
373	Quenya	J. R. R. Tolkien	1955
374	Sindarin	J. R. R. Tolkien	1955
375	Intal	E. Weferling	1956
376	Neulateinische Sprache	K. Pompiati	1956
377	Niuspik	J. Herpitt	1956
378	Pasigraphie	K. Obermair	1956
379	Radioglot	J. R. Te Winkel	1956
380	Romanid	Z. Magyar	1956
381	Translingua	E. Funke	1956
382	Euroglot	E. Ahlström	1957
383	Frater	Pham Xuan-Thai	1957

	Language	Author	Date
384	Luni	L. Znicz-Sawicki	1957
385	Picto	K. J. S. Janson	1957
386	Suma	B. Russell	1957
387	Unolok	H. Wilshire	1957
388	Geo	H. E. Salzer	1958
389	Globaqo	R. S. Jaque and	1958
		G. A. Jones	
390	Hesperyo	A. Lara	1958
391	Interling	T. Wood	1958
392	Mezhduslavjanski Jezik	L. Podmele	1958
393	City-Language	H. Emami	1959
394	Lalortel	R. N. Yetter	1959
395	Phonetic	C. H. Johnson	1959
396	Pikto	J. E. Williams	1959
397	Ande	A. W. Anderson	1960
398	Cacone	D. Sacks	1960
399	Delmondo	J. L. Mainprice (pseud.	1960
		E. J. Lipman)	
400	Lincos	H. Freudenthal	1960
401	Loglan	J. C. Brown	1960
402	Logography	B. Lipschitz	1960
403	Stipfone	A. Lallemand (pseud.	1960
		A. du Lothier)	
404	Neo	A. Alfandari	1961
405	Sollinga	A. M. Lichtgyeym	1961
406	Uneso	J. Nordin	1961
407	Unilo	V. Jørgensen	1961
408	Babm	F. Okamoto	1962
409	Eurolingva	H. K. J. Cowan	1962
410	Safo	A. Eckardt	1962
411	Utilo	A. R. Harrod	1962
412	ENI	M. Monnerot-Dumaine	1963
413	Espro	D. G. Rose	1963

	Language	Author	Date
414	Ladef	M. H. Michaylob	1963
415	Pocket Pasilex	C. Obermair	1963
416	Tunish	D. S. Blacklock	1963
417	Eksterlingui	J. K. D'Elcorecopo	1964
418	Eurolatin(e)	W. J. Visser	1964
419	Inga	B. Russell	1964
420	LoCoS	Y. Ota	1964
421	Neo-Esperanto	A. Lallemand (pseud. A. du Lothier)	1964
422	Oeropi	T. Mertens-van Gossum	1964
423	Sputnik	R. K. Verma	1964
424	Tungl	D. S. Blacklock	1964
425	Unilingua	R. Self	1964
426	Utoki	J. Manprice (pseud. E. Lipman)	1964
427	Zacno	D. A. Porter	1964
428	Euronord	A. J. Pilgrim	1965
429	Frendo	A. Churruca	1965
430	Liberanto	E. Kotar	1965
431	Nmtish	H. Irshad	1965
432	Novisimo	F. Sosdy	1965
433	Unilingua	N. Agopoff	1965
434	Anglo-Lat	R. Montero	1966
435	Ido Reformate	H. Pelligrini	1966
436	Lingvologia Lingvo	E. Hanhiniemi	1966
437	Zamalo (Zamenhof-Alting)	F. Alting	1966
438	Ilion	H. Milner	1967
439	Sekaigo	World Unification Movement	1967
440	Solinga	A. M. Lichtgyeym	1967
441	aUI	J. W. Weilgart	1968
442	Gloneo	R. S. Jaque	1968
443	ReNeo	N. D. Shyevchugov	1968

	Language	Author	Date
444	Unesal	E. Weferling	1968
445	El-Afrihili	K. Kumi Attobrah	1970
446	Geo-jezik	G. Zagoryel'sky	1970
447	Italiane Semplificate	H. Pelligrini	1971
448	Eurolengo	L. Jones	1972
449	Fasilfon	D. Carion	1972
450	Inglish (Basic English Improved)	L. Y. Le Bretton	1972
451	Mezdislav	B. Fahlke	1972
452	Paleneo	L. Charteris	1972
453	Vuldal	M. Hovey	1972
454	Koine Romai	V. de Gila	1973
455	Uni	E. Wainscott	1974
456	Gestuno	World Federation of the Deaf	1975
457	Instant World Language	A. Berendt	1977
458	Tsolyani	M. Barker	1978
459	Guosa	A. Igbinewka	1981
460	Vikto	B. Vilmos	1981
461	Glosa	W. Ashby and R. Clark	1982
462	SPL (Simplified Latin)	R. Dominicus	1982
463	Pacez	Y. Obana	1983
464	Klingon	M. Okrand	1984
465	Láadan	S. H. Elgin	1984
466	Unitario	M. Pleyer	1987
467	Lusane	L. S. Lopez-Negrete	1988
468	Lojban	Logical Language Group	1989
469	AllNoun	T. Breton	1990
470	Livagian	A. Rosta	1991
471	Vorlin	R. Harrison	1991
472	Azak	C. Grandsire	1992
473	Ehmay Ghee Chah	E. Hankes	1992
474	Ithkuil	J. Quijada	1995
475	Talossan	R. Madison	1995

APPENDIX A

	Language	Author	Date
476	Tepa	D. Elzinga	1995
477	Vela	B. Prist	1995
478	Verdurian	M. Rosenfelder	1995
479	Brithenig	A. Smith	1996
480	Ceqli	R. May	1996
481	Ilish	J. Henning	1996
482	Rikchik	D. Moskowitz	1996
483	Tokana	M. Pearson	1996
484	Rokbeigalmki	S. Belsky	1997
485	Draseléq	P. Flores	1998
486	Kēlen	S. Sotomayor	1998
487	Teonaht	S. Higley	1998
488	gjâ-zym-byn (gzb)	J. Henry	1999
489	Skerre	D. Ball	1999
490	Valdyan	I. Rempt	1999
491	Megdevi	D. Peterson	2001
492	Toki Pona	S. E. Kisa	2001
493	Ygyde	A. Nowicki	2002
494	Aeo	J. Tegire	2003
495	Idirl	J. Yench	2003
496	Nunihongo	J. Henning	2004
497	P@x'áãokxáã	E. Ohlms	2004
498	Þrjótrunn	H. Theiling	2006
499	Dritok	D. Boozer	2007
500	Proto–Central Mountain	J. Burke	2007

Language
Samples

Works on invented languages usually classify the languages into three categories. Languages like that of Wilkins, which are completely created from scratch, are called a priori languages. Languages like Esperanto, which take most of their material from existing natural languages, are called a posteriori languages. Languages like Volapük, which contain elements of both types, are categorized as mixed. There isn't always total agreement on which category a particular language should be in (especially for mixed languages), but you can usually tell what type a language falls under just by looking at it. Here are some examples:

A PRIORI:

Luftlandana (Larsson, 1893)

Ri napa luft byser hinsko. Napa ri spru freiste naj bar johrajb.

"We have invented a new language. We have seven moments of rest daily."

MIXED:

Bolak, La Langue Bleue (Bollack, 1899)

Ak vop sfermed pro spes maned, if om pobl to pobl, ne ei mnoka pfo an am lank.

"What an immense advantage for mankind, if from people to people we could communicate through the same language."

A POSTERIORI:

Medial (Weisbart, 1922)

Un Englo, un Franco ed un Deuto havit le taske pintir kamele. Le Englo voyajit ad Afrike for studiir le kamele in tisui doimie, le Franco gidit al zoologi jarden, ed le Deuto pintit on kamelo ex le profunde de sui psyke.

"An Englishman, a Frenchman, and a German were supposed to paint a camel. The Englishman traveled to Africa to study the camel in its habitat. The Frenchman went to the zoo, and the German painted a camel out of the depth of his psyke."

THE LORD'S PRAYER

One of the most commonly translated passages is the Lord's Prayer. For comparison, here are the first few lines in a variety of languages:

Scriptura Oecumenica (Carpophorophilus, 1732)

O baderus noderus ki du esso in seluma, fakdade sankadus ha nominanda duus, adfenade ha rennanda duus, ha folanda duus, fiassade felud in seluma, sik koke in derra.

Communicationssprache (Schipfer, 1839)

No Pera, wia ete Cielu, ta Noma sanctiferii, ta Royoma Ais arrivii; ta volonta färerii com Cielu änsi Terru.

Volapük (Schleyer, 1879)

O Fat obas, kel binol in süls, paisaludomöz nem ola! Kömomöd monargän ola! Jenomöz vil olik, as in sül, i su tal!

Weltsprache (Volk and Fuchs, 1883)

Not pater, vel sas in les cöles, ton nomen sanctöt, ton regnon venät, ton voluntat söt vam in le cöl, tam in le ter.

Pasilingua (Steiner, 1885)

Patro miso, quo er in coela, nama tüa sanctore, kingdoma tüa kommire, tüa willu fairore sur erda ut in coela.

Spelin (Bauer, 1888)

Pat isel, ka bi ni sielos! Nom el zi bi santed! Klol el zi komi! Vol el zi bi faked, kefe ni siel, efe su sium!

Lingua Komun (Kürschner, 1900)

Padre nose kuale tu ese in cielo, sante esa tue nómine; vena imperio tue; voluntá tue esa fate sur tera komo in cielo.

Idiom Neutral (Rosenberger, 1902)

Nostr patr kel es in sieli! Ke votr nom es sanktifiked; ke votr regnia veni; ke votr volu es fasied, kuale in siel, tale et su ter.

Spokil (Nicolas, 1904)

Mael nio kui vai o les zeal, aepenso lezai tio mita; veze lezai tio tsaeleda; feleno lezai tio bela, uti o zeal itu o geol.

Pan-Kel (Wald, 1906)

Sai Fat in sky, y sanu so nam; so land komu; so viy apsu up glob l sky.

Ulla (Greenwood, 1906)

Vus Patra hoo este n ciela, sankted este dus noma, dus rexdoma vene, dus desira esta färed n terra als tu este n ciela.

Nepo (Tscheschichin, 1913)

Vatero nia, kotoryja estas in la njeboo, heiliga estu nomo via; kommenu regneo via; estu volonteo via, jakoe in la njeboo, ebene soe na la erdeo.

Viva (Nesmeyanov, 1913)

Patr no ki es en ska, santanu to im, komu to regn, makru to vil ut en ska it on ge.

Qôsmianî (Beatty, 1922)

Mems patro qwe esip ir celestii, tom nomini a santificatap, tom regni venap, tom voliti fiatap aq ir celestii taleq or terri.

Novam (Touflet, 1928)

Patro nia que es nel sieli, vua nomo santificeveu, vua regno adveneu, vua volo fareveu sur il tero quale nel sielo.

Interglossa (Hogben, 1943)

Na Parenta in Urani: Na dicte volo; tu Nomino gene revero;

Plus tu Crati habe accido; plus u Demo acte harmono tu Tendo epi Geo homo in urani.

Maryala (Máriás, 1946)
Muy patra, ka jan en cölay, santages tu noma, alvene tu regna, ages tu vola cel en cöla ey en tera.

Zamalo (Alting, 1966)
ŋia padro, θiu estu in la cielo, saŋqtata estu wia nomom, venu wia regnom, oquru wia wolom na la tero, qiel in la cielo.

THE BABEL TEXT

These days, the inventors who create their languages for fun and art prefer to translate the story of Babel.

Verdurian (Rosenfelder, 1995)

Proše mižu: —Žaneno, tan satenam mážula er gorat, kiei finta attróue so syel er tan lažecom brac, pro dy řo ažlädam fne soa pera almea Ekaiei.

Then they said: "Come, let us build a town and a tower, whose top will reach the heavens; and let us get ourselves glory, so that we are not scattered across all the earth."

Teonaht (Higley, 1998)

Send eldwav ebra: "Mantets! Tesa-ilz lirifel-jo hadhhamats ta mehuen aid kempa ar Erahenahil, send rõ tyr aittearmats, ta vera listsõ hyny il takrem ro ssosyarem."

And they said: "Come! A city and tower let us build so that its head reaches to Heaven. And ourselves let us name, so that we get not throughout the earth our scattering."

Brithenig *(Smith, 1996)*

Affos ys ddisirent, "Gwath, gwan a eddiffigar yn giwdad per nu, cun yn tyr ke dang a llo chel, ke nu ffagen yn nôn per nu e sun ysparied rhen syrs feig lla der inteir."

Then they said, "Come, let us build a city for ourselves, with a tower that touches the heavens, that we make a name for ourselves and are not scattered over the face of the entire land."

Kēlen *(Sotomayor, 1998)*

ē teteñ ien hēja ñanna jamāonre pa jakōnōr ja ñi jōl rā anīstīli; ē teteñ ien hēja ñanna lewēra tō tūaþ wā ñi ñēim makkepōlien rā anmārwi āñ pēxa.

And they said to each other: We should make a city that has a tower that reaches to the heavens. And they said to each other: We should make our name so that we do not become scattered far among the world.

Skerre *(Ball, 1999)*

Eyan, eyik-ti "Katik saa kikenatin-wo a aran ni tates to sik tsiquos ena sakir kat rokerinsa a sise-we sas kikehaana-wo ya yiket i hasin i tahin."

Next, they said, "We should build a city and a tower that can go up to the sky so that our name will be remembered before we might be scattered to the entire surface of the world."

Rokbeigalmki *(Belsky, 1997)*

i uhmzu-guvdhab "ei! amzii-bolok fa'ailtzma sha'tzraap, i sha'wâjugôiyat ga'ghalu-a tzu-a ta'marom-a uzíí, i amzii-waz fa'ailtzma sem—fa'gaur nyeng amzii-kark la'lâurîluâmal-a."

and they said "hey! we'll build for ourselves a village, and a tower (lit. house of tallness) that its head in the heavens will [be], and we'll make for ourselves a name—so that we will not be scattered over the surface of the entire land."

Megdevi (Peterson, 2001)

pat za₄a₄u Doj, "j%₂6! noj paf noj midƐnlm tSapawa pat kirƐdlm, Ll-doj ?ApepltuT lƐnt Zi fezlz%₂6Z matsalA, pat gULo, noj paf noj mAkodZ%₂6Zlm bavalA, s%₂6mƐx noj karajiso gejn Zi sejL Zojzejs ?AbedZlsuT."

And said they, "Onward! Let's for ourselves a city build and a tower, which it the head of in the clouds will be, and at that time, we for ourselves famous reputations will have, lest we should be scattered throughout the whole Earth the face of."

Toki Pona (Kisa, 2001)

jan mute li toki e ni: "o kama! mi mute o pali e ma tomo e tomo palisa suli. lawa pi tomo palisa li lon sewi kon. o nimi pi mi mute li kama suli! mi wile ala e ni: mi mute li ken ala. mi mute li lon ma ali."

person many say this: o come! we many o work earth build building long object tall. head belonging to long object in above air. o name belonging to we many come big! we want not this: we many possible not. we many in land all.

Ithkuil (Quijada, 1995)

Çäwínn àköl šo ˇemm̀ u'çtîz˺ fačʰwa łôyú'¯ pâf kuł˅ šiwic' yöteîxoq ho'woftîc' winñ še ëktu'a s̪ałdoš.

Then they said let's make a town and a tower with its top part in the sky thereby potentially gaining notoriety and respect for ourselves lest we end up scattered across the face of this world.

Tepa (Elzinga, 1995)

huhawaqakkassa hanima etiqe ukaiqu kupine. huwaweletii pewalil-katta metasewe.

and we will build ourselves a pueblo whose top will reach to the sky; and we will be famous if we are scattered sometime throughout the region.

Ceqli (May, 1996)

hi jun pa bol, "ciq ven!—Gozi ben gozi fu bau han ceq, kai han turo kai toilsa xaq hu sta skai. hikai gozi fu tenho feimkiam por sam ke gozi be fentir ko kuljai hu sta to dunia."

and letter-pronoun-j past speak, "invite come!—I-you future build one city, and one tower and letter-pronoun-t separator-particle top which is-located-in sky. And you-I future have-become fame-name for-prevent that I-you passive spread-throw to all-place which is-located-in the world."

More samples of invented languages can be found at intheland ofinventedlanguages.com.

NOTES

Much of the information in this book comes from my own reporting. As much as I could, I have consulted the original works of the language inventors I discuss. The Library of Congress has a good collection of artificial languages, as does Princeton University and the University of Chicago. For the biographical information on Bliss, Weilgart, and Brown, I am indebted to the friends and family members who allowed me to interview them. They were incredibly open with me about memories that were sometimes painful for them. I am also grateful to the people who had the foresight to allow their basements and attics to be taken over by piles of documents for years, so that I could one day come along and dig through them. In this regard Shirley McNaughton, Bob LeChevalier, and Andrea Patten have provided me with indispensable help.

But, of course, I have also relied heavily on the work of others. What follows is a list of some of the secondary sources I have consulted and some suggestions for further reading.

General books about invented languages:

Umberto Eco, *The Search for the Perfect Language* (Blackwell, 1995).

Andrew Large, *The Artificial Language Movement* (Blackwell, 1985).

Marina Yaguello, *Lunatic Lovers of Language: Imaginary Languages and Their Inventors* (Athlone Press, 1991).

NINE HUNDRED LANGUAGES, NINE HUNDRED YEARS

For more about Hildegard von Bingen, see:

Sarah L. Higley, *Hildegard of Bingen's Unknown Language: An Edition, Translation, and Discussion* (Palgrave Macmillan, 2007).

The story of Joseph Schipfer comes from:

Norbert Michel, "Joseph Schipfer—Träumer oder Humanist?" *Beiträge zur Wallufer Ortsgeschichte* 1 (1993).

Information about Vela and Ben Prist is from:

Alan Libert, *Mixed Artificial Languages* (Lincom Europa, 2003).

JOHN WILKINS AND THE LANGUAGE OF TRUTH

Eco's book is particularly focused on this time period and contains a great deal of information about the historical background of the seventeenth-century language movement. Other books I have consulted for this section include:

Florian Cajori, *A History of Mathematical Notations* (The Open Court Publishing Company, 1928–29).

R. J. Craik, *Sir Thomas Urquhart of Cromarty (1611–1660): Adventurer, Polymath, and Translator of Rabelais* (Mellen Research University Press, 1993).

David Cram and Jaap Maat, *George Dalgarno on Universal Language: The Art of Signs (1661), The Deaf and Dumb Man's Tutor (1680), and the Unpublished Papers* (Oxford University Press, 2001).

James Knowlson, *Universal Language Schemes in England and France, 1600–1800* (University of Toronto Press, 1975).

Barbara J. Shapiro, *John Wilkins, 1614–1672: An Intellectual Biography* (University of California Press, 1969).

Joseph L. Subbiondo, *John Wilkins and 17th-Century British Linguistics* (John Benjamins, 1992).

LUDWIK ZAMENHOF AND THE LANGUAGE OF PEACE

For a very entertaining account of Solresol, see:

> Paul Collins, *Banvard's Folly: Thirteen Tales of Renowned Obscurity, Famous Anonymity, and Rotten Luck* (Picador USA, 2001).

This book also tells the story of George Psalmanazar, who in the early eighteenth century made up a language to perpetuate a hoax where he pretended to be a native of Formosa, and gave lectures all over Europe about his made-up exotic culture.

On Esperanto, see:

> Marjorie Boulton, *Zamenhof, Creator of Esperanto* (Routledge and Paul, 1960).
>
> Peter G. Forster, *The Esperanto Movement* (Mouton, 1982).
>
> Wendy Heller, *Lidia: The Life of Lidia Zamenhof, Daughter of Esperanto* (George Ronald, 1985).
>
> Pierre Janton, *Esperanto Language, Literature, and Community* (State University of New York Press, 1993).

Don Harlow maintains a very informative Web book about Esperanto at donh.best.vwh.net/esperanto.php.

On Hebrew, see:

> Jack Fellman, *The Revival of a Classical Tongue: Eliezer Ben Yehuda and the Modern Hebrew Language* (Mouton, 1973).
>
> Shlomo Izre'el, "The Emergence of Spoken Israeli Hebrew," in *Corpus Linguistics and Modern Hebrew: Towards the Compilation of the Corpus of Spoken Israeli Hebrew (CoSIH)*, edited by Benjamin H. Hary (Tel Aviv University, 2003).

CHARLES BLISS AND THE LANGUAGE OF SYMBOLS

On the rise of English and an analysis of how a language comes to world prominence, see:

David Crystal, *English as a Global Language* (Cambridge University Press, 1997).

Nicholas Ostler, *Empires of the Word: A Language History of the World* (HarperCollins, 2005).

For information about Elias Molee, see:

Marvin Slind, "Elias Molee and 'Alteutonic': A Norwegian-American's 'Universal Language,' " *Norwegian-American Studies* (forthcoming).

Molee's papers are held at the Norwegian-American Historical Association, St. Olaf College.

On the strange, strange life of Edmund Shaftesbury, see:

Janet Six, "Hidden History of Ralston Heights," *Archaeology,* May/June 2004.

For some good stories about Ogden, see:

J. R. L. Anderson and P. Sargant Florence, *C. K. Ogden: A Collective Memoir* (Elek, 1977).

K. E. Garay, "Empires of the Mind? C. K. Ogden, Winston Churchill, and Basic English," *Historical Papers, Communications Historiques* (1988), pp. 280–91.

The hieroglyphic example comes from:

Florian Coulmas, *The Blackwell Encyclopedia of Writing Systems* (Blackwell, 1996).

On how Chinese writing really works, see:

John DeFrancis, *The Chinese Language: Fact and Fantasy* (University of Hawaii Press, 1984).

For a good introduction to the linguistics of sign languages, see:

> Edward S. Klima and Ursula Bellugi, *The Signs of Language* (Harvard University Press, 1979).

On Gestuno, see:

> Bill Moody, "International Sign: A Practitioner's Perspective," *Journal of Interpretation* (2002), pp. 1–47.

If you'd like to see Bliss in action, the 1974 film *Mr. Symbol Man,* directed by Bruce Moir and Bob Kingsbury, can be ordered from the National Film Board of Canada.

JAMES COOKE BROWN AND THE LANGUAGE OF LOGIC

On Korzybski, see:

> Marvin Gardner, *Fads and Fallacies in the Name of Science* (Dover Publications, 1957).

> Michael Silverstein, "Modern Prophets of Language," University of Chicago, MS, 1993.

On Whorf, see:

> John E. Joseph, "The Immediate Sources of the 'Sapir-Whorf Hypothesis,'" *Historiographia Linguistica* 23, no. 3 (1996), pp. 365–404.

> Penny Lee, *The Whorf Theory Complex: A Critical Reconstruction* (John Benjamins, 1996).

> John Lucy, *Language Diversity and Thought: A Reformulation of the Linguistic Relativity Hypothesis* (Cambridge University Press, 1992).

> Michael Silverstein, "Whorfianism and the Linguistic Imagination of Nationality," in *Regimes of Language: Ideologies, Polities, and Identities,* edited by Paul Kroskrity (School of American Research Press, 2000).

For an interesting book about ideas and ownership, see:

> Ben Klemens, *Math You Can't Use: Patents, Copyright, and Software* (Brookings Institution Press, 2006).

Lojban information, including learning materials and grammars, can be found at www.lojban.org.

THE KLINGONS, THE CONLANGERS, AND THE ART OF LANGUAGE

The study of native Esperanto speakers referred to in the discussion of irregularity is:

> Benjamin K. Bergen, "Nativization Processes in L1 Esperanto," *Journal of Child Language* 28 (2001), pp. 575–95.

The story of Sebeok's analysis of the nuclear waste problem is in Eco's book. Sebeok's actual report, "Communication Measures to Bridge Ten Millennia" (1984), can be ordered from the National Technical Information Service (www.ntis.gov).

Information about Tolkien comes from:

> Humphrey Carpenter, *J. R. R. Tolkien: A Biography* (Houghton Mifflin, 1977).

Descriptions and histories of many conlangs can be found at www.langmaker.com.

APPENDIX A: THE LIST OF LANGUAGES

This list of languages is mostly culled from:

> Aleksandr Dulichenko, *Mezhdunarodnye vspomogatel'nye iazyki* (International Auxiliary Languages) (Valgus, 1990).

This book is at the Library of Congress and a few university libraries.

Dulichenko, in turn, has culled from:

> Louis Couturat and Léopold Leau, *Histoire de la langue universelle* (Hachette, 1903).

At many university libraries.

> Ernest Drezen, *Historio de la mondolingvo* (Ekrelo, 1931).

Very hard to find.

> Marcel Monnerot-Dumaine, *Précis d'interlinguistique générale et spéciale* (Librairie Maloine, 1960).

Held at many university libraries.

> Petr Stojan, *Bibliografio de internacia lingvo* (Universala Esperanto-Asocio, 1929).

Very hard to find.

APPENDIX B: LANGUAGE SAMPLES

The language samples were collected from original works, as well as from Dulichenko and from:

> Mario Pei, *One Language for the World* (Biblo and Tannen, 1958).

ACKNOWLEDGMENTS

The languages captured my interest; the people behind the languages reeled me in. If someone could figure out how to carve this amazing mountain of raw material into a story, I thought, what a great story it would be. I was foolhardy enough to think I was up to the task.

I was certainly not up to it when I began, but I was fortunate enough to have people who knew what they were doing on my side: my uncle Danny, who gave me the straight truth about my feeble early attempts, and my agent, Chuck Verrill, who knew exactly how to turn an *idea* into a *book*. Those early attempts benefited greatly from the editing pencils of Michele Mortimer at Darhansoff, Verrill, and Feldman; Allen Freeman and Jean Stipicivic at the *American Scholar*; and Michelle Wildgen at *Tin House*.

I owe an enormous debt of gratitude to my editor, Tina Pohlman, who is both a sharp-eyed professional *and* a cool chick. I am also lucky to count among my friends Dara Moskowitz and Dennis Cass, fabulous writers who are unnecessarily generous with their time and advice. I thank Cindy Spiegel and Julie Grau for taking me on and Mike Mezzo and Mya Spalter for seeing me through.

I received invaluable feedback and encouragement from

ACKNOWLEDGMENTS

Amanda Pollak, Michael Silverstein, and Nicole Juday. And the book would not have been possible without the many people who answered my questions and shared their stories with me: Shirley McNaughton, Ann Running, Paul Marshall, Douglas Everingham, Richard Ure, Ann Weilgart, Andrea Patten, John Clifford, Bob LeChevalier, Nora Tansky, Jennifer Brown, Joy Barnes, Evy Anderson, Hazel Morgan, Bob McIvor, Joseph Vandiver, Charles Robbins, Mark Shoulson, Marc Okrand, Lawrence Schoen, Louise Whitty, Humphrey Tonkin, Normand Fleury, Suzette Haden Elgin, Sarah Higley, and all the participants at the Esperanto, Lojban, Klingon, and Conlang conferences I attended.

None of this happens without good child care. For that I'd like to thank the entire staff of the Canaan Baptist Church day care, especially Ms. Linda Dubose, who was there from the beginning. Thanks also to Joey Dziomba and Arianna Neromiliotis at the community preschool of the Pennsylvania School for the Deaf for doing great things with small people.

And thank you, Derrick, Leo, and Louisa, for making life sweet.

INDEX

Abkhaz language, 290
Adam-Man Tongue, 148–49
Adams, John Quincy, 93
Aeo language, 286
Alley, Kirstie, 267
AllNoun language, 286
Alteutonik language, 144
Altutonish language, 144, 147
American Association for the
    Advancement of Science, 142
American Language, 144, 145
American Philosophical Association,
    142
American Sign Language (ASL),
    185, 186, 187
Amikejo, state of, 81
Amplifiki (band), 81
Amxrikai Spek (Foulk),
    137–38
"Analytical Language of John
    Wilkins, The" (Borges),
    59, 64
Anderson, Evelyn, 229–30
Anglic (Zachrisson), 137
Anglo-Franca language, 116
Anthem (Rand), 201
Antido I and Antido II languages,
    144

Ars signorum (Dalgarno), 74
artificial languages. *See* invented
    languages
artistic languages, 282–92
aUI language, 166, 178–81, 183–84,
    199, 291
Auli language, 116
Auxlang group, 98–99
Azak language, 286

Babm language, 14, 15–16
Bacon, Francis, 46
Balaibalan language, 89
Balta language, 107
Barron, David, 268
Basic English, 138–41, 142
Basic English (Ogden), 138
Basque language, 290
BBC, 140, 141
Beck, Cave, 33–34
Beermann, Ernst, 143
Beesley, Margrit, 155
Belafonte, Harry, 181
Ben-Yehuda, Eliezer, 117–18, 119,
    120, 121
Bialystok, Poland, 94–95
Bierce, Ambrose, 44

Bliss, Charles, 150, 153, 155,
157–59, 160–64, 165, 168–69,
173–78, 181–82, 183, 189–93,
194–96, 199, 202
Bliss, Claire, 161, 163, 164
Blissymbolics, 199, 202, 255–56,
257
Bliss's conflicts with users of,
173–77, 189–93
Bliss's promotion of, 163–64, 173,
181
Chinese writing and, 162, 168–69
constraints on interpretation of
symbols, 188–89
disabled children's use of, 153–54,
156–57, 174, 188–89, 193–94
invention of, 163
limited use worldwide, 193
modifications in accordance
with requirements of spoken
languages, 189
naming of, 164
purpose of, 162
syntax in, 236
system of symbol combinations,
155–56, 164–66
teaching manual for, 194–95
"true" and "natural" symbolism
issue, 183–84
Weilgart and, 181–82
Boozer, Don, 288–89
Bopal language, 107
Borges, Jorge Luis, 59, 64
Boyle, Robert, 22, 23
Brithenig language, 286
Brown, James Cooke, 206–7,
208–9, 211–12, 213–14, 216,
217–22, 223–24, 226, 227,
228–30, 250

Buck, Pearl, 181
Burgess, Anthony, 284
Burke, Jeff, 287–88

"calculus of thought," 36
Careers (board game), 213–14
Carnap, Rudolf, 210
Carson, Johnny, 181
Century of the Names and
Scantlings . . . , A (Somerset), 27
Chase, Stuart, 200
Chesterton, G. K., 44
Cheyenne language, 288
Chinese writing, 34, 46, 162,
168–72
Chomsky, Noam, 181
Churchill, Winston, 139–40, 141
Cinban language, 249–50
Clockwork Orange, A (Burgess), 284
Common Writing, A (Lodwick), 35
Communicationssprache language,
12–13
Compromiss-Sprache language, 144
computer programming languages,
258
Conlang (constructed language), 98,
99, 285, 287–90
Conlang (Listserv), 98
conventional agreement, 257, 258
Copernicus, 31
Coudenhove-Kalergi, Count, 137
Couturat, Louis, 149

Dagestanian language, 290
Dalgarno, George, 45–50, 51,
52–53, 73–75
Danish language, 84

Descartes, René, 36–37, 44
Dil language, 107
Diogenes the Cynic, 44
Doohan, James, 267
Dritok language, 288–89
Dynamic Language, 144

Eckardt, Andreas, 177
Ekskubalauron (Urquhart), 28
Elgin, Suzette Haden, 241–43, 245, 246, 247–49, 291
English language, 170
    Basic English, 138–41, 142
    female perspective and, 245
    irregularity in, 259
    as lingua franca, 135–37
    reforms targeting, 137–38
    Special English, 141–42
Esperantida language, 144
Esperantisto, La (magazine), 104–5
Esperanto Desperado (band), 81
Esperanto language, 255–56, 262
    artistry of, 291–92
    congresses of Esperantists, 82–85, 107–9, 112, 114, 116–17
    culture of Esperantists, 115–17, 129
    demonstration texts, 103–4
    dismissive attitudes toward, 98–99, 110–12
    homeland for, 81–82
    invention of, 94–98
    irregularity in, 258–60
    limited success, reasons for, 123
    national identities and, 112
    native speakers of, 84–85, 111
    nuances of, 113

peace in the world and, 129–30, 280
poetry using, 96–97
pronunciation of words, 83–84
public recognition of, 142–43
reforms to, 108–9
respectability issue, 124–26
rock music and, 81, 82, 129, 130–31
Schism among Esperantists, 99–100, 109
social network of Esperantists, 114–15, 130–31
Soros and, 126–27
spread of, 104–5
structure of, 100–103
syntax in, 236
Tonkin and, 127–29
unique terms in, 113–14
Esperanto Movement, The (Forster), 124, 126
Esperanto II language, 144
Esperido language, 116
Espido language, 116
Essay Towards a Real Character and a Philosophical Language, An (Wilkins), 25, 38
Euclid, 30–31
Europal language, 116
Europeo language, 116
Everingham, Douglas, 195

Faiguet, Joachim, 89
Finnish language, 268, 283
Foigny, Gabriel de, 284
folklore, 261
Forster, Peter, 124, 126
Foulk, Ruby Olive, 137–38

Frege, Gottlob, 210
French language, 79–80, 136
Freud, Sigmund, 178
Freudenthal, Hans, 212–13

Gagne, Paulin, 12
general semantics, 200–201
Geoglot language, 116
Germanic English language, 145
German language, 136
Gestuno sign language, 184, 187
Globaqo language, 98
Glosa language, 98
Glossolalia, 11
Godwin, Francis, 284
Gulliver's Travels (Swift), 29,
    284
Guugu Yimidhirr language, 290

Haakon, king of Norway, 147
Hawaiian language, 122
Hawking, Stephen, 154
Hayakawa, S. I., 200
Hebrew language, 95
    Modern Hebrew, 117–23
Henriksen, Kim, 81, 82, 83–85, 129,
    130
hieroglyphics, 34, 167–68
Higley, Sarah, 291
Hildegard von Bingen, 10–11,
    291
HolQeD (journal), 268, 292
Hom-Idyomo language, 98
Hooke, Robert, 22, 25
Hopi language, 204–5
Hungarian language, 268

Idiom Neutral and Idiom Neutral
    Reformed languages, 143
Idirl language, 262
Ido language, 98, 99, 109, 116, 136,
    263
Ile language, 116
Ilish language, 286
Ilo language, 116
imagistic symbolism, 184–89
Institute of General Semantics, 201
Interlingua language, 98, 99,
    209–10, 263
International Auxiliary Language
    Association (IALA), 209
international languages, 135, 136,
    137, 142. See also Esperanto
    language
International Sign Language, 188
Internet, 262–63
invented languages
    artistic languages, 282–92
    characteristics of, 6–7
    claims made about, 16
    convention and, 257
    earliest documented language,
        10–11
    existing languages as basis for,
        88–90
    fad for languages in 1600s, 26–29
    Freudian explanation for, 149
    history of failure, 12–16, 262
    industrialization and, 88
    Internet and, 262–63
    large-scale adoption of language,
        conditions for, 122–23, 262
    mathematical approaches, 30–37,
        43–45, 49
    purpose of, 11–12
    radical words and, 46–49

universal real character and, 46
See also specific languages
*Invention and Discovery That Will
Change Our Lives, The* (Bliss),
158
irregularity in languages, 258–60
Ispirantu language, 116
Ithkuil language, 290

Jakobson, Roman, 209
Janson, Karl, 177
Japanese language, 270, 286
Jespersen, Otto, 149
Jewish people, 117–23
Jones, Sir William, 89

Kepler, Johannes, 31–32
Klingon Dictionary, The (Okrand),
272, 280
Klingon language, 263
as agglutinating language, 268–70
appeal for speakers, 281
artistic vision of, 282
conference of speakers, 7, 8–9,
273–78, 292–93
conversation using, 273
creation of, 266–67, 270–71
inconsistencies in, 279–80
learning the language, 9, 271,
276–78, 292–93
lexicon of, 276, 277
low status of speakers, 3–4
new vocabulary for, 278–79
number of speakers, 272–73
ownership of, 228
phonological system, 266, 268
pronunciation of words, 265–66

purposelessness of, 280–81
sophistication of, 267–68
spellings in, 265–66
verb-agreement system, 270
Klingon Language Institute (KLI),
4, 9, 268
Klingons of *Star Trek,* 264–65
Korean language, 270
Korzybski, Count Alfred, 200–201,
202
Krankor, Captain, 273–74

Láadan language, 290, 291
clarity and validity issues, 246–47
failure as experiment, 248–49
female perspective conveyed by,
243–48
grammar and dictionary of, 243,
248
invention of, 242–43
lesbianism and, 248
Lojban and, 249
purpose of, 241–42
Láadan Network, 243
Language Creation Conference,
287–89
Language in Culture (book), 206
language invention. *See* invented
languages
language/thought question, 72–73
language's alleged bad influence
on thought, 199–203
natural languages and, 256
social science approach to, 203
Whorfian hypothesis, 203–6,
234, 250–51
Lapenna, Ivo, 124–26
Latin language, 68–69, 89

League of Nations, 125, 136
LeChevalier, Bob, 215–16, 221–26, 234, 249
LeClerq, Jean-Marc, 129, 130
Leibniz, G. W., 25, 36, 43, 71, 79
Leslie, John, 126, 127
Lessons in the Art of Acting (Shaftesbury), 148
Lincos: Design of a Language for Cosmic Intercourse (Freudenthal), 212–13
Lingua Ignota language, 10–11
Lingua Internazional language, 144
Lingue International language, 144
linguistics, 5
Lingvo internacia (Zamenhof), 97–98, 100
Lingvo Kosmopolita language, 144
Locke, John, 25, 142
Lodwick, Francis, 34–36, 37, 43
Logical Language Group (LLG), 226
logic in language, 210–13, 231–32. *See also* Loglan language; Lojban language
Loglan Institute, 214, 217, 220
Loglanist (journal), 216–17, 221
Loglan language, 229–30, 251–52, 255–56
    culture of, 250
    development of, 216–17, 219–23
    funding for work on, 217–18
    grammar and dictionary of, 219
    as human-computer interface, 220
    logic/language alignment in, 210, 211–12
    marriage vows using, 215–16
    "mind-expanding, thought-facilitating" effect, 228–29
    ownership issue, 223–25, 226–27
    purpose of, 206–7
    scientific orientation, 208–9
    scientific reviews of, 219
Logopandecteision (Urquhart), 28
Lojban language, 230, 257, 262
    complexity of, 232–34
    conference of Lojbanists, 234–35, 238
    conversation using, 238
    cultural neutrality of, 239–40
    culture of, 250
    English influence, danger of, 238–39
    invention of, 225, 226, 227
    Láadan and, 249
    practical benefits of using, 251
    syntax in, 235–38
Lord of the Rings trilogy (Tolkien), 282–83, 284
Lott, Julius, 143–44

Maimieux, Joseph de, 80
Man in the Moone (Godwin), 284
Maori language, 122
Marshall, Paul, 193–94
Martinet, André, 209
mathematical notation, 30–32
mathematics of language, 32–37, 43–45, 49, 73
    logic in language and, 210–11
McNaughton, Shirley, 154–55, 156, 157, 158–59, 173, 174, 176, 190, 191–93, 194
Mead, Margaret, 181

Meaning of Meaning, The (Ogden and Richards), 200
meaning transmission, 260–61
Mekeo language, 239
Mr. Symbol Man (film), 176–77, 190
Modern Hebrew, 117–23
Mohawk language, 286, 287–88
Molee, Elias, 144–47
Mondialo language, 144
Mondlingu language, 116
Mondlingvo language, 116
Monopanglosse language, 12
More, Sir Thomas, 284
Morris, Alice Vanderbilt, 209
Mundelingva language, 116
Mundolingue language, 144
musical scale, 87–88
Mutsun language, 270

Nal Bino language, 107
Napoleon I, Emperor, 80
Native Tongue (Elgin), 242, 243
natural languages, 4–5
  conventional agreement and, 257, 258
  flexibility and power of, 256, 258
  fuzziness of meaning in, 258
  irregularity in, 258–60
  language/thought question and, 256
  meaning transmission and, 260–61
  negotiation to avoid misunderstandings, 256–57
  shortcomings of, 11–12
Navajo language, 248
negotiation to avoid misunderstandings, 256–57

Nepali Sign Language (NSL), 185–86
Neuro-Linguistic Programming, 201
Neutra, Richard, 178
Newspeak language, 202
Newton, Isaac, 25
Niger-Kordofanian language, 290
Nimoy, Leonard, 267
1984 (Orwell), 201–2
Niu Teutonish language, 144, 146
Nov-Esperanto language, 144
Novial language, 98, 99
Novilatiin and Novilatin languages, 143
nuclear waste warning messages, 260–61
Nunihongo language, 286

Ogden, C. K., 138–39, 140, 141, 142, 200, 202
Okamoto, Fuishiki, 14, 15–16
Okrand, Marc, 266–67, 270–71, 272, 277, 278, 279–80, 282
Onion (satirical paper), 272
Orba language, 107
Orwell, George, 201–2, 203
Ostwald, Wilhelm, 149
ownership issue regarding languages, 223–25, 226–28

Paneuropean Union, 137
Paramount Pictures, 228
Pasigraphie language, 80
P@x'áãokxáã language, 285–86
Peano, Giuseppe, 149
Perfektsprache language, 116
philology, 89–90

philosophical languages, 44, 73. *See also* Wilkins's language
Picto language, 177
Pikto language, 177
Piron, Claude, 115–16
Pirro, Jean, 86
Plato, 43
"Politics and the English Language" (Orwell), 203
Portuguese language, 136
Prist, Ben, 13
Pure Saxon English language, 144, 145

Quenya language, 284
Quijada, John, 290

radical words, 46–49
Ralstonism health food cult, 148
Rand, Ayn, 201
Ray, John, 22
Reform-Neutral language, 143
Richards, I. A., 200
Rikchik language, 286
Roget, Peter, 65, 71–72
Roosevelt, Franklin D., 140
Rosenberger, Woldemar, 143
Royal Society, 21, 23–24
Ruggles, James, 90–93
Running, Ann, 151–53, 154
Russell, Bertrand, 163–64, 210
Russian language, 136

Safo language, 177
Sapir, Edward, 203, 209
Saussure, René de, 144

Schipfer, Joseph, 12–13
Schleyer, Johann, 105, 106–7, 291
Schoen, Lawrence, 271
Schwartz, Jacob, 110–11
Schweitzer, Albert, 181
Science and Sanity (Korzybski), 200
Scientia International (newsletter), 209–10
Sebeok, Thomas, 260–61
Semantography (Bliss), 155, 158, 163
Shaftesbury, Edmund, 148–49
Shah of Iran, 181
Shaw, George Bernard, 277
Shoulson, Mark, 4, 7–8, 9, 273, 275, 276, 278
sign languages, 184–88
Simplo language, 116
Sindarin language, 284
Skinner, B. F., 181
Solresol language, 86, 87–88, 290
Somerset, Edward, 27
Soros, George, 126–27
Soros, Tivadar, 126
Spanish language, 270
Special English, 141–42
Spectroscopia Molecular (journal), 209
Spelin language, 107
Sudre, Jean François, 87–88
Swadesh, Morris, 209
Swahili language, 286
Swift, Jonathan, 29, 284
symbol languages, 150, 166–72, 177–81, 183–84
   imagistic symbolism, 184–89
   relationships between concepts, expression of, 34–37
   See also Blissymbolics
synonyms, 60, 62–64

Tansky, Nora, 215–16, 217, 219, 223, 224, 225–26, 234
Terre australe connue (Foigny), 284
thesauruses, 65–67, 71
thought. *See* language/thought question
Times Higher Education Supplement, 110–11
Toito Spike language, 144
Toki Pona language, 286
Tolkien, J. R. R., 282–85, 291–92
Tolstoy, Leo, 104
Tonkin, Humphrey, 127–29
Turkish language, 270
Tutonish language, 144, 145–46
"tyranny of words" idea, 199–203
Tzeltal language, 290

Ubykh language, 290
Ulla language, 116
UNESCO, 126
Universal Character, The (Beck), 33–34
Universal-Esperanto language, 144
Universalglot language, 86–87
Universal Language, A (Ruggles), 90–93
Uropa language, 116
Urquhart, Sir Thomas, 27–29, 31, 32–33, 34
Utopia (More), 284

Vela language, 13
Verkehrssprache language, 144
Voice of America, 141
Volapük language, 105–7, 263, 291
Vonnegut, Kurt, 181

Wakashan language, 290
Waldheim, Kurt, 181
Wallis, John, 25
Walsh, Birrell, 221
Weilgart, John Wolfgang, 166, 178–79, 180–82, 183–84, 199, 291
Weixlgärtner, Arpad, 178
Welsh language, 283
Whorf, Benjamin, 203–6
Whorfian hypothesis, 203–6, 234, 250–51
Wilkins, John, 21–25, 46, 49–50, 167, 291
Wilkins's language, 255–56, 257, 290
  absurdity of, 59
  categorization of everything in the universe, 38–43
  conceptual precision as drawback of, 67
  destruction of original manuscript, 22
  disorienting effect on user, 58, 64
  grammar of, 68–69
  idiosyncratic nature of, 44–45
  index to, 53
  Latin influence, 68–69
  pronunciation of words, 52, 68
  purpose of, 24
  scientific community's reception of, 24–25
  synonyms, handling of, 60, 62–64
  syntax in, 236
  as thesaurus, 65–67
  thought and, 73
  transcendental particles of, 62
  translation of English into, 59–65, 67–70

Wilkins's language (*cont.*)
  as unusable, 71, 72
  word/referent relationship, 51–53, 56–57
  word search in, 53–57
Williams, John, 177
women's language. *See* Láadan language
Word Magic, 139, 200
World Federation of the Deaf, 184
Wren, Christopher, 22

Yench, John, 262
Yiddish language, 119

Zachrisson, Robert, 137
Zamenhof, Aleksander, 130
Zamenhof, Klara, 97, 98
Zamenhof, Ludwik, 94–98, 100, 101, 102, 103, 104, 108–9, 118–19, 130, 143
Zamenhof, Marcus, 95, 97

11/27